SUSPICIOUS
MINDS

SUSPICIOUS MINDS

The Triumph of Paranoia
in Everyday Life

IAN DOWBIGGIN

Macfarlane Walter & Ross

Toronto

Macfarlane Walter & Ross

37A Hazelton Avenue

Toronto, Canada M5R 2E3

Canadian Cataloguing in Publication Data

Dowbiggin, Ian Robert, 1952-

Suspicious minds : the triumph of paranoia in everyday life

Includes index.

ISBN 1-55199-035-0

1. Paranoia. 2. United States – Politics and government – 1993- .

3. United States – Social conditions – 1980- .

4. Canada – Politics and government – 1993- .*

5. Canada – Social conditions – 1980- .

I. Title

JA74.5.D68 1999   302'.17   C99-930916-1

Macfarlane Walter & Ross gratefully acknowledges financial support for its publishing
program from the Canada Council for the Arts, the Ontario Arts Council, and the Government
of Canada through the Book Publishing Industry Development Program.

Printed and bound in Canada

CONTENTS

ACKNOWLEDGMENTS

D URING THE RESEARCHING and writing of this book, I have had the pleasure of discussing paranoia – or "delusional disorder" – with a number of psychiatrists and historians of psychiatry, including William F. Bynum, Ann Dally, Kenneth Kendler, Mark Micale, Alistair Munro, Roy Porter, Sonu Shamdasani, Edward Shorter, and David Wright. Whether any of them would agree with all the conclusions reached here is doubtful; nonetheless, I have learned a great deal from each one. I'm also grateful to the Wellcome Institute for the History of Medicine for hosting me as a research fellow in the fall of 1997, enabling me to pursue my studies further and providing me with a galaxy of interesting and informed people to chat with.

Five colleagues in particular deserve special thanks. Since I met him in 1986 in Dallas, Texas, Wilfred M. McClay has been a splendid friend, sympathetic listener, and unerring critic when I needed it most. To Gillis Harp, an equally steadfast friend, I owe more than he probably realizes. At the

University of Prince Edward Island, Gilbert Germain has always been willing to discuss political theory with me; even if I haven't made it obvious, his views have influenced me deeply. Philip Davis, a true scholar, has likewise helped me clarify my ideas, as has Henry Srebrnik, whose readiness to share his own research with me proved to be indispensable. If there are any errors of commission or omission in this book they are my responsibility entirely.

Gary Ross of Macfarlane Walter & Ross was instrumental in his own way, first encouraging me to go ahead with this project and then providing me with invaluable advice and support along the way. Both he and Barbara Czarnecki are to be commended for their thoughtful and careful editorial work.

As always, words cannot express the debt I owe to my wife, Chris, and our children, Beth and Christopher. To me, they are the measure of all things wonderful.

INTRODUCTION

BACK IN 1964, in the midst of the United States presidential election that saw Lyndon Johnson crush Arizona senator Barry Goldwater, Richard Hofstadter wrote a book titled *The Paranoid Style in American Politics*. Normally university professors don't attract much attention, but Hofstadter was different. His book started a debate that is still heating up. The debate is over a mental disorder that was once thought to afflict only a tiny percentage of the population. The disorder is paranoia. Its place in contemporary society and culture is the subject of this book.

Hofstadter defined the "paranoid style" as a mode of expression used by certain political figures throughout American history. This style is characterized by "heated exaggeration, suspiciousness, and conspiratorial fantasy." The "paranoid spokesman in politics" wields power because he views the world as fundamentally hostile. Rather than singling himself out as "the individual victim of a personal conspiracy," the paranoid spokesman is able to mobilize support for his cause because he manages to collectivize his conspiratorial delusions. He succeeds in convincing others that they too share his victimhood at the hands of history. He appeals to those voters who don't simply "see conspiracies or plots here and there in history" but "regard a 'vast' or 'gigantic' conspiracy as *the motive force* in historical events." "History *is* a conspiracy" to the paranoid.

If Hofstadter hoped that his warnings would eliminate the paranoid spokesman from history, then clearly he was wrong. As this book argues, the paranoid spokesperson, far from disappearing from politics and society, has become a powerful presence in late twentieth-century America and Canada. Politicians and public figures, men and women, increasingly use the vocabulary of paranoia, punctuating their speeches and writings with the themes of persecution, hostility, resentment, self-righteousness, and moral indignation. Others cultivate a confessional, self-revelatory style appropriate for an age obsessed with psychology and a citizenry convinced that sensitivity and caring are more important than wisdom and good judgment. Still others fantasize about a coming New World Order orchestrated by the United Nations that will enslave us all. Indeed, what distinguishes Hofstadter's day from ours is that political paranoia has become common coin in recent years. A sort of inflation of paranoid rhetoric has set in.

What also distinguishes Hofstadter's time from ours is that political paranoia with its emphasis on conspiracy and persecution is no longer a monopoly of the political right. When Hofstadter described the paranoid style in politics in the mid-1960s, the White House and Congress were busy creating the "Great Society," opening "New Frontiers," waging "War on Poverty." Sweeping reforms in welfare, social security, health care, and civil rights legislation were under way. The memory of John F. Kennedy's presidency lived on, firing the imaginations of young and old in the U.S. The country appeared to be in the able hands of a liberal managerial elite. McCarthyism had been crushed. Only isolated, socially marginalized groups refused to welcome these changes, nursing their anti-intellectual resentments as history passed them by. To Hofstadter, paranoids were the last echoes of a populism that simply didn't know when to quit.

Much the same was happening in Canada. In Ottawa the federal Liberal Party officially changed the country from a nation of "two solitudes," French and English, to one based on a reconciliation of the two linguistic, so-called founding groups. Pierre Trudeau was on the verge of becoming prime minister and for a brief, sun-kissed moment appeared to embody a nation's thirst for optimism. Quebec's Quiet Revolution was under way, marking the province's transition to a modern, urban, industrial, and secular region. Preparations were being made for Expo 67 in Montreal, after World War II the grandest Canadian national project of the twentieth century. Expo was an extraordinarily successful World's Fair that electrified Canada with its exciting and sanguine visions of the future. People had great confidence in government-managed reform, in technocratic expertise. Back then Americans and Canadians had faith that progress, prosperity, justice, and happiness were not just possible but inevitable. There was a widespread belief that the state could tackle and solve social problems, that government could run things well, that technology was the answer. Conservatism was out, statist liberalism and its grand expectations were in.

Nothing seemed to demonstrate this more acutely than Johnson's landslide victory over Goldwater. To liberals like Hofstadter, political paranoia was "most evident on the extreme right wing," the expression of frustrated Goldwater conservatives, Republicans, McCarthyite anti-Communists, and fringe elements like the John Birch Society. Hofstadter obviously felt that if Americans had anything left to fear from political paranoia, it was from a bunch of decisively defeated and increasingly marginal right-wing fanatics. They were all that stood between America in the 1960s and Utopia, or so he believed.

Thirty years later it's hard to imagine how things could be more different.

Far from declining, paranoia is alive and well. By the mid-1990s the confidence of the mid-1960s had collapsed like a house of cards. Hofstadter had no inkling that political paranoia was about to get a powerful jump-start from some unlikely quarters. Just around the corner was the counter-cultural upheaval of the late sixties, the New Left movement with its university unrest, mass anti-war marches, "street theater" protests, and ritualistic celebration of anti-establishment violence. Political and popular culture today has inherited much of the confrontational, adversarial, and polarizing rhetoric and thinking of those turbulent years. Everything from everyday language to race relations and the relations between the sexes has been poisoned by ingrained distrust and suspicion.

One casualty of this process has been big-government liberalism, now a discredited political philosophy. State socialism is worse off, buried amid the rubble of Communism's collapse in eastern Europe and the debt-ridden ruins of Keynesian economics in the 1990s. Although many North Americans still want government to tackle social and economic problems, few believe any longer that government has the expertise or resources to solve them. In Canada the Trudeau vision of a nation united by official bilingual and bicultural policies is in tatters, if not ruins. This crisis of confidence has undermined the notion of community itself. The paranoid mentality feeds on the perception that the ties that normally bind society together are disintegrating, and seeks desperate remedies to heal the rifts, but to no avail. By compounding widespread sentiments of inveterate diversity and mutually exclusive interests, the paranoid's nostrums only make matters worse.

Paranoia is now bipartisan, having grown to encompass the whole political spectrum. Worldwide the paranoid style can be found both on the political right and on the left. Indeed, the political left may be beating the right at the paranoia game, as seen in its recent embrace of political correctness. American political commentator Daniel Pipes argues in *Conspiracy* (1997) that – because of their better credentials, greater sophistication, wider

4

access to the media and genuine power, and other factors – leftist figures like Noam Chomsky, Pierre Salinger, Jesse Jackson, Gloria Steinem, and Oliver Stone leave the militias and the Liberty Lobby far behind. Nothing could be more telling about paranoia's reach into the corridors of power than Hillary Rodham Clinton's 1998 outburst on network TV about a huge "right-wing conspiracy" out to destroy her and her husband.

Paranoia has become mainstream, an equal-opportunity employer, ignoring race, creed, color, and class. People have been responding with alacrity to the paranoid message, evidence that there is a deep taste among ordinary citizens for the smorgasbord of delusions peddled by pushers of paranoia. Sensing this popular taste, political, social, and cultural leaders pander to it, creating a kind of vicious circle. Judging by recent history, the circle is widening alarmingly.

Since Hofstadter's era, the paranoid style has ceased to be simply a weapon used by politicians to win votes. It's been transformed into a kind of psychological complex shared by millions of men and women. The paranoid frame of mind has seeped into popular consciousness to a degree that would have appalled Hofstadter. Paranoia, with its delusions of persecution, conspiracy, and grandeur, has become the ideal mental reaction to millennial times. It appeals to those who fear that catastrophe is just around the corner, who feel as if their personal autonomy is slipping away under pressure from circumstances beyond their control. They imagine themselves isolated, insecure, defenseless, uncertain, stripped of moral certainties, locked in some enormous struggle with agencies they cannot readily see but whose existence they dimly sense. Paranoia appeals to those who worry that the traditional narratives that gave meaning to history are spiritually and intellectually bankrupt and have to be replaced by other systems of thought. As such, paranoia addresses the fundamental human need for a worldview that situates seemingly random events in a coherent scenario: in other words, an ideological faith.

The collapse of once reliable narratives like liberalism and Communism has made the 1990s a time of particular soul-searching, a dramatic turning point in modern history. The political left is in disarray, grievously disunited by identity-group politics. Conservatism, despite its impressive electoral victories in the 1980s and 1994, may also be breaking up into its various factions. The failure of the Reagan presidency to forge a new political consensus in the U.S. paved the way for the vacuous and "compartmentalizing" Bill Clinton to capture the White House. The utter collapse of the Progressive Conservative coalition led by Brian Mulroney in Canada enabled Jean Chrétien's policy-bankrupt Liberal Party to seize power in what may be the last gasp of a geriatric federalism. Recent Canadian attempts to "unite the right" have done little to disguise the fact that conservatism's sectarianism is as great as ever. The dissolution of the traditional political narratives leaves a vacuum that paranoia is quick to fill. Little did Hofstadter know that instead of closing a chapter of history he was really documenting the beginning of a new one.

This, then, is a book about the power of delusions, what psychiatrists call incorrect beliefs. Paranoid delusions are powerful because they are seductive and addictive. They can numb, charm, tranquilize, or thrill the human mind. The paranoid, in the words of the American novelist Thomas Pynchon, is captive to an "orbiting ecstasy." Though it's possible to advance a good cause using paranoid terminology, paranoid delusional thinking, as the term suggests, leads far more often to bad consequences than to good. Delusions are dangerous because they resist reality-based testing. Paranoid delusions rest on the conviction that "appearances deceive." Such an attitude makes delusions impervious to the normal process of falsification and verification. "'Appearances deceive' is a passport to bad judgment," Daniel Pipes notes.

Like Hofstadter, I do not use the terms "paranoia" and "paranoid" in a strictly clinical or reductionist sense. I use them to refer to "a way of seeing the world and of expressing oneself." By that, I don't mean to imply that all persons whose views are described as paranoid suffer from a certifiable mental disorder warranting treatment. In all likelihood, the vast majority don't. In using these words I am instead describing more metaphorically than medically what I believe to be an elementary condition of the human psyche, a kind of original mental sin that is fated to afflict human history to one degree or another. How much influence paranoia will wield in future depends on many factors. Perhaps the most important is the leadership of our elites in government, academia, the arts, education, business, labor, and the entertainment industry. Their examples will largely determine whether respect for wisdom, prudence, charity, selflessness, natural justice, and human dignity – the antidotes to paranoia – will flourish.

In any case, the question of diagnosing paranoia as a medical disorder or as a symptom of another illness is one I happily leave to trained psychiatrists. Who should or shouldn't be seeing a psychiatrist is a question I am unqualified to judge. That said, we are now, thanks to about two centuries of modern psychiatric literature on paranoia, in a better position than ever to recognize a delusion for what it is. We also benefit from the history of the thirty or so years since Hofstadter wrote his book. Unlike Hofstadter, who limited his discussion of paranoia to its style, we know that paranoia can be judged by the *content* of its delusions as well. What paranoids believe is just as important as the manner in which they express their opinions. We also know that delusions crop up in everyday life, that otherwise sensible, sane, and law-abiding people have them. Today, more so than in Hofstadter's time, people's minds are swayed by the kernel of plausibility in every popular delusion. Thus, paranoia is an apt and useful way to describe conditions that may have nothing to do with an actual emotional illness.

This feature of modern society is gaining increasing notice. Books on political paranoia and the rash of conspiracy theories have been published recently. Academics get together at conferences to discuss paranoia. Rarely a day goes by without seeing or hearing the words "paranoia" or "paranoid."

They have become some of our favorite terms of derision and defamation. We seem to recognize readily the dangers of paranoid consciousness but are unable to defend ourselves against it. Though we appear at best dimly aware of it, paranoia is on everyone's mind.

Trends such as these confirm that paranoia has emerged from the closet as an issue of vital importance as the twenty-first century dawns. Nowadays paranoid psychology is catching and represents an unfortunate reversion to outdated forms of thought. What marks the last years of the twentieth century is that more and more people are becoming aware of this fact.

Paranoid thinking shows few signs of receding, and things could be getting worse. The way the world is constructed today fosters paranoia. Digital information technologies with their powers of instant communication and menacing potential for exhibitionism and electronic stalking provide paranoids with tremendous playgrounds. The scare over the Y2K computer "bug" reflects the terror engendered by the specter of telecommunications systems out of control. It also mirrors the religious and secular fears associated with the millennium. These factors, combined with the indelible legacy of the 1960s and the irresponsibility of North American elites, guarantee that the twenty-first century will begin no differently than the twentieth century is ending.

CHAPTER ONE

The Age of Paranoia

E RNST WAGNER was a troubled, suspicious soul. A German schoolteacher who lived at the beginning of the twentieth century, Wagner was convinced that other men knew he was a frequent masturbator and discussed it behind his back continually. Worse still, he believed they knew about an act of bestiality he had apparently committed earlier in life. These thoughts tormented him daily, though no one seemed to notice. He finally reached his breaking point one night in 1913. That evening he murdered his wife and four children by slitting their carotid arteries while they slept. The next night Wagner, having run to a neighboring town, set fire to several houses. When the inhabitants ran from their flaming homes Wagner opened fire on the male villagers, killing eight and severely wounding twelve others before he was apprehended. After being arrested, tried, and convicted, Wagner lived out the rest of his life in an asylum for the insane. He survived to witness Hitler's coming to power, and his last days were spent applauding the Nazis' anti-Semitic policies. His mental status never deteriorated like a schizophrenic's, confirming that his condition constituted a separate and distinct disease. That disease is paranoia.

Almost a century later, Wagner's delusional psychology is very much alive. It surfaces periodically in its most grotesque forms in events such as those surrounding Professor Valery Fabrikant of Concordia University. For Fabrikant, August 24, 1992, was a day of reckoning. After years of bureaucratic wrangling, he had just learned that the university would not grant him job-security tenure. On that warm summer day, wearing clip-on sunglasses and a dark blue suit, Fabrikant walked into Concordia's Henry F. Hall Building in Montreal concealing two loaded weapons in a brown leather bag.

Just after three o'clock Professor Michael Hogben, president of Concordia's faculty association, stepped into Fabrikant's ninth-floor office in the mechanical engineering department. Hogben was nervous, knowing full well Fabrikant's campus reputation for being litigious and sullen. Seating himself, Hogben produced a letter telling Fabrikant that because of charges that he was harassing staff, his visits to the faculty association's office were being restricted. Fabrikant's answer was to produce a .38-calibre pistol and fire three shots. One bullet hit Hogben in the head. A second lacerated his heart. A third went through his lower back. Hogben collapsed, bleeding to death on the floor while still clutching the letter.

Minutes later Fabrikant barged into the office of Jaan Saber, another colleague. Saber was on the phone to his wife. As Saber's wife listened in horror, Fabrikant fatally shot him in the head and stomach. Fabrikant left Saber's office, lurching down the corridor. There he met Elizabeth Horwood, a secretary. He shot her in the thigh before she was able to lock herself frantically in an office.

Still Fabrikant wasn't finished. In front of an astonished fellow professor, Fabrikant shot Phoivos Ziogas, chairman of Concordia's electrical and computer engineering department. Ziogas's wound to the abdomen was mortal and he died a month later.

Finally, Fabrikant encountered civil engineering professor Matthew Douglass at the office of the dean of engineering. Douglass protested when he saw Fabrikant aiming his gun at a secretary, and Fabrikant shot him four times. Belying the notion that his act was a crime of passion, Fabrikant fired one .25-calibre bullet while standing over Douglass, who was bleeding to death on the floor.

Thus, when Fabrikant later left campus under police escort, two of his colleagues in the engineering department were dead and two mortally wounded. A fifth had been shot and wounded. Few who knew Fabrikant were entirely surprised. He had had a long history of idiosyncratic, deceitful, abusive, and violent behavior in both Canada and the Soviet Union. Besides issuing death threats, he had sometimes referred to himself as the next Isaac Newton, the illustrious seventeenth-century physicist. But what colleagues remember most about Fabrikant were his persistent allegations that they were persecuting him, either by denying him tenure or by stealing his research.

Fabrikant's murders are important for reasons that transcend his disturbed personal life and psychology. Though relatively few paranoids are driven to murderous extremes, his case vividly illustrates in microcosm paranoia's significance for North Americans at the end of the twentieth century. Fabrikant was a refugee from the Soviet Union, perhaps the most paranoid political regime in all history. As an immigrant he was particularly vulnerable to the stress that triggers paranoid fears and suspicions. Literally hundreds of complaints filed by and against him filled his personnel dossier from 1988 to 1992. He was a self-anointed victim, the consummate griever. He combined these traits with a grossly inflated self-perception. He thought himself a unique genius, surrounded by scoundrels and fools. Quick to appreciate the paranoid potential of the Internet, he spent long hours typing his frustrations into what the Montreal *Gazette* called "his own private international broadcast network." His resort to murder also highlights the close connections between paranoid ideologies like Communism and Nazism and the twentieth-century acceptance of violence as a political solution. In addition, it's no coincidence that Fabrikant, a university professor, believed himself a victim of harassment within the one North American institution that today nurtures some of the most paranoid of all trends, such as the victimology movement, gender feminism, lesbian and gay "queer studies," and Afro-American "critical race theory."

Whether Fabrikant was certifiably deranged is a matter of speculation, but his outbursts and his crime certainly raise questions about what paranoia is and has been clinically. As a medical term, "paranoia" dates back at least to classical antiquity. The word "paranoia" derives from the Greek words for "beside" and "mind," meaning "out of mind" or "thinking amiss." The ancient Greeks and Romans used the word to refer to mental illness generically. However, it wasn't a technical term in medicine until the nineteenth century. Before 1800 those who exhibited paranoid delusions were normally diagnosed as melancholic. With the emergence of modern psychiatry in the nineteenth century and the dramatic rise of industrial, urban living, paranoia became a topic of compelling interest to psychiatrists. They built up a huge literature chronicling the ravages of the disease in the lives of countless men and women.

Since the early twentieth century paranoia has gradually lost its popularity amongst psychiatrists. In recent decades many have been proclaiming it a rare condition, responsible for only a tiny percentage of psychiatric cases. Some might imagine that paranoia, like hysteria, is itself disappearing as a medical diagnosis. The term "paranoia" has been dropped altogether in the 1994 edition of the psychiatrists' "bible," the American Psychiatric Association's *Diagnostic and Statistical Manual of Mental Disorders* (*DSM*). Since delusions of grandeur and persecution occur in a variety of disorders, including schizophrenia, alcoholism, severe depression, tertiary syphilis, and

Alzheimer's disease, psychiatrists traditionally have been reluctant to admit that there is such a thing as true paranoia. Many prefer to attribute paranoid symptoms to other diseases. Other psychiatrists maintain that some delusions are more properly defined as symptoms of obsessive-compulsive disorder or mood disorders like depression.

Reports of paranoia's demise, however, may be premature. A small group of psychiatrists in Europe, Canada, and the United States are struggling to both retain and expand the paranoia diagnosis, now called "delusional disorder" (DD). One Canadian psychiatrist claims that the incidence of DD in the general population may be as high as one to two percent – in other words, as frequent as schizophrenia. Another estimate has it that more than 10 percent of mental hospital admissions are for paranoid states. Determining the actual number of clinically paranoid people in society is probably impossible. Even paranoids like Fabrikant tend to be able to function in society. Frequently they are well educated. Unlike those with more debilitating mental disorders like schizophrenia or depression, paranoids often hold down jobs, pay taxes, raise families, partake in personal friendships. Many refuse to seek medical help in the first place, preferring to nurture their delusions in private. They distrust anyone who doubts the reality of their delusions, especially physicians, and often receive medical treatment only after committing outlandish or criminal acts. What is beyond question is that many emotional disorders involving paranoid delusions go undetected until it's too late.

As some psychiatrists admit, the recorded cases of delusional disorders may simply be the tip of the iceberg. The psychiatrists David Swanson, Philip Bohnert, and Jackson Smith have written, "For every fully developed case of paranoia in our mental hospitals there must be hundreds, if not thousands, who suffer from minor degrees of suspicion and mistrust; whose eyes are blighted by this barrier to human harmony; and who poison the springs of social life for the community." There is a whole class of people who are not considered to be mentally ill, who often are not treated by psychiatrists, who are frequently described as paranoid, yet whose prognosis is generally favorable. According to the 1994 *DSM* they suffer from "paranoid personality disorder." This class of people is opinionated, touchy, and hostile. Lacking a sense of humor, defiant of established institutions and authority, and often imagining they are physically sick, they accept nothing at face value and are fascinated by the search for hidden meanings. As one 1970 psychiatric textbook stated, "The paranoid reads more between the lines than he sees in the lines themselves, thus overlooking the obvious." No wonder paranoids are typically injustice collectors, relentlessly believing that misfortune is never accidental or deserved but is always due to the malevolence of others. Their presence, depressingly familiar to many of us, testifies to the inroads paranoia has made into modern society.

Paranoid thinking is based primarily on a belief in delusions. Paranoid delusions make sense to otherwise reasonable people, not just clinically ill individuals, because they ordinarily contain a kernel of truth. They are, in the words of the *DSM*, "non-bizarre" delusions, those "involving situations that occur in real life, such as being followed, poisoned, infected, loved at a distance, or deceived by a spouse or lover, or having a disease." However, even the psychiatric profession admits that judging whether a delusion is bizarre can be subjective. "One person's *bizarre* is another person's *strange but plausible*." It's as if psychiatrists themselves are losing their nerve when it comes to saying what is and isn't a delusion. If they won't say, what hope is there for the rest of us?

These psychiatric reservations reflect the fact that in our turn-of-the-millennium world almost anything goes. Even Fabrikant had a few supporters at Concordia, including loyal students and one political science professor who called him "the Albert Einstein of mechanical engineering." And as the 1994 Arthurs inquiry into abuses of academic research at Canadian universities concluded, there may in fact have been some substance to Fabrikant's claim that his colleagues were stealing his ideas. Paranoia, write Robert S. Robins and Jerrold M. Post, authors of *Political Paranoia*, "is seldom a complete delusion. It is typically a distortion of a truth." As the saying goes, even paranoids have real enemies. Or just because you're paranoid doesn't mean you aren't being followed.

The foremost type of delusion in paranoia is a belief in conspiracies. The paranoid is a master systematizer. He has a strong, distracting suspicion that people are harassing or persecuting him. Over time this feeling grows into a full-fledged conviction. He starts racking his brains for the answers to questions like: Who is persecuting me? Why? How are they persecuting me? What do they want? Before long he's spun out an elaborate theory that seeks to explain his emotions and answer these questions. By this time he's convinced himself that he's become the target of a huge conspiracy that will use any means to make his life miserable and possibly injure him. He imagines that his enemies are using his radio, TV, telephone, microwave, and other appliances to get at him. Once he accepts this notion, it becomes imperative that he spend his life in a state of hyper-alertness and heightened vigilance, never resting for a moment lest he miss any of the innumerable signals that might reveal the plotters and the dimensions of their conspiracy. He naturally turns inward, adopting a defensive and antagonistic attitude toward the rest of society. Inevitably, this hostility provokes hostility in others, confirming his initial suspicions. He becomes trapped in a web of circular reasoning, heeding only "the demon within." In other words, once paranoids begin to construct their systematic worldviews, they are on a long descent into madness.

But paranoia isn't just a belief in conspiracies. Historically, paranoid delusions have not been restricted to delusions of persecution. The paranoid mentality is far more subtle and complex than that. Once you believe you are the target of a grand conspiracy it's only a small step to believing that people are doing this to you because you are special, inordinately gifted and blessed. You might even surmise that you're a unique agent of God entrusted with a special message to other, less favored mortals who persist in misunderstanding you. It's no wonder that paranoids sometimes claim magical, miraculous powers that go far beyond any parlor tricks. Charles Manson, found guilty in 1969 of conspiracy to murder seven victims, including the actress Sharon Tate, predicted a coming war to the death between American blacks and whites. He also claimed he could fly, levitate buses, charm rattlesnakes, and perform healing miracles. As a paranoid you conclude that people are jealous of your inventive, intellectual, prophetic, or amorous skills. After all, why would they go to such lengths to harm you if they didn't resent you? Just as Fabrikant imagined himself terribly maligned and harassed as well as the next Isaac Newton, so paranoids often combine fears of persecution with delusions of grandeur. Their sense of self-importance can be extraordinary. Quips the writer Susan Sontag, "I envy paranoids; they actually feel people are paying attention to them."

By stressing the belief in conspiracy and persecution, then, we run the risk of missing the full significance of paranoid psychology. The paranoid mentality is not only addictive; it's truly multidimensional, manifesting itself in myriad ways. Alongside delusions of persecution and grandeur, paranoids can suffer delusions that they are infested with bugs, that famous people are in love with them, that they are grotesquely misshapen, that they are sick from a mysterious virus. Hypochondriacal paranoids have delusions of physical symptoms that can't be verified by physicians' workups. They often become so obsessed with their conditions that they quit their jobs and devote all their time to studying their ailments. In fact, it's possible for someone to be deluded on almost any subject under the sun.

Thus, on a limited number of subjects paranoids erect complex and sophisticated systems of thought. The multilayered and non-bizarre complexity of much delusional thinking today is both deceptive and seductive. It's typical of overly abstract thinking, the triumph of logic over common sense. Abstract thinking when unchecked, as it often is nowadays, frequently ends in paranoia.

The tendency to invent new words is another sign of paranoid psychology. As long ago as the turn of the twentieth century psychiatrists noted that a symptom of paranoid thinking is the propensity to invent neologisms, especially those that sound philosophical or scientific. The paranoid's neologisms turn vagueness and imprecision into assets. Though the exact meaning of a paranoid's chain of ideas may be elusive, the chain looks exquisitely subtle. The weakness of paranoid thinking becomes obvious only after a few minutes' conversation or reading. But this quality makes delusional reasoning perfectly suited to the late twentieth-century mind, which is – thanks to the electronic media – easily bored, impatient, incapable of sustaining attention. We are dazzled by the momentary persuasiveness of the paranoid's mental gymnastics. Paranoia is intellectual spectacle passing as profundity and masking ignoble passions. It's the ultimate serious Woody Allen movie. The writer G.K. Chesterton was close to the truth when he said that the paranoid doesn't lack reason; if anything, he lacks "everything except his reason." The paranoid is what the intellectual turns into when he falls in love with his own sophistication and erudition and discards the ballast of morality, common sense, and empirical experience.

Paranoia has become epidemic because paranoid views strike a chord deep in the public's belief systems. As the novelist and science writer Arthur Koestler once remarked, a "paranoid streak" is inherent in human beings. Based on what scientists are now arguing about the biological roots of paranoia, it is safe to say that mistrust, fantasies of self-importance, and fears of conspiracies and persecution are embedded in the neurological wiring of our brains, waiting to be activated by persuasive paranoids. Who can remember *not* being frightened at some point and falling prey to the suspicion that something or someone was out to get us? Of course, in the overwhelming number of instances there was nothing "out there." The real demon hides in the recesses of our own brains.

Thanks to neurophysiological research we can locate the paranoia demon in an area of the mammalian brain made up of neurons and hormone-secreting structures called the limbic system. Current research suggests that the delusions of paranoia are caused by overactivity of the neurotransmitter dopamine within the limbic system. The product of more than two million years of evolution, the limbic system governs the reactions involved in survival, including what the psychiatrist Ronald K. Siegel has called "the four 'f' words of survival: feeding, fighting, fleeing, and fornicating." Since these activities are central to survival, it's little surprise that paranoid suspicions can be triggered so easily.

Epidemic paranoia plays on this primal nature of suspicion. Next to fear, suspicion may be the most communicable, contagious attitude. From an evolutionary standpoint paranoid delusions are the atavistic relics of basic instincts and thought formations that served an adaptive purpose when life was precarious, a residue of primitive existence when human technology did little to protect people from the natural elements. These mental conditions may once have helped people to survive. Aggression and anger could be said to have been adaptive at some earlier stage of evolution. But what worked in the jungle frequently doesn't work in civilization. Society has become safer and more secure over the course of history. It has also become more sophisticated and complex, with people more interdependent than ever. Unfortunately, the history of civilization has moved far faster than our capacity to change biologically. Our primitive impulses to react in paranoid ways have not been eliminated yet by natural selection. The interdependence fostered by modern society helps to trigger these primal anxieties, never far from consciousness, about our relative powerlessness. When these fears are encouraged, paranoid delusions can break out. We worry about the power wielded by others to do us harm. We begin to imagine that unseen forces are manipulating our lives and insidiously robbing us of our personal autonomy. In this respect paranoia offers a graphic example of how nature and nurture intersect. Paranoia's origins and foundations are rooted deep in our biology.

The psychiatric literature abounds with examples pointing to this congenital aspect of paranoia. A recent case of a high-ranking European civil servant, told to me by a psychiatrist, also vividly illustrates both the relative invisibility of paranoia and the tenacity of delusions. For years this official held an important bureaucratic post, convincing friends, family, and co-workers that he was successful and stable. There was one flaw in his makeup, however; he imagined himself to be an ideal model for artificial limbs. For years he studied anatomy and surgery texts, until one day he proceeded to amputate his leg. When the operation went sour and he began to lose a lot of blood he came to medical attention. Presumably no one had suspected he was laboring under this delusion until the moment he lopped off his leg.

Other paranoids are all too visible. The litigious (or "querulous") paranoid, for example, according to the psychiatrist Robert Lloyd Goldstein, "repeatedly hales opponents into court to demonstrate to all the world that he has been wronged. Such individuals resort to the legal system to defend themselves against the many injustices that are being inflicted on them. They use the legal system as a vehicle to act out delusional concerns and retaliatory fantasies against their enemies, often with fanatical determination and vindictiveness ... Not infrequently, the paranoid's victims find themselves enmeshed in a protracted nightmare of litigation without end. In the process, the rational, legitimate objectives of the court system may be lost sight of and defeated."

Fabrikant himself went through seven lawyers, four of whom he insisted were saboteurs. He demanded that assault charges be filed against a security guard for physically mistreating him and that libel charges be laid against *Le Journal de Montréal* for describing him as insane. In 1995 he sued Concordia University for $900,000 plus legal costs for threatening his life, claiming his rampage was an act of self-defense. The case went all the way to Canada's Supreme Court, which in early 1999 decided not to hear his appeal. As one lawyer complained, Fabrikant was "jamming the system." Litigious paranoids like Fabrikant indulge their delusions by tying up the courts until they are finally ordered to undergo psychiatric tests. The huge rise in litigation over the last few decades may in fact be tied to the way our legal system invites paranoids to take the objects of their delusions to court.

Descriptions of other litigious paranoids underscore the mischief they perform. One was a fifty-year-old attorney specializing in tenants' rights. His paranoid personality was finally unmasked when he served as the main prosecution witness in a trial charging other lawyers with conspiracy and attempting to cover up the gruesome murder of a tenants' rights organizer who had been the victim of a vicious chainsaw attack. He testified eloquently and passionately that powerful landlord groups were responsible for the organizer's death and that he himself had received threatening letters claiming he would be next. It came out in court that he had a long history of making these kinds of accusations against other lawyers, clients, and magistrates. After a court-ordered psychiatric examination, it was concluded that he had an ingrained tendency to view all events in his life, even seemingly ordinary ones, as the result of conspiracies hatched by others out to get him. Manifesting the typical paranoid symptoms of hyper-vigilance and acute suspiciousness, he was barred from practicing law indefinitely.

Then there is the case of a man charged with slashing the throat of his work supervisor, whom he had suspected of conspiring with other employees to kill him. Like Valery Fabrikant, he was convinced that the court system was stacked against him and that ultimately no lawyer could be trusted to represent him fairly. Having attended one year of law school he was further convinced he ought to represent himself. Though he was sure he could unmask the truth in court, he was instead referred to an assessment for competency to stand trial and, not surprisingly, found to be out of touch with reality and the true nature of the legal proceedings. His case and those of countless other litigious paranoids show that paranoids are particularly attracted to the legal system, seeing it as a drama-laden arena in which injustice and their persecutors can be revealed for the world to see. Unfortunately, they often ruin the lives of people who are forced to share in the harrowing litigation that paranoids thrive on.

Those with delusional disorder can also suffer from pathological jealousy. Jealous delusional disorder seems to afflict men disproportionately. Men suffering from conjugal jealousy suspect their spouses or lovers of infidelity and interpret everything imaginable as confirmation of their delusions. They may employ private investigators to spy on their spouses or they may perform the surveillance themselves, hiding in closets and under beds in an effort to substantiate their theories. In other instances they may confront their wives with their accusations, subjecting them to humiliating scenes. One twenty-nine-year-old jealous husband insisted on searching his wife's vagina for evidence of sexual relations with other men. The usual culmination of such events is a volatile domestic situation in which physical violence is likely.

Women are prone to a different, less violent form of delusional illness. The psychiatric literature records many cases of women who construct delusional fantasies about loving high-profile figures. The targets of delusionally jealous patients' affections can be famous individuals, like members of the Royal Family, or simply people whom the patient could not realistically expect to mix with socially. One woman, a fifty-five-year-old, married white female, illegitimate, alcoholic, and poorly educated, with an unhappy childhood and equally miserable marriage, became convinced that a highly placed, good-looking male physician at the hospital where she worked was deeply in love with her. She based her views on the belief that he conveyed

21

his feelings to her through secret signals, such as nodding his head. After she left her job she thought he continued to communicate with her telepathically. At times she would feel his hand on hers, or feel his leg pressed against hers. When confronted with the fact that he had never openly declared his love for her, she replied that he resorted to subterfuge to spare his wife and children. Over time, her delusions became so strong that they obsessed her day and night. To try to control her mounting amorous attraction to this man, she increased her alcohol consumption until she eventually came to psychiatric attention. In other patients, these erotomanic delusions are more serious. Sometimes patients imagine themselves to be carrying the child of their supposed lover. If they are not hospitalized, they frequently badger the objects of their passions. They incessantly telephone or try to arrange face-to-face encounters, all the while stalking their alleged lovers. When it becomes clear that the paranoid's feelings are not being reciprocated, resentment and anger may follow, endangering lives.

The damage done by paranoids to innocent people is all too clear in divorce and custody proceedings. The explosion in family law cases in recent years has opened up a fertile battleground on which paranoids can launch relentless attacks against their spouses or other relatives. One such paranoid was a thirty-five-year-old schoolteacher. Convinced that her husband and others had sexually abused her two children, she spent two years in court, during which time her husband was barred from the marital home, refused visitation rights with the children, and driven into personal bankruptcy in an effort to vindicate himself through the courts. During the proceedings it emerged that she had coached and browbeaten her children to give evidence against their father. Like many people today, she was eager to believe that child molestation was not just a reality but an everyday occurrence in most people's lives. She also viewed the courts as the place where she could get even. In this instance the law unmasked her delusional theories. In other cases the results are not nearly so fortunate.

Yet another type of delusional disorder crops up in certain patients. This variety of emotional illness is sometimes referred to as the somatic subtype of delusional disorder, meaning patients have delusions about their bodies. In years gone by physicians have used terms like hypochondriasis, parasitosis, or dysmorphophobia to describe patients with these symptoms. Such patients may believe their bodies are misshapen, ugly, deformed. Or they might think they are ill, or that their skin is crawling with insects. In most cases there are no other symptoms. What makes them controversial today is that these conditions have close links to the more publicized eating disorders anorexia nervosa and bulimia, or chronic fatigue syndrome, or the conviction that one incorrectly inhabits the body of the opposite sex. People with these beliefs harbor strong opinions that something isn't right with their own bodies, that in a sense their bodies are making them miserable.

People who imagine that they are infested with bugs or that some aspect of their physical appearance is seriously amiss often go undiagnosed by psychiatrists. They are so distraught that they instead consult dermatologists, entomologists, plastic surgeons, or pest control specialists in a frantic attempt to cure their problems. Those suffering from the delusion of infestation believe that small creatures such as lice, vermin, or maggots live and thrive on or in their skin. While no reliable data are available, there is reason to assume that the incidence of this kind of delusional disorder was associated with the rising popularity of cocaine as the drug of choice in the 1980s. Tests with primates have shown that administering stimulants around the clock causes primates to scratch, pick, and dig at their skin with fingernails until they rip flesh off their bones and even amputate their own fingers. Some cocaine addicts behave similarly, occasionally chewing off fingers in search of bugs.

The delusion of infestation starts with a variety of physical sensations: tingling, pricking, itching, creepy feelings in the skin, or perhaps a burning, flushing, or numbing sensation. If the delusions persist, a person can go from considering the sensation *"as if* something were crawling in my skin" to thinking that "something *is* crawling in my skin." Hallucinations can develop in which the patient actually begins seeing the pests themselves. By this stage patients frequently become desperate and start scratching so badly that wounds appear on their skin. Patients have been known to take dissecting instruments to their own bodies to attempt to remove the sources of infestation surgically.

Equally troubled are the men and women who suffer from "the distress of imagined ugliness," what the psychiatrist Katharine Phillips has named "body dysmorphic disorder" (BDD). In her book *The Broken Mirror* (1996) Phillips has chronicled many cases of BDD in men and women who are pre-occupied with an imagined defect in appearance, usually having to do with the nose, skin, hair, or genitals. Living within a culture that celebrates impossibly high standards of fitness and beauty encourages this kind of obsession. Sometimes the preoccupation can focus simultaneously on several body parts, or it can include different body parts at various times. The common thread to all BDD delusions is that they are "distressing, time-consuming, and generally difficult to resist or control." Patients may spend hours each day worrying about their imagined defects, made all the worse by the fantasy that other people are staring at and talking about them. One twenty-eight-year-old single white man started worrying at age eighteen about his thinning hair. Others, including four dermatologists, reassured him that it wasn't noticeable, but he couldn't stop fretting. He became socially withdrawn, unable to study and go to school, and worked only part-time. He sought psychiatric care only after his girlfriend said their relationship was jeopardized by his obsession.

Other cases of BDD have more serious consequences. One twenty-seven-year-old single, unemployed white woman had been so anxious and obsessed about supposed facial acne, scars, and veins since the age of fifteen that she attempted suicide and had to be hospitalized. Before her attempt she had spent her days continually checking mirrors and repeatedly asking her mother, whom she lived with, about her face. Time and again she applied makeup to her imaginary defects, often picking at her skin with pins, though she knew that only made her look worse. She saw countless dermatologists, one of whom described her as "a beautiful woman with perfect skin." Dropping out of high school, she withdrew from socializing and dating. For an entire year she refused to leave the house while her distress and sense of isolation mounted. Aware of her condition, she called herself "every dermatologist's nightmare." "Some of my dermatologists are probably seeing therapists because of me," she lamented.

The most controversial of all the conditions tied to the somatic type of delusional disorder is chronic fatigue syndrome (CFS), or myalgic encephalomyelitis. CFS is invariably non-fatal. Its exact cause is unknown, but it leaves its victims debilitated. CFS patients generally feel tired, too exhausted to play, perform everyday chores, go to work. They complain of both localized and diffuse aches and pains. Because its symptoms often mimic those of influenza and frequently strike middle-class, urban, fast-track professionals, it was nicknamed the "yuppie flu" when it first surfaced in the 1980s. Although the data aren't conclusive, conventional wisdom is that CFS afflicts more women than men.

A vocal, activist CFS sufferer is Mary Schweitzer, professor of history and women's studies at Villanova University, near Philadelphia. Once a prolific scholar, full-time teacher, and avid skier, today she spends most of her time in bed, using her laptop computer and Internet hookup to disseminate information on CFS. She rarely leaves home. She traces the onset of her symptoms to 1990, but she didn't collapse until October 1994. After struggling to finish the semester she went on medical leave. Ten months of fighting with her insurance company followed, with the company ultimately agreeing to pay long-term disability benefits. Obviously politicized by her struggles, she now attacks critics of CFS, such as the English literature professor Elaine Showalter, while trying to raise awareness of the syndrome.

What strengthens the link between paranoia and CFS is the possibility that CFS patients' interpretations of their disability may rest on a delusion. CFS patients and their defenders are still groping for the kind of scientific evidence they need to transform it into a bona fide disease. To this point CFS has yet to make the transition from "syndrome" to full-fledged, certifiable "disease." (According to Hillary Johnson, an American journalist, a syndrome is "a collection of uniquely presented symptoms and physical signs for which a cause has yet to found," while a disease is "a manifestation of illness for which medicine has an explanation ... as well as a scientifically sound explanation of the patho-physiology.") AIDS, for example, is now considered a disease because it has been linked to the HIV infection. CFS, however, shows no consistent abnormalities that are observable and measurable.

None of this daunts the CFS movement. When the narratives of its members encounter skepticism, as they often do, CFS defenders inside and outside medicine become defensive. They liken CFS to AIDS on the basis of the resistance both initially met. They allege cover-ups in government agencies and charge the medical establishment with self-interest when it questions CFS. As Showalter notes in her book *Hystories* (1997), conspiracy theories abound among CFS patients and advocates.

In another age the convictions of CFS patients would have been diagnosed as hypochondriacal delusions. That label isn't entirely fair since it implies that CFS is primarily psychological, opening up CFS sufferers to the charge that "it's all in their heads." In fact the symptoms CFS patients exhibit are very real. They feel pains in their legs, arms, and stomachs, and aches in their heads and joints. How can anyone say their weariness is imaginary? But the fact that they experience these sensations doesn't mean the sensations are any more "real" than those felt by people with delusions of infestation. What further distinguishes hypochondriacs from CFS patients is that hypochondriacs sometimes have the insight to suspect that their conditions aren't genuine. CFS patients, on the other hand, tend to be true believers. They seek affirmation for their complaints in the form of recognition from organized medicine that CFS is not simply depression or a delusional disorder but is linked to abnormalities in the brain and immune system. If they have doubts about the reality of their condition, they aren't saying. In other words, CFS patients' rights organizations would be impossible without a society and culture that sympathetically affirms similar activist movements.

Thus, the recent history of CFS shows how it bridges the more debilitating delusional disorders and the paranoid psychological states shared by countless men and women today. There is a continuum between severely delusional patients and a large group in society with milder, less bizarre beliefs. This situation, while acute lately, is not entirely new. Historically, there has been a fascinating, complex resemblance between paranoid phantasms and the convictions held by many religious, political, and cultural leaders. In particular, the psychology of paranoia has had much in common with that of charismatic prophets and their followers. Recognizably paranoid delusions can be traced back as far as the origins of Christianity with the rise of competing religious philosophies such as Manichaeanism and Gnosticism. Central to both pagan cults was the belief that the world was locked in a ferocious battle between two diametrically opposing forces. In their own minds cultists were those few persons gifted enough to see this hidden truth and destined to triumph in the end. In the meantime, they were fated to be horribly persecuted by an enemy of gigantic proportions. These and similar cults attracted many brilliant but disturbed followers who through cunning and ambition used ruthless means to achieve power.

As time wore on, these currents merged with millenarian fantasies that spawned numerous peasant revolts during the Middle Ages. Based on biblical prophecies of a final struggle between Christ and Antichrist, political paranoia fed the imaginations of dispossessed and suffering men, women, and children right down to the nineteenth century. In the last two hundred years, the original paranoid mentality has become mainly secularized with the arrival of Nazism, Communism, and other extremist ideologies. These paranoid ideologies claim that all of history can be reduced to a conflict between groups, in Communism's case between social classes, in Nazism's between races. On one side is normally an innocent but endangered group; on the other is a group whose own pitiless, unscrupulous tactics justify its utter destruction. To the Communist, the working class is perfectly entitled to annihilate its mortal adversary, the exploiting ruling class. To the Nazi, the Jews and other ethnic groups deserve the same fate. These totalitarian ideologies promise swift deliverance from present problems. Despite (or perhaps because of) their secularization they have authorized the worst instances of social engineering in human history. In Cambodia's killing fields, in Stalin's gulag, in Mao's Great Leap Forward and Cultural Revolution, and in Hitler's Final Solution, political paranoia has exacted a fearsome toll. Literally millions have perished in the name of totalitarian paranoia; many more have been imprisoned or analogously humiliated. With the defeat of Nazi Germany in 1945 and the collapse of Communism in eastern Europe in 1989–1991, some may think that the paranoid trends in these political movements have disappeared, but echoes of political paranoia reverberate in the 1990s. Neo-Nazis in central Europe continue to flex their muscles, drawing on a popular fascination with Nazi memorabilia. Ethnic hatred drives people to butcher their neighbors in Balkan lands like Kosovo. The latest news from Russia and some former Soviet-bloc countries tells us that Communist politicians can still get elected and exert influence. The lingering popularity of Joseph Stalin among some Russians is a sobering reminder that the past is not quite dead.

As paranoid themes have played increasingly influential roles in the political history of modern times, so paranoia has fascinated countless scholars, poets, novelists, and playwrights, some of whom have described it as a peculiarly modern way of thinking. Descriptions of paranoia, such as the paranoid jealousy in Shakespeare's *Othello*, had already surfaced before the nineteenth century. But modern paranoia received a powerful shot in the arm from the philosopher Jean-Jacques Rousseau (1712–1778), whose writings in the late eighteenth century combined a taste for revolution and counter-cultural politics. Rousseau, perhaps best known for *The Social Contract* (1761), could be called both the first modern hippie and the first modern paranoid, if only because his turgidly self-indulgent autobiography anticipated the kind of wearisome confessional spectacle popularized by today's TV talk shows and celebrity memoirs. In his posthumously published *Confessions* he lashed out at virtually all of France, accusing his countrymen of spying on him, censoring his writings, and generally damaging his reputation. Near the end of his life he sought to have one of his manuscripts placed upon the high altar of the Notre Dame cathedral in Paris. Fittingly, his last book was a quirky environmentalist account of his veneration of nature and his hatred for human society. By his death Rousseau had turned his back on culture, science, and technology. If mail bombs had been invented in the eighteenth century, he might have been the first Unabomber.

Rousseau began a trend that has shaped the course of the modern history of ideas and culture. Numerous nineteenth-century writers have described paranoid states of mind in literature. Examples of paranoid characters in modern literature include Stendhal's Julien Sorel in *The Red and the Black*, Melville's Captain Ahab in *Moby Dick*, and Dostoyevsky's "The Underground Man." The Russian novelist Gogol captured the psychological condition of someone suffering from paranoid grandiosity in his short story "The Diary of a Madman." Flaubert did the same in his novel *Madame Bovary*, documenting with unerring accuracy a paranoid's escape into the titillating world of her own erotic delusions and fantasies.

But no nineteenth-century writer did more to make paranoia a conventional literary style than the playwright August Strindberg. Strindberg, whose dramas are undergoing a revival today, was undoubtedly paranoid himself. Enormously talented but insanely jealous of his wives, he led a life punctuated by rhythmic bouts with paranoia. He worried that even his best friends were conspiring to poison his food and pump noxious gases into his home. He plunged into mystical philosophy, wrote seriously about alchemy, dabbled in witchcraft, and accused his fellow playwright Henrik Ibsen of plagiarism, all the while convinced that invisible powers were working to frustrate him. In 1897, during a sane interval in his career, he described his descent into madness in *Inferno*. When Strindberg received a letter from the philosopher Friedrich Nietzsche, himself no stranger to paranoid delusions, the playwright signed his reply, "The One and Only God."

The twentieth century has seen an acceleration of paranoid literature. The writings of Franz Kafka are riddled with paranoid motifs. In English-language literature World War I proved a critical watershed, introducing what the critic Paul Fussell has called "paranoid melodrama." Paranoid melodrama relies heavily on adversarial tension, oversimplified oppositions, psychological polarization. Complex characterization is absent in this literary form, replaced by demonization and a relentlessly binary vision that sees sharply defined antithesis everywhere. Much of this outlook derives from the outpouring of literature during and after World War I. Writers like Robert Graves, Wilfred Owen, Siegfried Sassoon, and Edmund Blunden told and retold their stories about serving as soldiers in the trenches. Their wartime experiences made them think like paranoids, teaching them to be chronically suspicious of others and their motives. They came to doubt everything they read, detect conspiratorial lying behind every official statement, oscillate between boundless cynicism and blind idealism. Their psyches remained on a war footing long after official hostilities ended. They were unable to disengage themselves mentally from wartime's death, destruction, obscenity, jingoism, and propaganda. For them there was no emotional closure, no psychological armistice. And this mental trait has afflicted the intelligentsia ever since. It has persisted well into the post–World War II era. Since 1945 writers like Norman Mailer (*The Naked and the Dead*, 1948) and Joseph Heller (*Catch-22*, 1962), though setting their novels in World War II, have merely rehashed the images and themes of the "Great War."

One of the greatest post–World War II novelists of the twentieth-century paranoid literary imagination is Thomas Pynchon. Author of the acclaimed novels *V* (1963), *The Crying of Lot 49* (1966), and *Gravity's Rainbow* (1973), Pynchon is now as famous for his militantly reclusive habits as he is for his writings. Not only are his novels about paranoia, he himself has lived a paranoid existence for years. (It was only in 1997 that Pynchon was apparently photographed, having erected a gigantic wall of secrecy around himself, a remarkable achievement in today's paparazzi-crazy world.) Of all his paranoid novels, *Gravity's Rainbow* stands out. It begins near the end of World War II just as Nazi Germany's new V-2 rocket and the atomic bomb are ushering in the era of nuclear missile technology. Its principal hero is an American lieutenant named Tyrone Slothrop. He is assigned to a fictitious organization modeled after the British Special Operations Executive, whose main functions during World War II were espionage and sabotage. Slothrop's organization is housed, appropriately enough, in a former mental hospital. Slothrop is believed to have been programmed in infancy to get erections before a rocket attack, so his initial duties are to use his supposed gifts to predict the dispersal pattern of V-2 rockets falling on London. His trials and tribulations, for the most part surreal and fantastic, are designed to demonstrate Pynchon's basic point that "everything is connected." Discovering these connections beneath the visible surface of things leads to the discovery of myriad plots intended to give the plotters power over the rest of the population. In *Gravity's Rainbow* the war and its politics are "all theater," a means for distracting people from "the needs of technology" and big international businesses. In this view we are all cogs in a huge machine.

We all occupy coordinates in mammoth information systems. As Slothrop's personal history shows, conspirators have exerted power over us since earliest childhood. Paranoia thus becomes a natural form of thinking and feeling. It becomes necessary for one's sanity, so to speak. Paranoia is indeed total awareness, the pathway to real wisdom. It's a desirable mental state, according to Pynchon, for its opposite, "anti-paranoia, where nothing is connected to anything, [is] a condition not many of us can bear for long."

Pynchon's great endeavor in *Gravity's Rainbow*, as one critic has suggested, is to redeem paranoia, strip it of its pathological features, make it respectable. Is this why he has become such a counter-cultural hero, the darling of those who allege that multinational corporations and international cartels with their all-encompassing information systems really run the world? Ultimately Pynchon's point is not political. *Gravity's Rainbow* isn't a celebration of the little guy, the "lovable slob" like Slothrop who struggles to live and love in defiance of corporate impersonality. His thesis is darker and more anarchic than that. The old leftist theory that the common man is noble and embodies the hope for a better future is a myth. It's too late for that kind of sentimentality. Paranoia is universal: it's the very nature of existence in the twentieth-century world. Freedom will soon be extinguished because the technical means of control will then be capable of connecting us all in one enormous web. In Pynchon's mind, all traditional forms of protest and subversion are outdated. Revolutions are no longer possible. Protests, no matter how large, are quickly forgotten. They just leave the old paranoid systems in place. There's nothing left to do but indulge our literally fictional personal entertainments.

Pynchon's bleak, dystopic novel is not the last literary word on the subject. In *Underworld* (1997) Don DeLillo has written a work of fiction that updates the paranoia theme. *Underworld* and *Gravity's Rainbow* serve as bookends to an era that began in the 1960s and is peaking in the 1990s. If *Gravity's Rainbow* depicts the paranoia generated by a world entering the age of nuclear missile technology, *Underworld* depicts the paranoia of a world exiting the Cold War with its ominous threat of atomic annihilation. But the message of *Underworld* is no happier or more hopeful. If anything, it's more horrific. Paranoia hasn't been declining as the millennium approaches. It's actually getting worse.

Underworld describes what happens to a variety of American characters between the 1950s and the early 1990s. Its two chief characters are Nick Shay and Karla Sax, she a celebrity performance artist, he a white-collar employee of a huge waste management corporation. They meet in an early scene set in 1992, but their lives and those of the many other characters are braided together intimately all the way back to the moment when the novel opens. It's October 1951. Frank Sinatra, Jackie Gleason, and Toots Shor are sitting together in the Polo Grounds, attending the famous Brooklyn Dodgers–New York Giants playoff baseball game decided by Bobby Thomson's dramatic home run in the ninth inning. But baseball wasn't the only thing happening that day. As DeLillo writes, "This game was related to something much bigger." Also there to watch Thomson's "shot heard round the world" was FBI boss J. Edgar Hoover, who learns at that moment that the Soviets have detonated their first nuclear bomb, the *other* shot heard around the world.

The narrative, such as it is, occurs on two levels: the history of the actual ball Thomson hit, and the history of the Cold War. Life for an entire generation of Americans would never be the same after this fateful autumn day in 1951, DeLillo is saying. A new era of paranoia had begun.

Not only is *Underworld* a novel about paranoia, its very form and organization are paranoid. Sprawling, rambling, episodic, ambitious, mesmerizing, often frustrating, *Underworld* is fraught with a raw, hallucinatory tension. Its characters come and go as the novel flits from one location to another, back and forth in time. One moment the reader is in the Bronx in the early 1950s, the next at a nuclear testing site in contemporary

Kazakhstan. DeLillo mimics the paranoid's essentially ahistorical, overly selective way of ordering the past. He also re-creates the paranoid's perception of others as cartoonlike, surreal and stereotypical, at once indistinct and grotesque, alive but unbreathing, possessing flesh and blood yet lacking heart and soul. Rarely do the men and women in the novel come alive; they are more like ethereal presences than solid, grounded personalities. They are ill defined, outlandish, yet strangely unmemorable. They float from one scene to another, appearing and disappearing abruptly and inexplicably.

It's only as the novel nears its end that the web that ties *Underworld*'s individual stories together grows visible. The novel culminates in a scene that captures the 1990s taste for miracles, this decade's thirst for superstition and supernaturalism, and its disdain for conventional rules of thinking. A crowd gathers after dark to catch a glimpse of a recently murdered young girl's image on a billboard in the war-zone-like Bronx. Was it real or merely an illusion produced by a passing commuter train's lights bouncing off the billboard? The question is meaningless in the age of paranoia. "Everything is connected," writes DeLillo, echoing Pynchon. As one critic has noted, the novel's "immense size has to do with the paranoid vision's inability to stop collecting connections." In the end we are besieged by forces beyond our control, DeLillo insists, "lines of intersection that cut through history and logic and every reasonable layer of human expectation."

The 1990s world DeLillo describes is a paranoid nightmare, his version of Orwell's *Nineteen Eighty-Four* (1949), a world of international capital, transnational media, hostile takeovers, electronic sex. Distrust and unhappiness are plentiful, money means nothing any more, violence is easier and out of control, sameness rules, affecting "everything from architecture to leisure time to the way people eat and sleep and dream." People sense that a watershed in history has been crossed but don't know how to describe it. They "can't understand how the last decade of the [twentieth] century looks worse than the first in some respects. Looks like another century in another country." People are fearful and anxious in the 1990s, DeLillo is saying, because they see themselves unprotected amidst a high-tech bombardment more sinister than the nuclear threat ever was. They feel as if their skin has been flayed, exposing their insides to millions of penetrating and manipulating electronic signals. They feel excoriated, invaded, violated.

The great metaphor for the paranoid 1990s, *Underworld* says again and again, is the Internet, "where everybody is everywhere at once," yet where one can hide in the midst of everyone else, "unseen" but still "there." A place that isn't a place, a site that isn't a site, space without boundaries inhabited by millions who can't see each other but know they're there. DeLillo affirms that we're living in the wake of a mammoth revolution in communications technologies that has destroyed our traditional theories of geographical space. The computer with its simulations and programs is just one of a host of appliances that have uprooted us cognitively. VCRs, cable TV, CDs, glossy magazines have joined the computer to produce a rapid-eye-movement sequence of "on-the-fly images." As we flip and zap, our fantasies and the images we view become curiously united; the old subject-object distinction breaks down. Subjectively we are fragmented, de-centered, out of space and yet in it. Boundaries crumble, frontiers are breached. We become paranoid, unable to separate ourselves from other people and things. To visualize today means to see and feel what the paranoid sees and feels. When DeLillo's characters interactively enjoy "Nude Dancing on the Information Highway" they participate in the virtual reality of the paranoid.

No wonder DeLillo much prefers the good old paranoia of the Cold War. In conventional fiction the Cold War would serve as some kind of background to the isolated and personal lives of a handful of characters. Not in *Underworld*. Its characters internalize the twists and turns of the Cold War without being terribly conscious of it. *Underworld*'s characters eat, drink, and sleep it. Cold War paranoia invades their sinews and nerves.

Yet some, oddly, grow to love the effects of this fusion between personal and global history. Even if the Cold War faceoff between the two super-powers meant Armageddon was whisker-close, "you could measure things. You could measure hope and you could measure destruction." Other characters wanted the Cold War to keep going. "It's the one constant thing. It's honest. It's dependable." Nick Shay, the least paranoid of *Underworld*'s characters, fondly remembers the Cold War, "when I was alive on the earth, rippling in the quick of my skin, heedless and real . . . when I walked real streets and did things slap-bang and felt angry and ready all the time, a danger to others and a distant mystery to myself." The sensibilities of youth resonated all the more strongly when you knew every minute could be your last and everyone else's.

When the Cold War begins to wind to a halt life becomes drained of meaning. It becomes hard to breathe, says DeLillo. His characters dread the end of the Cold War's exhilarating paranoia. One character says that "when the tension and rivalry come to an end, that's when your worst nightmares begin. All the power and intimidation of the state will seep out of your personal bloodstream" and "other forces will come rushing in, demanding and challenging." Once the threat hanging over the planet is gone, one becomes "the lost man of history." Without the consoling fictions of the atomic age, each of us is alone in the 1990s with our fears, hatreds, and anxieties.

Underworld may be the most important English-language work of fiction to appear in the last decade. What makes it remarkable is that it captures the subtly powerful terror so many feel in the 1990s. People today sense "the loss of personal presence" and scramble frantically to rescue personality from its banishment to the realm of mythology. They labor fruitlessly to recover it, sampling everything in a Sisyphean struggle gone mad, stripped of all redeeming values, shorn of all concrete reference points, as all paranoid endeavors are. DeLillo is right, then, in arguing that with the end of the Cold War we have become the lost children of history.

By contrasting this paranoia to Cold War paranoia, however, DeLillo runs the risk of becoming the Oliver Stone of fiction. Both Stone and DeLillo ultimately absolve the paranoia of yesteryear. They conveniently forget Pynchon's insight that in paranoid politics there are no real heroes and villains, because all politics is a charade, a stage play full of sound and fury, signifying nothing. Just as Stone pines for the days of John F. Kennedy's Camelot, so DeLillo longs for a time when issues were clear-cut, when friend and foe were obvious, when it actually made sense to be paranoid. During the Cold War you knew who your enemy was and, as one of *Underworld*'s characters says, you could get 40,000 people out to protest around an air force base. DeLillo despairs of the present day, seeing in it an entirely new age, a time pregnant with disasters beyond our imaginations. Like other people who cast their eyes back nostalgically to the fifties, sixties, and seventies, he believes you had to be crazy *not* to be paranoid back then.

Perhaps the real terror behind 1990s paranoia, then, is the sneaking suspicion that good old paranoia is now a liability. In the final analysis it serves no useful purpose. The fall of Communism and the resurgence of free-market capitalism seem to have settled all the grand-scale philosophic debates of the twentieth century, making for a sobering spectacle to millions accustomed to seeing the world clearly divided into two hostile camps. Not only has Communism's collapse undermined the credibility of socialism in general, it has posed a huge question mark for many of the other grand narratives of history. Whether historical narratives are about the progress of reason and freedom, the eventual victory of the working class, or the triumph of nation-building, they depend on fundamental differences, crystalline distinctions, stereotypical enemies. There are still enemies out there, but they turn out to be pretty mundane compared with the demons we were willing to believe in earlier. Often they're also hard to pinpoint, which makes the entire process of demonization all the more anxiety-filled. Though wars continue, nations disintegrate, and diplomats broker cease-fires and peace agreements, "a certain furtive sameness, a planing away of particulars," in DeLillo's words, looks to be growing. People feel a sharp need to believe in overarching theories of the past. They need to believe that history is moving in the right direction. Otherwise the present just doesn't make sense. The last thing they want to find out is that, cosmologically speaking, history is headed nowhere. Such a realization can be disillusioning and frightening. The path of least resistance lies in inventing new demons, or resurrecting old ones and elevating them to new heights of infamy. This is what many people have been doing in recent years. Without the comfortable scapegoats and villains of earlier times, they find new ones that help to justify old-fashioned paranoia. This new form of paranoia has a special hysterical edge to it, perhaps because of an unconscious recognition that there's no reason for it. And nowhere is this more evident than within the "political correctness" movement of recent years. In a desperate attempt to shore up an old paranoid paradigm, its adherents have replaced the villainous, exploiting, bourgeois capitalist with the white, heterosexual, environmentally careless male. The risible efforts of the PC crowd to condemn the latter are matched only by the tolerance today's society extends to paranoid causes.

Nonetheless, many still believe that people are right to be paranoid today because they have a lot to be fearful about. Indeed, expectations about the future have plummeted over the last few decades. But is this because our world is changing too rapidly, because advances in technology and shifts in traditional definitions of employment and social roles are fundamentally disorienting? Is it because of currents in popular sentiments and emotions that mirror genuine changes in modern life? Or is it because of the leadership of the "new elites" whose influence over society's major institutions, corporations, and media enables them to shape popular ideas, tastes, and attitudes?

Certainly there are grounds for today's alienation. People rightly worry about jobs and the economy. They worry about making ends meet at a time when the gap between rich and poor is widening and the size of the middle class is shrinking. As they reel from the effects of corporate downsizing, middle-aged baby-boomer adults in the 1990s especially fear that the standards of living enjoyed by their parents are receding tantalizingly out of reach. They also worry about crime, addiction, education, homelessness, health care, the environment. Canadians have legitimate reasons to worry about national unity. The data tell us we live in the richest society in history. But then we turn on the TV or read the newspaper and see that other modern societies like Yugoslavia and the Soviet Union have crumbled, leaving ruin, poverty, and anarchy behind. Anxiety abounds and suspiciousness escalates, as people fret that the same things could happen here.

At the same time, however, today's paranoia cannot be reduced simply to economic, social, or political circumstances. As disorienting as the recessions of the 1980s and 1990s have been, they are nothing next to the depression of the thirties or, more recently, the horrific economic conditions of Boris Yeltsin's Russia. In Canada, it's true, the drop in average after-tax income during the 1990s has been the worst since the Great Depression. But the unemployment rate by the end of 1998 had fallen to its lowest level since 1990. The economic statistics from the United States in the mid-1990s have been even more impressive. Per capita after-tax income actually rose 9.5 percent between 1990 and 1998. These data were enough to help re-elect the feckless Bill Clinton, one of the least impressive presidents in U.S. history and a man millions of Americans don't trust. If economic issues have helped to engender the paranoia of recent years, they can hardly be called the most decisive causes.

Similarly, if socioeconomic conditions have fueled 1990s paranoia and caused greater impoverishment, surely paranoia would be most visible at the grass roots of society. Unquestionably, paranoia thrives at this social level. As Daniel Pipes has shown, anti-Semitism still enjoys a resilient popularity among some North Americans. Fears of grand international conspiracies, often featuring Jewish financiers orchestrating the lives of ordinary

Americans, seem to touch a nerve in the public consciousness. The success of books like Pat Robertson's *The New World Order* (1991) and the popularity of people like the TV commentator and Republican Party presidential hopeful Pat Buchanan mirrors the widespread belief that organizations like the United Nations and the International Monetary Fund are out to harm American taxpayers, "the designated fall guys of the New World Order," in Buchanan's words. The notorious militias, who share the same vocabulary if not the same methods, are as grassroots as you can get.

But the truly striking phenomenon of millennial paranoia is how readily it afflicts society's opinion-making elites, those who should know better, such as today's "New Class." To the Canadian author Kenneth McDonald this "New Class" includes "political clergy, union leaders [especially white-collar unions], the government-paid staffs of women's groups and francophone and ethnic associations, university professors, senior civil servants, human rights and language commissioners, senior businesspeople, print and electronic journalists, writers and actors and playwrights." Nowadays it is surprising to find paranoid themes woven into the thinking of many academics, actors, artists, writers, politicians, and other celebrities. Even bankers, brokers, consultants, engineers, and systems analysts, people we assume are primarily practical and pragmatic, are not immune to the paranoid psychological style. Oliver Stone, Gloria Steinem, Oprah Winfrey, Ted Turner, Shirley MacLaine, John Ralston Saul, to name just a few: all are educated and none is impoverished; indeed, they generally enjoy affluence and fame. Some are genuinely powerful, influencing the flow of money and information across borders, running philanthropic organizations and institutions of higher learning, or directing huge media corporations that dominate the terms of public debate and discourse. But that hasn't stopped its members from acting and sounding like the descendants of the millenarian charismatics who fired the paranoid imaginations of medieval peoples. Instead of demystifying paranoia, they abdicate their responsibilities by indulging it.

They foist their own alarmist versions of reality on the public. As we'll see in the next chapter, TV shows repeatedly project paranoid images, encouraging us to believe we're all essentially luckless and powerless victims, solitary misfits adrift in a cold, menacing universe, vulnerable to unpredictable twists of fate or the malevolent schemes of others. People, they tell us, are right to be paranoid. Rather than subjecting cultural paranoia to reality testing, our elites prefer the nihilistic notions which say that politicians are all the same, religion is nothing but a neurosis, everyone's in it for themselves, we all have our own agendas.

This variety of cynicism, dubbed "debonair nihilism" by the American philosopher Allan Bloom, holds that everything is simulation. But if everything's simulation, there's no "real" out there; no original is being copied. In the paranoid's mentality, old boundaries and polarities vanish so that it's impossible to make universal judgments. Everything admirable can be dismissed with a simplistic slogan or formula. The very idea of reality is in question. As Christopher Lasch shrewdly observed in *The Revolt of the Elites and the Betrayal of Democracy* (1995), those who make their living as "symbolic analysts" – for example, processing data or creating visual images for the entertainment and advertising industries – "inhabit an artificial world in which simulations of reality replace the thing itself." They are the natural leaders of a paranoid society. Little wonder that people turn to Hollywood for political commentary and moral judgments.

Such an attitude is infectious. We have become knee-jerk debunkers, constantly sniffing the wind for telltale signs to confirm our cynicism and suspicions. Sadly, about the only thing people commonly believe in is paranoia itself, the need to maintain an ironic, hostile, and distrustful distance, ready to half believe everything and to fix conviction in nothing. Just as paranoids believe only their own delusions and refuse to accept anything else at face value, so they seem content to assume the existence of things they can't see, touch, taste, or smell. Irony and gullibility go hand in hand with acute suspicion in the paranoid mind. Today's paranoid is inveterately suspicious but not really skeptical, alternating between a boundless, almost sweet trust and a judgmentalism as severe as that of a fire-and-brimstone Puritan preacher. The paranoid subjects things and people around him to a fiercely dismissive hostility but falls captive, strangely, to some of the worst nonsense in recorded history. Thus, the age of paranoia, though character-ized by rampant doubt and cynicism, paradoxically coincides with the end of skepticism, the loss of the critical ability to discern truth from falsehood. Skepticism isn't suited to the flitting quality of the paranoid mind. Today's mainstream paranoid says, "I treat the people and things around me with humorous, hip disdain. I withhold my admiration from what I am expected to honor. I reserve it for the things that don't make sense." How else to explain why we pay more attention to Shirley MacLaine the New Age guru than Shirley MacLaine the performer?

In this millennial day and age, when expert prophecy and trend-spotting are huge industries, it is all the more important that we recognize these features of paranoia. The following chapters document how these aspects of delusional psychology have made inroads into society, politics, government, education, movies, music, literature, and the legal system; how they have affected the relations between the sexes and the races. If this book does one useful thing, it will help to reinstate the virtues of common sense and informed, natural reason. Nothing in history is inevitable, and paranoia is no exception. Only a full and open debate over its causes and effects will stem its advance.

CHAPTER TWO

Politics,
Race, and
Electronic Culture

I F YOU'RE LOOKING for 1990s paranoia look no further than the TV comedy program *Seinfeld*. *Seinfeld* revolved around the experiences of the New York City resident Jerry Seinfeld, played by the stand-up comedian of the same name, and his friends Elaine, Kramer, and George. *Seinfeld* was popularly billed as the comedy program about nothing, but that's not quite true. It *was* about something. It was about paranoia. That an estimated 150 million North Americans tuned in to watch it each week speaks to the peculiar attraction the paranoid mentality exerts on the popular mind.

No *Seinfeld* character demonstrates this more than Jerry's close friend George Costanza. Brilliantly played by Jason Alexander, George is – to put it mildly – difficult to get along with. Only in the world of television sitcoms could someone like George actually have friends. Beneath his genuinely funny exterior, he's superbly suited for the paranoid 1990s. Living in a self-consciously psychological age, he has learned to doubt his own sanity.

Though he's able to function in society, he knows enough about psychiatry to suspect that he too is sick. As he tells Jerry in one episode: "Do you ever just get down on your knees and thank God that you know me and have access to my dementia?"

George swings erratically from one obsessional idea to another, seized either by fears that he is the consummate loser or by hilarious delusions of grandeur. He is suspicious, moody, short-tempered, anxious, manipulative, blundering, hostile, combative, competitive, self-hating. At the same time he's perpetually plotting to get dates, make a quick fortune, right some apparently egregious wrong, or evade the hysterical influence of his bizarre parents. When he does seem to succeed, his perverse personality ensures that whatever he touches ultimately turns to dross. He strikes the mother-lode by landing a job in the New York Yankees' front office, where he works for George Steinbrenner, a dysfunctional human being in his own right.

Lady Luck next shines on him when he meets and gets engaged to a rich and beautiful young woman. She dies after licking toxic wedding invitation envelopes he himself ordered because they were inexpensive. George's reaction? He hardly misses a beat, showing neither remorse nor disappointment. He displays both an uncanny emotional detachment from and an unhealthy obsessional interest in certain aspects of reality, the sign of a true psychotic. He shares with Jerry and his other friends what a psychiatrist has called "affective deadening," the inability to react to ordinary people and things. When he should feel guilty or desperately unhappy he shows almost no emotion. Yet insignificant things torment his mind. He is a fine example of a paranoid, able to function in everyday life but hamstrung by an extremely selective sensitivity. A true paranoid personality, he is always looking for hidden messages and meanings.

George is hardly alone on *Seinfeld*. Every episode depicts mishaps and misfortune that strike one or more characters in the show. Hopes are incessantly dashed. Carefully thought-out plans regarding money, sex, revenge, and power repeatedly go awry. Lurking in the background but ever ready to make an appearance are lesser-known characters like the tyrannical Soup Nazi; Newman, the disturbed and gleefully malicious postman; and Bania, the obnoxious stand-up comedian, to say nothing of George's own neurotic, bickering, and interfering parents. Together these characters constitute a small universe, a world calculated to subvert emotional stability. Their florid personalities, played to hilarious extremes by *Seinfeld*'s talented actors, make up the show's dark underside.

Of course, *Seinfeld*'s paranoid dimensions would prove nothing if similar themes did not pervade much of today's popular culture. *Seinfeld*'s characters resemble many of the other hapless and idiotic characters on other TV shows. Homer Simpson of *The Simpsons*, Hank Kingsley of *The Larry Sanders Show*, Matthew on *News Radio*: all evoke laughter thanks to imaginative scriptwriting. But in the cold light of day they are figures destined to do the wrong thing in a world geared to punish them remorselessly. They inhabit a paranoid universe that inevitably denies them gratification, which only drives them to scheme and obsess all the more. Fittingly, Homer Simpson has become a kind of Internet cult figure, with over 10,000 Webpages devoted to him. Fans wonder if the signature sounds he makes – such as his "Mmm's" – actually convey paranoid messages.

Even a comedy as seemingly innocent as *Friends* makes a similarly somber point. The six main characters float through life, in and out of relationships, apparently getting nowhere in either professional or emotional terms. The show self-consciously attempts to depict life as it appears to its many twenty-something fans who find the concept of a future problematic. Superficially, security and stability can be found living among like-minded friends. But the subliminal message of the show seems to be that nothing provides the real bedrock on which to ground a meaningful, productive existence. This marks the biggest difference between the early TV sitcoms of the 1950s and 1960s and the successful sitcoms of the 1990s. For Ralph

Kramden of *The Honeymooners* the lesson he seemingly had to learn in every episode was to renounce his big plans and accept his lot in life as a humble bus driver and loving husband. For the characters of *Seinfeld* and *Friends* there is no similar solution. No matter where they turn, their environment scuttles all their dreams and hopes. *Seinfeld*'s message is that there is no hope. There is no point embracing normality because normality is impossible in a paranoid world. It's the Cosmo Kramers and George Costanzas who stand a chance, if only because they have learned that the only way to survive in a paranoid universe is to be paranoid yourself, to indulge your delusions.

The theme of a menacing world looms larger in the popular "hard news" and tabloid shows of the 1990s, like *Hard Copy*, *48 Hours*, *Inside Edition*, and *America's Most Wanted*. These shows seek to describe what life is really like out on the streets but also, significantly, in the homes of the nation. The shows give the impression that there is no haven in a heartless world, to borrow Christopher Lasch's phrase. The dangers of society infiltrate the ostensibly safe precincts of our homes, disabusing us of one of our few remaining consolations: that we can erect barriers around our families and loved ones, protecting them from the threatening forces of society.

Like all paranoid delusions, this notion has some truth to it. With TV's 100-plus-channel universe and the Internet and its cybernetic world of innumerable messages, many of them unwelcome, society does indeed make its way into our intimate lives in ways that people could not have imagined half a century ago. In the words of the singer/songwriter David Byrne of the rock group the Talking Heads, turning on the TV means the world rushes into our living rooms. The Internet goes a step further than TV. It gives paranoids access to other paranoids around the globe and lets the paranoia of Internet addicts into our homes.

Movies too reflect the paranoia at the end of the millennium, especially the pervasiveness of conspiratorial thinking. The advertisement for the 1998 thriller *The Spanish Prisoner* read "Can You Really Trust Anyone?"

Appropriately enough, a summer hit of 1997 was Mel Gibson's *Conspiracy Theory*. "An idiosyncratic action picture," in the words of the *Vanity Fair* writer Cathy Horyn, *Conspiracy Theory* features Gibson playing "a half-nutball cabbie who sees spooks around every corner." The movie's story is based on the popular theory that assassins like Lee Harvey Oswald, the likely killer of John F. Kennedy, were part of CIA experiments. *Conspiracy Theory* picks up on a favorite Hollywood motif that stretches back at least to the Watergate era of the 1970s and movies like *The Parallax View*, *The Conversation*, and *All the President's Men*. The conspiracy theme never really died and continued sporadically up to the 1990s, perhaps best captured in Oliver Stone's overwrought conspiracy film *JFK* (1991). *JFK* single-handedly rejuvenated the national obsession with the Kennedy assassination. The fact that it was nominated for eight Academy Awards indicated that the film's conspiracist allegations made few in Hollywood blink. Stone is just another in a long line of Hollywood moviemakers since the 1960s who not only indulge the public taste for conspiracy theories but appear to believe in them as well. As Stone himself admits, "I've come to have serious doubts about Columbus, about Washington, about the Civil War being fought over slavery, about World War I, about World War II and the supposed fight against Nazism and Japanese control of resources... I don't even know if I was born or who my parents were." Stone goes a step further and celebrates the paranoid imagination. "Paranoids have the facts," he says seriously, codifying the popular late twentieth-century notion that in such a mixed-up world it both helps and is natural to be paranoid.

Paranoia has crept more subtly into other current popular films. The *Batman* series, including the evocative *Batman Forever*, emphasizes the dark and haunting elements in the old Batman story, carrying it well beyond a simple good-guy/bad-guy scenario and the campish, send-up *Batman* TV show of the 1960s. The 1990s Batman is a disturbed, haunted man with a traumatic past. He fights twisted, psychotic villains against the backdrop of a nightmarish, surreal Gotham City tyrannized by criminals and headed by impotent forces of law and order. Though *Batman, Batman Returns,* and *Batman Forever* have a tongue-in-cheek, even humorous quality, thanks in large measure to the performances of the actors Jack Nicholson, Danny DeVito, Jim Carrey, and Tommy Lee Jones, there is no mistaking their serious message. Their producer, Tim Burton, and the creative teams behind these films depict a dystopic world that mirrors the one in which many people believe themselves to live. It is a world in which democracy has failed, traditional political institutions no longer function, and personal freedom means license to terrorize fellow citizens. Nations are run by sinister individuals and agencies plotting to disenfranchise, impoverish, and control the common folk. In the frightening, lawless, and nocturnal atmosphere surrounding the Batman legend the millennial fears and apocalyptic anxieties of our society find popular expression.

The same could be said for TV shows like *The X-Files* and the aptly named *Millennium.* Both shows offer a brew of conspiracy, the occult, and the paranormal, elements that often intersect in today's paranoia. The third book of published *X-Files* scripts is entitled *Trust No One. The X-Files* spotlights the careers of two FBI agents, Mulder and Scully, who are assigned unsolved cases involving the supernatural. Many of their investigations deal with what fans of the series call "the Mythology." This is a plot to hide the truth about aliens visiting the Earth and the existence of a powerful organization dubbed "the Syndicate," which is secretly working with alien colonizers to produce hybrid alien-human clones. The show piles mystery on top of mystery, thanks to the presence of characters like Cancer Man, who may or may not be Mulder's father. Given its pervasive atmosphere of paranoia, it was only a matter of time before *The X- Files* dealt with the JFK assassination, arguably the favorite topic for conspiracy theories. Sure enough, a November 1996 episode featured an army captain who killed Kennedy on orders from his military superiors.

In *Millennium* a consultant with special mental powers works for an independent agency that investigates occult-like crimes. Fittingly, like Batman, he has been severely traumatized by horrors earlier in his life, enabling him to see things others cannot. In these programs the world increasingly takes on the appearance of a gigantic battle between right and wrong, good and evil, sin and innocence, light and darkness. Since the human psychological tendency is to take the side of persecuted righteousness in such struggles, it's little wonder that viewers respond to such storylines. Paranoia thrives in the "adversary culture" where estrangement, alienation, anger, fear, and suspicion abound.

In movies like *Pulp Fiction* (1994) the criminal underworld is populated by an outlandish cast of characters virtually running amok, beyond the reach of the law. But the movie that best mines this paranoid vein is John Woo's *Face/Off*, a box-office hit of 1997. *Face/Off* is the story of the epic conflict between a homicidal, maniacal, and utterly amoral terrorist, played by Nicholas Cage, and an anti-terrorist operative for the U.S. government, played by John Travolta. Set in modern-day southern California, the film conveys the widespread impression that post–Oklahoma City America is perpetually threatened by highly organized terrorists or criminals. In a macabre twist, *Face/Off*'s protagonists literally switch faces, leaving Travolta's character helpless as his terrorist foe assumes his identity. The reversal of roles plunges all the other characters into a horrific dilemma. No one knows who's who until a frenetic and violent final scene sorts things out. In the meantime suspicions, doubts, and fears multiply like germs. No one can trust anyone else.

A concept typical of paranoid popular culture is that government law enforcement agencies unwittingly aid the terrorist cause, underscoring the notion that, rather than being part of the solution, they are instead part of the problem. Paranoia has poisoned even the inner sanctum of the family. Wives can't be sure who their husbands are. Like Oliver Stone, children

can't be sure who their real fathers are. When the terrorist manages to infiltrate the government agent's family and encourages the daughter to take
drugs, *Face/Off* highlights the terrible fears that beset so many parents
today. The terrorist embodies the specter of adults unrestrained in their
physical desires, libidinously eyeing children, ready to destroy the civilities
families have tried so hard to erect. Because he's also a stranger who has
deviously penetrated the home, he further embodies the threat society poses
to these same parents who worry about the influence of drugs and pornography on their children. *Face/Off* ends as do many contemporary Hollywood
films, when private citizens take the law into their own hands to save their
families and their country.

Face/Off and movies of that ilk indicate that in paranoid, late twentieth-
century society North Americans distrust government. This distrust of government and politicians can lead to apathy on the part of the electorate, an
indifference born of resignation about what goes on in Washington or
Ottawa. People couldn't care less as long as it doesn't directly affect them.

But apathy isn't the only thing that stems from distrust of government.
A refusal to believe anything governments say is common. People are perpetually smelling a cover-up. A widespread view is that government is a
covert agency that is conspiring to make us miserable. Few across the political spectrum are immune to this demonization of government. In the minds
of some Americans government is out to enslave them. To others government
is literally out to kill them one way or another. Conspiracy theorists not only
refuse categorically to accept what the evidence suggests, they actually
believe that their form of reasoning is the normal and natural way to think.
Sean Lennon, son of the former Beatle John Lennon, told the *New Yorker*
magazine in April 1998 that the U.S. government was behind his father's
slaying in 1980. John Lennon, of course, was shot by Mark Chapman in
front of the singer's Manhattan apartment building. Chapman claimed he
was influenced by the J.D. Salinger novel *The Catcher in the Rye* and a

voice in his head telling him to "Do it! Do it! Do it!" Sean Lennon disagrees. His evidence? His father was "a countercultural revolutionary, and the government takes that kind of shit really seriously historically." In a leap of paranoid logic, Lennon jumps from that plausible statement to the unwarranted conclusion that this is proof the government must have killed him. Anyone who believes Chapman was "just some crazy guy who killed my dad for his personal interests is insane, I think, or very naive, or hasn't thought about it clearly." Sean Lennon has, so much so that he can't understand how others don't see what he sees.

Sean Lennon's suspicion about his father's death is hardly original. It derives from a form of theorizing dear to the counter-cultural left. It applies to the deaths of figures like JFK, Robert Kennedy, and Martin Luther King. The thinking goes something like this: all these people posed one threat or another to the status quo and died violently; therefore, they must have been murdered by a government conspiracy. The theory is extremely serviceable since it can be extended beyond political individuals to artists, musicians, and writers with cultural clout, like John Lennon. Lennon himself was paranoid enough to tell an activist in 1972 that if anything happened to him or his wife, Yoko Ono, it wouldn't be an accident. Supporters of Sean Lennon's theory argue that Chapman was a kind of CIA-controlled "Manchurian candidate," a reference to the 1962 film about Communist brainwashing that, significantly, enjoyed a revived popularity recently.

Even Bob Marley, the reggae singer who died of brain cancer in 1981, is the subject of a conspiracy theory. The CIA, it is alleged, injected Marley's toe with a secret carcinogen after he suffered a soccer injury in 1977. The motive? Marley sided publicly with Michael Manley, the anti-American Jamaican prime minister, rather than the CIA's favorite, Edward Seaga, who was far more friendly toward the U.S. Widely considered far-fetched, conspiracy theories about Marley's and Lennon's deaths drew little attention for years. Now, in the paranoid nineties, they're experiencing a second or third life.

Perhaps the most graphic example of conspiracist paranoia is the militia movement. The militias became notorious in the wake of the April 1995 terrorist attack on the Alfred P. Murrah Federal Building in Oklahoma City, an incident that killed 167 people. Timothy McVeigh, a former Army enlisted man, was arrested and eventually convicted of making and igniting the bomb responsible for the explosion. During his trial in 1997, information leaked out that McVeigh agreed with the views of the militia movement. Like many in the movement, he held the federal government responsible for the April 1993 assault on the compound of David Koresh's Branch Davidian cult near Waco, Texas. For fifty-one days the FBI and the Bureau of Alcohol, Tobacco, and Firearms laid siege to the ranch. When the siege ended, seventy-five of Koresh's followers were dead, including Koresh himself and twenty-five children. McVeigh's plot to blow up the Oklahoma City federal building was apparently devised in retaliation for the Waco fiasco.

The connection between McVeigh and the militias was strengthened during his defense attorney's final speech to the jury during the penalty phase of the trial. His lawyer hinted that sentencing McVeigh to death would simply provoke the Montana and Texas militias into unleashing more violence like that seen at Waco and Oklahoma City.

As of 1995 there were established militia groups in at least thirty-nine American states. They are made up of men and women convinced that elected politicians and their bureaucracies are part of a mammoth conspiracy to rob ordinary citizens of their rights and freedoms. A key freedom, the U.S. militias claim, is their right to bear arms as guaranteed by the Constitution. Without it, the militias insist, they are defenseless against the coercive powers of a government that, among other things, wants to alter the chemical composition of citizens' blood as a prelude to imposing a New World Order headed by the United Nations and funded by Jewish bankers. The militias compile what they think is overwhelming evidence that events such as the murder of Martin Luther King, Edward Kennedy's accident at Chappaquiddick, the death of Bill Clinton's friend Vincent Foster, and the JFK assassination are all linked. At the time of McVeigh's sentencing the militias even claimed the Oklahoma City bombing itself was a huge plot by the Clinton administration to crush them. Militia fax networks asserted that there were actually two separate bomb blasts, ten seconds apart, disproving the single-bomb theory. To the paranoid rumor-mongers on the World Wide Web, McVeigh was just another Lee Harvey Oswald, a hapless fall guy mixed up in a gargantuan government conspiracy.

The personalities behind the militias come alive in Michael Kelly's 1995 *New Yorker* article on Bob Fletcher, a breathtakingly bizarre member of a small, flamboyant organization called the Militia of Montana. Fletcher lives with other members of his militia group in the northwestern corner of Montana awaiting the coming apocalyptic confrontation with the forces of the New World Order. He expects that when the final battle occurs he and his militia allies will face as many as "one hundred million troops." "They'll come out of the ground! They'll come from submarines! They'll come from air drops! They'll come from everywhere!" he rambles in interviews. "I'm the same as everybody else in this country," Fletcher tells a reporter, "I got into this because I got screwed, big time."

Like Timothy McVeigh, who allegedly told his lawyers that the government had planted a surveillance microchip in his buttocks during the Gulf War, Fletcher claims to be a victim of government espionage and harassment; in Fletcher's case, he says, it's because he came close to the inside story about the Iran-Contra affair, when American arms were sold to Iran in order to finance the Nicaraguan Contras. But it would be wrong to imagine Fletcher as a paranoid perpetual loser, some homeless street person whose ravings evaporate unheard in the air. As late as 1990 he actually ran for Congress as a Democratic Party candidate in Florida. The fact that the Democratic Party was willing to back him illustrates clearly that Fletcher's brand of paranoia is a lot closer to the political mainstream than most imagine. Nor is it something limited to the fringes of the Republican Party.

The Democratic Party was also the chosen home for Fletcher's fellow political paranoid Lyndon LaRouche. Born in 1922, and originally a Marxist, LaRouche sought the Democratic nomination for the presidency in 1996. He appears frequently on public access television and has a well-used Website on the Internet. Political commentators agree that there is no unifying trope to his ideas other than his paranoia. He preaches conspiracy, pure and simple. In fact, his theories of conspiracy cast suspicion on so many people and things that his views may be *too* paranoid for his own credibility. As observers have noted, LaRouche spreads blame for the world's ills so far and wide that he fails to emphasize race, religion, and economic exploitation, the three "great engines of human conflict" beloved by conspiracy theorists.

LaRouche's and Fletcher's links to the Democratic Party belie the fashionable belief that political paranoids are to be found only on the so-called political right. This belief appeared in several editorials in the wake of the Oklahoma City bombing. Editorialists accused Newt Gingrich and other congressional conservatives of encouraging McVeigh and like-minded extremists to resort to violence as a political solution. The Republicans, of course, have their well-publicized examples of paranoia theorists in Pat Robertson and Pat Buchanan. Both men subscribe to variations on the same theme of a New World Order conspiracy being hatched and managed by the Council on Foreign Relations, the Trilateral Commission, the United Nations, the International Monetary Fund, and the like. Robertson kept most of his paranoid theories quiet during his run for the Republican nomination for the presidency in 1988, but in 1991 he revealed his thoughts in his book *The New World Order*. Still, the examples of Robertson, Buchanan, LaRouche, and Fletcher, as well as the presidential candidate Ross Perot in 1992 and 1996, confirm that paranoia is not the monopoly of any one political party or location on the political spectrum. It touches the hearts and minds of people with a wide variety of political views and allegiances.

Further evidence that paranoia crisscrosses customary political borders is the case of the Unabomber, Theodore Kaczynski, arrested in 1996.
"Unabomber" was the name U.S. law enforcement officials gave to the
person they suspected of a series of mail bombings that over some seventeen years killed three people and injured twenty-nine. Kaczynski, a
Harvard graduate, ended his promising career as a mathematician at the
University of California at Berkeley in 1969 when, without explanation,
he opted for the life of a recluse holed up in a six-by-six-foot cabin in the
wilds of Montana. In early 1998, to escape the death penalty, he pleaded
guilty to thirteen charges in exchange for a sentence of life imprisonment
without possibility of release.

Kaczynski might never have been caught if the *Washington Post* and the
New York Times hadn't published his 35,000-word manifesto in 1996. The
manifesto, the wording of which tipped off his brother that Kaczynski was
in fact the Unabomber, had all the marks of a paranoid mind. It was a
monotonous environmentalist diatribe full of grievances against modern
technology and reflected the lifestyle of its author, a grudge-nursing, wild-
haired man who had retreated from society and his family. Kaczynski was in
all likelihood certifiably mentally ill with paranoid symptoms; that was the
opinion of a court-appointed psychiatrist who diagnosed him as a paranoid
schizophrenic, much to Kaczynski's initial displeasure. In a courtroom
tantrum Kaczynski threw his pen while rejecting his lawyers' "mental
defect" defense. Like other paranoids, Kaczynski refused to disown his writings. He saw himself as a uniquely gifted seer, an inspired prophet with the
obligation to tell society it was going astray and needed to wake up before it
was too late. He too viewed the legal system as just another agency out to
persecute him.

The Unabomber case underlines what the Fabrikant case showed: out
of context, paranoids' grievances and protests have a certain uncanny
credibility. One of the names on the Unabomber's list of intended targets

discovered by the FBI was the Houston psychiatrist Stuart Yudofsky. Yudofsky, who studies the links between genetics and aggressive and violent behavior, never received a letter or mail bomb, but published references to his work had caught the Unabomber's eye. Yudofsky's research has troubling implications. Yudofsky himself has suggested that it may soon be possible to screen people who are biologically prone to violence and thus reduce the crime rate.

This specter of science interfering with the fundamental liberties of human beings is troubling to most citizens. Then again, so are the militias' concerns about the power of the state. The ineptness of the assault on the Branch Davidian compound was a good example of the way law enforcement personnel can badly mismanage a touchy situation. What set the paranoia of the Unabomber apart from the worries of ordinary men and women was the all-consuming interest he took in the topic, his senseless resort to violence, his desperate tone of urgency, and his perception that it was now or never to get his message across. Above all, it was his self-perception as a lonely, uniquely blessed prophet, destined to lead mankind to salvation by smiting the wicked. To the Unabomber, to most paranoids, the "power process" is shut off from the vast majority of people. As he wrote in his manifesto, "When one does not have adequate opportunity to go through the power process the consequences are ... boredom, demoralization, low self-esteem, inferiority feelings, defeatism, depression, anxiety, guilt, frustration, hostility ..." In that respect Kaczynski was no fool. He was not wrong that increasing numbers of people felt this way. But he was wrong that these sentiments were necessarily an accurate reflection of reality, an understandable reaction to society. And he was certainly misguided when he, like the militias, advocated violence as the only alternative left to the responsible citizen. His thinking was typical of how normally intelligent and well-educated people can begin with a reasonable idea and then spin out a fantastic chain of logic. Each stage in the logical sequence looks sensible, but in its entirety Kaczynski's mental process betrayed his extremism and detachment from reality.

THEODORE KACZYNSKI may have hated modern society, but modern society has provided a communications technology that serves paranoia brilliantly. The number of conspiracy magazines is grotesquely impressive; they include *Paranoia*, *Flatland*, *The New Federalist*, *Behind the Barricades*, *Conspiracy Update*, and *The Probe*. There are also publishing houses that traffic in conspiracy theories. For paranoia addicts there are computer databases and Internet addresses that dispense "information" that could variously be described as populist, survivalist, and anti-government. Electronic mail, discussion groups, and the World Wide Web are like heaven on earth for paranoids who with relative anonymity can transmit and receive all kinds of information. In such a huge electronic network the paranoid eventually finds what he's looking for and people he can talk to. This can be enormously gratifying as it helps to dissipate the loneliness and isolation paranoids acutely feel.

At the same time, though, the Internet reinforces countless delusions, including some of the most dangerous. In the United States, where the first amendment to the Constitution protects free speech, there are Websites for militia men and militia women, JFK assassination fanatics, Holocaust deniers, and hatemongers of all stripes. According to the Simon Wiesenthal Center, a prominent Nazi-hunting organization, in 1997 there were 600 racist sites on the Net, up from 300 in 1996. Among them were thirty-five American militia sites. The Anti-Defamation League in the United States puts the number of white-supremacy Websites alone at 250. Ernst Zundel, a Holocaust denier in Toronto, fled Canada's tougher anti-hate laws and moved his Website to California a few years ago.

The list doesn't stop with the lunatic fringe. Noam Chomsky, the celebrated linguist and radical leftist at the Massachusetts Institute of

Technology, who inveterately blames the U.S. government for every domestic and international crisis, has several sites on the Internet. With the tenacity of a real paranoid, Chomsky compulsively argues that there is a sinister purpose behind every American foreign policy. When he finds himself alone in his charges, he accuses the media of complicity in a U.S. government plot to cover up the facts. He still speaks before overflow campus crowds, as he did in September 1998 at the University of Calgary. In a long, rambling speech, Chomsky accused the United States of trying since 1945 to impose a "world order" designed to crush economic nationalism across the globe and serve the interests of "transnational corporations and the bureaucracies that they control."

Cyberspace enables paranoia to grow exponentially. Increasing numbers of predisposed minds tap into the information highway, and what happens next is a classical case of infectious paranoia. A conspiracy theory that might remain virtually unknown can become almost overnight not only well-known but accepted as fact. If it hadn't been for the Internet, for example, the theory that TWA Flight 800 had been shot down inadvertently by a U.S. Navy missile in July 1996 might never have seen the light of day. Thanks to the Internet and its enthusiasts, it became international news. Esteemed figures like Pierre Salinger, former press secretary for presidents Kennedy and Johnson (who also contends he caught his wife in bed with Robert Kennedy), defended this theory. Thus, in cyberspace people discover that many other individuals – some well-known – share their paranoia, removing doubts that such views were silly in the first place.

Conspiracy and cover-up themes on the Internet have also centered on the death of Kurt Cobain, Nirvana's lead singer, who was to Generation-Xers not unlike what John Lennon was to their parents. Cobain was found dead in 1994 in his home near Seattle with three times the lethal amount of heroin in his blood and a shotgun blast to the head. Sixty-eight fans were so distraught over the news of his death that they committed copycat suicides.

Since the day Cobain's body was discovered Internet sites have buzzed with discussions of the suspicious circumstances surrounding his death. In their 1998 book *Who Killed Kurt Cobain? The Mysterious Death of an Icon*, the Montreal-based writers Ian Halperin and Max Wallace added fuel to this paranoid fire. As Halperin and Wallace document, almost from the beginning of the investigation there had been rumors that Cobain had been murdered and that his widow, the actress and singer Courtney Love, was somehow involved. Though the police ultimately ruled his death a suicide, questions abound. Why were there no fingerprints on the gun? Why were there no fingerprints on the box of shotgun cartridges or on the pen used to write his farewell note? How could he have shot himself with enough heroin in his blood to render him unconscious within seconds? Suicide, or murder? Even the authors can't make up their minds. What is certain is that their book will do nothing to stop Internet addicts from speculating about the singer's death.

The tragic death of Diana, Princess of Wales, and Dodi Fayed in August 1997 also lit up the Internet with conspiracy theories. Paranoids tend to ignore most facts, focusing on anything that appears out of the ordinary. Conspiracy theorists pounced on the following: Diana's death was not reported until four hours after it happened; it took place underground, a convenient place to rig something to look like an accident; Diana had dispensed with her bodyguard while in Paris; the night she died witnesses reported hearing an explosion shortly before the screech of tires, but there was no mention of an explosion in subsequent media reports. Paranoids refuse to believe in accidents, so invariably they ask: Who benefits? The answers ranged from the Royal Family (the favorite culprits) to the arms industry to Diana's jealous allies in the campaign against land mines. Others claimed she faked her death to get out of the media spotlight and live in seclusion. In the Arab world, figures such as Libya's leader, Muammar Gaddafi, said the British and French secret services executed Diana and

Dodi Fayed "because they were annoyed that an Arab man might marry a British princess."

The paranoid possibilities of the Internet are plainly visible when it comes to stalking. The Net not only provides a medium through which stalking can be performed with relative ease, it also heightens fear of stalking by encouraging victims of stalkers to speak out. Stalking is a deliberate course of action that causes other people to be afraid, a favorite activity of lovelorn paranoids caught up in the delusions of erotomania. It can include verbal threats, letters and notes, repeated phone calls, hanging-up calls, hiding outside someone's home, and harassing the victim's friends, family, and coworkers. But "cyberstalking" is now approaching epidemic proportions too, in the form of online harassment carried out primarily via computer network communications. Net harassment shows up in unsolicited e-mail, chatrooms, Usenet postings, Webpage guestrooms. In response, anti-cyberstalking, self-help Websites have sprung up, like "Women Halting Online Abuse" (WHOA), which claims to offer "a safe cyber-room of our own." Though many anti-cyberstalking Websites stress that there are big differences between cyberstalking and simply rude or annoying behavior, the repetitious references to online harassment tend to confuse the two activities. A kind of panic ensues which merely stimulates further discussion and greater fears.

Paranoid trends have also been reinforced by the explosion of talk radio across the continent in the last decade or two. Paranoid talk radio has blossomed so much in recent years that Rush Limbaugh is now considered a moderate, compared with someone like Chuck Harder. As of 1995, almost 300 radio stations in the U.S. carried Harder's daily three-hour show titled *For the People*, up from a mere handful in 1987. More than fifty TV stations aired daily half-hour videotaped versions of his radio program. More than 40,000 listeners paid a minimum of $15 yearly to belong to his organization, also called For the People. In addition, Harder publishes a biweekly thirty-two-page newsletter. He calls his network "the workingman's PBS" and describes it as "non-partisan, middle of the road." "Our goal," he states, "is to save the middle class, save the little guy."

But Harder sounds suspiciously like Bob Fletcher. Among the guests Harder has welcomed to his show are Ken Adams, state information officer of the Michigan Militia, and Eustace Mullins, a Holocaust denier. Harder himself dispenses a steady stream of xenophobia and New World Order rhetoric that seems to play well with his largely rural and white audience. But his ideas reach out and touch minds beyond the political right. A regular guest on his show is Dr. Sidney Wolfe, a vehement enemy of the tobacco lobby and "one of the left's most ardent advocates," in the words of *The Nation*, a radical left magazine that ought to know. Harder not only has the consumer activist Ralph Nader on his show by phone each week, he has used muckraking material from *The Nation* to substantiate his conspiratorial theories. Though President Clinton is a frequent target of his derision, Harder has also slammed NAFTA and GATT and is no admirer of Bob Dole or Newt Gingrich.

Nor are the militias. Newt Gingrich is "part of the problem," declares Bob Fletcher. To the paranoid fringe, the leaders and members of the Republican "Contract with America" are in bed politically with the Rockefellers, the Freemasons, and the whole "eastern establishment" to outlaw the Constitution and build a New World Order. Gingrich's association with the futurists Alvin and Heidi Toffler and the fact that his half-sister is a lesbian feminist activist are often cited as evidence of his surreptitious liberalism and internationalism.

These recent signals of growing paranoia have convinced increasing numbers of commentators that, when it comes to paranoia, the old political categories of right and left no longer have any meaning. Michael Kelly has called this phenomenon "fusion paranoia." Lately, he writes, "views that have long been shared by both the far right and far left ... have come together, in a weird meeting of the minds." Consider the case of the American investigative reporter Seymour Hersh, a darling of the political left and the journalistic equivalent of Oliver Stone. Hersh won a Pulitzer Prize in 1970 after breaking the story of the My Lai massacre during the Vietnam War. He has won numerous other awards as a muckraking journalist. His books include one on Henry Kissinger's role in the downfall of Chilean president Salvador Allende in 1973 and another on the downing of Korean Airlines Flight 007 in 1983. Most of his journalism has been tinged with conspiratorial theories about skulduggery, cover-ups, and clandestine operations. When it came to My Lai he was right. Lately he's been more wrong than right. He was one of many prominent figures, including the journalist Christopher Hitchens and Hodding Carter, assistant secretary of state under President Jimmy Carter, who gave credence to the "October Surprise" theory about the 1980 presidential election. This theory alleges that Ronald Reagan struck a secret deal with Iran's leaders to keep American hostages in Iran until after the election, thereby scuttling Carter's electoral chances. It wasn't until a congressional inquiry found no evidence to support such a notion that its backers quietly retreated.

Hersh's most recent bestseller, *The Dark Side of Camelot* (1998), a searing look at John F. Kennedy in power, takes his paranoia a step further. JFK, Hersh writes, was an addict and a cheat who stole the 1960 presidential election, had been married before he wed Jacqueline Bouvier, cooperated with the Mafia, prolonged the war in Vietnam, and provoked the Cuban Missile Crisis of 1962. JFK's brother Bobby had an affair with Marilyn Monroe. There was more, but essentially Hersh writes that JFK was a president sullied by deep corruption and fraud.

Some of what Hersh says is unoriginal. Many of the "revelations" of *The Dark Side of Camelot* have been mentioned by other authors. What sets Hersh's account of the Kennedys apart is the unremittingly negative picture he draws of JFK and Robert Kennedy. He appears to be saying that everything bad you thought about the Kennedys was true. Thanks to his paranoid tunnel vision Hersh was unthinkingly willing to accept any piece of evidence discrediting the Kennedys. Not surprisingly, he ended up being royally duped by forgers who insisted they had documents proving that Monroe blackmailed JFK. Allegedly she agreed never to talk about her relationship to JFK, or his links to organized crime, in return for $100,000 per year for a trust for her deranged mother. The trouble was that these documents were bogus. If the producers of ABC Television hadn't had the documents checked themselves, Hersh would have gone on network TV to announce them.

Any other journalist, having been similarly deceived, might have paused to reflect on what he was doing. Not Hersh. He proceeded to write the book without the information. Predictably, his book drew innumerable hostile reviews. At least one reviewer likened him to Oliver Stone. Hersh, in retaliation, has used the paranoid's logic: if you don't agree with me, you must be out to get me. Thus, he's dismissed all objections as a pro-Kennedy conspiracy designed to stifle him.

Kelly's thesis of a "fusion paranoia" that links left and right makes even more sense when we compare militia rhetoric and the discourse of revolutionary student and black groups of the late 1960s. Indeed, the ancestry of a lot of today's paranoia can be traced back to that decade. The militias of the 1990s assert their territorial independence, their freedom from governments' policing powers, and their right to defend themselves with arms when governments send their troops in to reinforce these powers, as they did at Waco. The student radicals of the 1960s, like Tom Hayden, former husband of the actress Jane Fonda and now a California state senator, talked basically the same language. They similarly called for the establishment of "free territories" throughout the country, the harboring of fugitives from the law, and the paramilitary training of revolutionary activists dedicated to exporting revolution to the rest of American society. There was no mincing of words about the willingness of revolutionaries to use weapons to achieve their goal. They preached the violent overthrow of the "military-industrial complex" by waging "an American form of guerrilla warfare." "We are now facing a whole range of crises," a typical student revolutionary tract of 1970 read, "any one of which could permanently and profoundly alter the course of American history and threaten our individual lives and freedoms."

Revolutionary groups like the Weathermen and the Students for a Democratic Society (SDS) meant what they said. They kidnapped, held up banks, and planted bombs that took lives. Tom Hayden, meet Timothy McVeigh. The big difference between the two is that McVeigh's chances of becoming a state senator or marrying an acclaimed actress are considerably slimmer than Hayden's ever were.

Michael Novak, now a conservative theorist, remembers being appointed dean of students in 1968 at the State University of New York at Old Westbury. There, in the midst of the chaos that had descended on so many campuses across North America, the university administrators had abolished grades and curriculum requirements. Students were represented at every level of campus decisionmaking. But these concessions, paradoxically, seemed to fuel student radicalism. As student power waxed, belief in imaginary plots unaccountably flourished. "There was a sort of insanity on that campus," he recalled recently. "We had some psychologists stay with us and they just could not believe the paranoia. There were bomb scares; my children were threatened. People were living out radical fantasies, but since there were only radical students there, there was no one to rebel against."

A favorite tactic of radical students was the non-negotiable demand. Based on the delusion that one's political opponents were consumed with bad faith and ulterior motives, the non-negotiable demand rejected the possibility of compromise. Members of the SDS stressed the utter polarization of viewpoints. Their goal was to force people to choose among irreconcilable options. The only choices were utter capitulation or struggle to the death. The paranoid theory of polarization guaranteed that there could be no claims to political neutrality. But if there was no such thing as neutrality, no such thing as a barrier between the private and the public, then the personal was indeed the political.

Many today think that the cause of student outrage in the 1960s was the Vietnam War. But other countries like Canada, France, Italy, and Germany that weren't directly involved in the war had similar student rebellions. Clearly the generational factor was crucial: baby-boomers entered early adulthood during the sixties and headed off to college in unprecedented numbers. There they constituted a critical mass of young people facing almost no enemies other than what their own imaginations could conjure up. What exactly sparked these student revolts remains a matter of considerable debate. What is beyond dispute is their paranoid roots.

Others who witnessed campus antics during the 1960s came away with similar conclusions. Indeed, a comparison of today's paranoid vernacular with that of the campus radicals of the sixties and with that of Nazi students in 1930s Germany makes for sobering reading. The Nazi analogy may sound far-fetched; for too long people have tried, reprehensibly, to discredit opponents by associating them with Adolf Hitler. Clearly the student radicals of the 1960s were not admirers of Hitler's preaching. But there were paranoid elements common to both political movements, as Robert Bork argues in *Slouching Towards Gomorrah* (1996). The Nazi students who did so much to poison the politics and climate of ideas in German universities, like the New Left students of the sixties, believed themselves engaged in a titanic battle against a fundamentally unjust and corrupt "system." In both cases the system was supposedly propped up by a decadent but still resourceful parliamentary democracy. Being on the correct side in this struggle meant self-confidence in one's own righteousness and good will, no matter what furious tactics were employed, such as demonization of one's enemies. The New Left called police and the Nazi youth called Jews the same thing: "pigs." There was no middle ground possible. You were either part of the "movement" or you were irredeemably evil and benighted. You were either part of the solution or part of the problem. Like the Nazi youth, the sixties students had no positive or sharply defined vision of the future. They only knew they had to overthrow the "system." The very experience of revolution, in other words, was their aim. Violence, despite hippie lip service paid to "love," was glorified as part of this process. In the 1960s the "streets" were to be cleared for "the people." In the 1930s they were to be cleared for the brown-shirted battalions of the Hitler Youth.

Back in the 1960s black radical groups were preaching an equivalent message about independence, autonomy, and violence. White student radicals time and again sided with Black Panther activists like Huey Newton and Eldridge Cleaver. Leftist young whites either justified or hid the facts about Panther murders and sex crimes. They also averted their glances when Panther language turned anti-Semitic. The Panthers and their white allies openly expressed their admiration for Mao's Communist China and proclaimed the need for an independent "New Afrika" in the American South. This, they brazenly declared, could be achieved only through guerrilla warfare. America, leftist and Panther theory stated, was too rotten to be reformed any other way. Though hopelessly corrupt, it was still too powerful to change without armed insurrection. Like so much of sixties paranoid rhetoric, the black activists' discourse posited a world divided irrevocably between a white racist power structure and a totally victimized and innocent underclass. This underclass had finally recognized the dimensions of its oppression and was prepared to fight back with extreme measures.

If these paranoid themes sound familiar to readers in the late 1990s, they should. Despite data that document the socioeconomic gains of African Americans since the 1950s, paranoia has gripped many U.S. blacks as the millennium approaches. Ironically, black separatism and Afrocentrism are actually serving an inclusivist purpose. They're enabling blacks to assimilate into the paranoid mainstream of white America. In 1990 a poll of African-American New Yorkers revealed that 10 percent believed that AIDS "was deliberately created in a laboratory in order to infect black people." A further 19 percent said that it "might possibly be true." Another 25 percent believed the U.S. government "deliberately makes sure that drugs are easily available in poor black neighborhoods in order to harm black people." These data alarmed many observers, including black journalists. Clarence Page, a columnist for the Chicago *Tribune*, remarked: "There's a lot more talk about conspiracy than there used to be. You could call conspiracy theories about AIDS and drugs fringe ideas, but they seem to have a large following among the black intelligentsia. And it's present at the grass roots too. You find it at all levels." Many African Americans believe they live in a totally racist country. Camille Cosby, the wife of the comedian Bill Cosby and the mother of Ennis Cosby, murdered in 1998, accused America of teaching her son's killer – a Ukrainian immigrant – to hate blacks.

One of the earliest examples of African-American paranoia was the reaction to the assassination of the civil rights leader Martin Luther King Jr., murdered in April 1968 in Memphis, Tennessee. Though the consensus is that King was killed by James Earl Ray, who hoped to collect a $50,000 bounty allegedly offered by segregationists, King's family has never been persuaded that this was true. King's widow, Coretta Scott King, and her four children think that Ray was the pawn of plotters who included Lyndon Johnson, the FBI, the military-industrial complex, and the Mafia. In the past their efforts have led to three official investigations, including one by the House of Representatives in the late 1970s that lasted more than two years and cost over $5 million. In 1998, on the thirtieth anniversary of the assassination, Mrs. King requested a national commission of inquiry with the power to grant immunity from prosecution. What she got from Attorney General Janet Reno was an agreement to review new information and evidence.

Conspiracy theories surrounding King's assassination rely heavily on four points. The first is that it is hard for some to accept that such a formidable public figure, an emphatic opponent of the Vietnam War and passionate advocate of civil rights for blacks, could have been shot by the venal and amateurish Ray acting alone. Second, Ray pleaded guilty to escape the death penalty, his trial lasted only two hours, little evidence was presented against him in court, and he recanted his confession shortly after. Third, Ray insisted all those years that ballistic tests would show that the gun found at the murder scene was planted there to incriminate him. Finally, a lawyer acting on Ray's behalf has produced two handwritten notes that supposedly confirm the existence of the person Ray said was the real villain in the assassination. Though the FBI denies it vehemently, the lawyer accuses the agency of concealing this information.

Thus, a review by the U.S. Justice Department of allegations such as these would be most welcome, if only out of respect for Mrs. King and her late husband's legacy. Should the findings conflict with scenarios built on the reality of plots and counter-plots, however, it's unlikely that conspiracy theories about King's murder will end there. Not only do conspiracy theories help people make sense of terrible tragedies like the King and Kennedy killings, they also keep King's memory alive, an important consideration for America's black leaders.

While paranoid suspicions about King's murder have simmered over the years, black anger and resentment of whites exploded into full public view when the verdict in the criminal case against O.J. Simpson was announced in 1995. The trial itself should have stood as ringing proof of the folly of conspiracy theories. Instead it merely fed black paranoia. First, Simpson spent a fortune to assemble the best defense team money could buy. Then his defense team spun an elaborate conspiracy theory aimed at titillating the minds of a largely minority-group jury. Capitalizing on paranoid logic, which says all appearances can be discounted, his attorneys dismissed the prosecution's formidable forensic evidence that Simpson had murdered his ex-wife and her friend. The Los Angeles Police Department doctored the evidence, his attorneys alleged, because it wanted to frame Simpson. Why? Because of racial hatred. The vast majority of black commentators applauded his acquittal. Some argued that even if Simpson were guilty, his acquittal was justified as revenge for historical white unfairness to African Americans.

The Simpson affair was followed by the Million Man March to Washington, D.C. Organized by the Black Muslim leader Louis Farrakhan, whose anti-Semitic and Afrocentric views have been widely publicized, this spectacle was a further shock to white sensibilities. Farrakhan holds whites responsible for the deaths of literally millions of blacks, African and African-American alike. He traces the high rates of AIDS among blacks to white genocidal intentions. Jews, he claims, gave the world Communism, capitalism, and World Wars I and II. They financed Hitler, they dominate the media, and since 1932 they've controlled the White House. His followers in the Nation of Islam freely distribute the notorious *Protocols of the Elders of Zion*, cited the world over as proof of a Jewish conspiracy to rule the globe, but in actuality a forgery concocted by anti-Semites in France and Russia at the end of the nineteenth century.

Then in August 1996 the *San Jose Mercury News* ran a story that the CIA had condoned the sale of crack cocaine by Contra-connected Nicaraguan drug traffickers and thus was responsible for the widespread use of crack in south-central Los Angeles. The *New York Times*, the *Washington Post*, and the *Los Angeles Times*, three of the most reputable newspapers in the country, quickly investigated the story and dismissed its findings. But that didn't satisfy many black leaders, including Congresswoman Maxine Waters, a California Democrat. Even when the *Mercury News* pulled its reporter off the Nicaraguan drug story, she continued to harp on the notion of a CIA conspiracy. Waters, as fine an example of paranoia-mongering as there is, has also called the Los Angeles riots after a jury acquitted white policemen of beating Rodney King, a black man, a "civil uprising," and she charges the "white press" with trying to undermine the National Association for the Advancement of Colored People (NAACP). During the height of the debate in the U.S. House of Representatives on whether to impeach President Bill Clinton, Waters accused the "right-wing Christian majority" of "trying to take over this nation." When white female recruits at a U.S. Army training base in Maryland charged that two black staff sergeants had raped them, she called the women and the army officials who prosecuted the sergeants racist.

With her propensity to see racist conspiracies everywhere, Waters sounds suspiciously like a militia member. But before we write off Waters as a Bob Fletcher lucky enough to get elected to Congress, a marginal figure without political clout, it is worth knowing that her views on the *San Jose Mercury News* story were shared by African-American luminaries like Jesse Jackson and the comedian Dick Gregory. Waters is a member of the powerful House Judiciary Committee that voted to impeach President Clinton, much to her displeasure. In 1996 she was also named chairwoman of the Congressional Black Caucus. This promotion gave her a highly visible platform from which to launch her favorite debating weapon: accusations of racism.

The spate of church burnings across the United States between 1995 and 1997 highlighted the way people like Waters have made political paranoia on race issues respectable. Between January 1995 and May 1997, according to a federal task force, 150 burnings, bombings, or attempted bombings of houses of worship of all sorts took place. The task force discovered that black churches were not in the majority of those set afire, that racial bigotry was only one of several motives behind the incidents, and that no conspiracy was responsible. These findings confirmed what a handful of journalists had reported at an earlier date, including the fact that fires at both black and white churches had sharply *decreased* since 1980. Nonetheless, to people like Waters these crimes were part of a huge racist conspiracy, signaling a vicious new era in white violence against blacks.

Waters was not alone in her peddling of paranoia. Her eagerness to express outrage was shared by political figures like President Bill Clinton, Hillary Rodham Clinton, Vice-President Al Gore, and Abraham H. Foxman, the national director of the Anti-Defamation League, all of whom rushed to hasty and wildly inaccurate conclusions before all the evidence was in. Their consensus was that the burnings showed that America was dangerously close to undergoing its own Holocaust or a rash of ethnic cleansing on a scale comparable with the genocide in Bosnia or Rwanda. That they got away with this hyperbole proves that paranoia goes a long way in today's politics and is not localized in the woods of Montana or the plains around Waco. It also indicates how intimidating paranoid politicians have become. Staffers admit Waters's own Democratic Party is afraid that questioning her exaggerations simply invites accusations of racism. It's easy to see, then, why she and like-minded demagogues get away with paranoia in 1990s politics.

Much of the suspicion of white intentions that Waters exploits stems from the growing belief in the black community that integration as a solution to racial prejudice has been a failure. Black militancy over attempts to end affirmative action also reflects the loss of African-American faith in integration and the principles of race-blind, individual justice. During the 1990s more and more North Americans have come to realize that affirmative action (or employment equity, as it's also called) is unfair. Originally launched in the United States in the midst of the civil rights movement of the 1960s, affirmative action was designed to address black grievances over past racial discrimination in matters such as employment, promotion, government benefits and contracts, and school admissions and outcomes. These policies were clearly intended to be temporary. Senator Hubert Humphrey, one of affirmative action's original backers, assured skeptics that affirmative action would not discriminate against whites.

But affirmative action has proven to be neither temporary nor color-blind. If anything, its supporters today insist that it's needed more than ever. And despite vehement disclaimers from its admirers, affirmative action has been transformed from an outreach program to a quota program of racial preferences.

Affirmative action has enjoyed a remarkable persistence since its inception. Bureaucracies created to enforce it have tenaciously erected an elaborate theoretical edifice that until recently has succeeded in disguising its shortcomings. The theory states that women and minorities have suffered relentless, systemic discrimination. Like many paranoid belief systems, this one has some basis in historical reality. But paranoid theories of history are unremittingly one-sided and fail to recognize that the past is not monolithic nor seamless. History simply can't be reduced to a battle between the victimized good and the victimizing bad. Nor can history's conflicts be settled by the kind of social engineering favored by those enamored of paranoid interpretations of the past. Paranoid theories about history are usually based on some facts; their exquisite selectivity is what enraptures their followers.

Such is the case with affirmative action. Its supporters ignore the advances made in the last few decades by the very groups who continue to benefit from it. First-hand experience with both the individuals and the mechanisms responsible for enforcing affirmative action says otherwise. Practice teaches that it rapidly ends up rewarding those who aren't discriminated against by penalizing innocent individuals who have never discriminated.

The paranoid elements in the affirmative action movement are all too evident in the way its members turn on those blacks who dare to question it. One black who has challenged affirmative action is the California businessman Ward Connerly. As a regent of the University of California, Connerly led the successful campaign to end race- and gender-based affirmative action policies throughout the state's publicly funded university system. An indication of how skewed these policies were is the fact that in the first year without affirmative action at U.C. Berkeley's law school, black admissions fell by 81 percent and Hispanic admissions by 50 percent. Clearly, until then underqualified candidates had been admitted in large numbers. Connerly then spearheaded the fight to get Proposition 209 – which called for the end of affirmative action throughout state and local government and education – on the ballot in California in 1996. Californians endorsed Proposition 209 by 54 to 48 percent. Over the course of this campaign Connerly was the butt of vicious attacks, especially from other blacks. Journalists, cartoonists, and civil rights leaders called him an "Uncle Tom," a "lawn jockey," a "front man for the white right," or an ally of the former Ku Klux Klansman David Duke. In the heated, paranoid world of demonizing racial politics, Connerly is a traitor to his race. But which race? Connerly himself is of African, French, Irish, and Choctaw descent and is married to an Irish-American woman. Their son is married to a Vietnamese American. "What racial box on the university admission form is their child supposed to check?" he asks.

Racially oriented affirmative action is just one chapter in an ongoing paranoid drama that has enveloped the black community in America. For example, in December 1996 the school board in Oakland, California, unanimously approved a two-page resolution declaring black English, or Ebonics, a formal language. The announcement was greeted by howls of protest from various groups and individuals, including some blacks.

Ebonics is typical of the paranoid 1990s, but it's hardly new. Like so many of today's paranoid beliefs, the idea behind Ebonics has been around since the 1960s. It's been taught to California black students since 1989. Ebonics is defined as the teaching of the mother tongue of African Americans at the elementary, secondary, and post-secondary schools. It's taught not as a bridge to English for disadvantaged black children but as a language in its own right. It essentially legitimizes what passes today for the vernacular spoken by many black children and adolescents. Teachers are encouraged to use "rap" diction and "playin' the dozens" (black male verbal confrontation) in classrooms, praising students by shouting "Shonuff" and "Ooooo-weeee," and favoring "mumble reading." In Ebonics, students' language skills are never questioned as long as students do not protest. But then, what child would want to?

Ebonics is based on the argument from history. African language systems, the Oakland school board resolution reads, "are genetically based and not a dialect of English." Ebonics enthusiasts insist that when African slaves came into contact with English-speaking groups in the American and Caribbean worlds they did not adopt the language of their oppressors. Instead, they created a distinctive language from their own west African linguistic traditions. Race, in other words, is destiny.

Ebonics is simply a slightly updated variation on the theme of black separatism, another self-congratulatory myth that pits African Americans against white Americans and "Eurocentric" ideologies. Ebonics is poised to replace the now-discredited myth Alex Haley constructed in his 1967 bestseller *Roots*. Today we know that Europeans were just one interested party in a mammoth intercontinental slave trade that included Muslims and black African chieftains. We also know about black ethnic cleansing against other blacks in Congo, Rwanda, Nigeria, and Sudan. Thus, it's hard to believe in Haley's view of an idyllic pre-colonial Africa or in an Africa today whose peoples are united among themselves and tied spiritually to American blacks thanks to a common race and culture. Afrocentrism is another of today's several paranoid myths that parade as serious, scholarly interpretations of history.

It may be true, as the American author Jim Sleeper has argued, that black "race consciousness" deludes Americans into ignoring "the quest by black Americans for acknowledgment and belonging in our national life." He calls it "the most powerful epic of unrequited love in the history of the

world." Perhaps. But like all race-based ideologies, Ebonics exerts a myste-
riously magnetic attraction on the human mind. The tragedy of black racial
consciousness is that it also builds on the paranoid perception that a group's
self-identification rests on its implacable and irreconcilable differences from
another racial group.

The paranoid rhetoric of identity-group politics hasn't been used to
serve just African-American purposes. Gay activist groups too have learned
how to play the paranoia card by exploiting fears of AIDS. When AIDS first
emerged in the early 1980s its high incidence among male homosexuals
triggered a campaign of denial among gays. They were particularly aggressive in trying to silence any efforts to draw attention to the data that highlighted this link. Gays lobbied furiously to foil attempts to screen donors for
HIV-positive blood. They generally tried to ignore the stark realities of the
disease. When the facts became impossible to deny in the mid-1980s, gay
activists, in conjunction with some epidemiologists, began changing their
tune. The message was altered to read: everyone is at risk from AIDS and it
will soon be the plague of the century. Those who continued to insist on
more than a casual connection between homosexuality and AIDS were sometimes subjected to virulent protests. In December 1989 ACT-UP (AIDS
Coalition to Unleash Power), a radical gay group, interrupted Mass at St.
Patrick's Cathedral in New York City by shouting down John Cardinal
O'Connor during his sermon with cries of "Murderer." On another occasion
ACT-UP demonstrators interrupted the ordination of priests in Boston by
pelting a newly ordained priest and his elderly mother with condoms.

Were AIDS activists discredited by these antics? Quite the opposite.
Funding for research into AIDS escalated, thanks to celebrities like Elizabeth
Taylor and events like "walks" for AIDS. At the 1994 Academy Awards cer-
emony the actor Tom Hanks, accepting an Oscar for his role in the movie
Philadelphia, wept while referring to AIDS victims as "angels in heaven." By
1997 funding for AIDS research at the National Institutes of Health was

US$1.5 billion, second only to cancer ($2.2 billion) and exceeding the amount spent on heart disease ($1.4 billion). Never in the history of disease has so much been done so quickly with so little gratitude.

In 1997 it was also clear that the predictions made over a decade earlier remained unfulfilled. No AIDS epidemic has occurred in the United States or Canada. In 1995 twelve times more Americans died of cancer and seventeen times more of heart disease than died of AIDS. In Canada, AIDS-related deaths have probably plateaued; AIDS is in eleventh place among the causes of death, behind cancer, heart disease, motor vehicle accidents, and diabetes. The average Canadian is as likely to die in a commercial air crash as die of AIDS. "The plain fact," writes the *Globe and Mail,* "is that not all North Americans are equally at risk." But Ottawa's Federal Centre for AIDS keeps telling Canadians that heterosexuals, along with homosexuals, intravenous drug users, and hemophiliacs, are equally at risk to contract AIDS.

Thus, the debate over AIDS these last two decades reveals the respectability of paranoia-mongering. On hot-button issues we are remarkably tolerant of not just exaggeration but outright falsehood. Even when we know better, we seem prey to arguments that reduce complex matters to simplistic tropes. Good versus evil, them versus us: these are concepts ideally suited to a society that likes to think in apocalyptic, millenarian terms.

The same could be said for diseases other than AIDS. Indeed, there is a culture of alarmism that envelops the whole issue of epidemic illness in today's society. Books like Richard Preston's *The Hot Zone* (1994) and Laurie Garrett's *The Coming Plague* (1994) and movies like *Outbreak* have spread the fear that a huge, global series of infectious epidemics is impending. Citing evidence of new antibiotic-resistant diseases localized in the jungles of Africa, some virologists are predicting a Black Death–like calamity. Others are more cautious, but even they are uneasy. As the Nobel Prize–winning biologist Joshua Lederberg asked in Garrett's book: "Are we better off than we were a century ago? In most respects we are worse off. We have been neglectful of the microbes and that is a recurring theme that is coming back to haunt us."

Like most anxieties Lederberg's is not bizarre. Disease control authorities in Western countries have to be vigilant about lethal viruses escaping from laboratories or jumping from animal hosts to human beings. These things have already happened and potential disasters have been averted only by public health officials using extreme measures. But the notion that we are worse off today can't stand the light of empirical evidence. If the wars against illnesses like cancer and heart disease have produced only modest victories after decades of enormous spending on research, perhaps it's because we mistake the struggle to cure disease as a war in the first place. When we do, we succumb to plague paranoia. If we imagine ourselves in such a war it's easy to become defeatist, to resort to the environmentalist explanations of Laurie Garrett. In her otherwise fine book she contends that the headline-grabbing viruses of the past twenty years can be blamed on human irresponsibility. Like the fundamentalist preacher who claims God is using AIDS to punish homosexuals for their sins, Garrett thinks the "coming plague" is our just deserts for destroying the globe's rainforests and jungles. In her view microbes existed harmoniously with natural and human hosts for centuries. Then rapacious human beings upset this idyllic balance with encroaching civilization. In other words, we deserve everything we get. We are a species that is little more than a parasite on the planet. Our fate is no more worthy of consideration than that of the cockroach. As Malcolm Gladwell wrote in *The New Republic*, this alarmist "new virus paranoia" is "a terrifying super-virus of our own creation, a mutant hybrid of cold war apocalyptics, biblical moralism and environmental fire and brimstone."

Such sensationalism about millenarian scenarios gradually wears down our defenses against the deep-rooted human tendency to indulge paranoia. Whether the warnings are about a New World Order, government takeovers or cover-ups, imminent holocausts, or plagues, we are bombarded left, right, and center, making it hard to detect paranoia. Our threshold for tolerating paranoia has dropped steadily in recent years. At the same time, our critical ability to extract the kernel of truth from paranoid theories dwindles. So when the more benign forms of apocalyptic paranoia come along, we fail to see them for what they are.

This certainly applies to the current interest in "self-esteem" approaches to education as well as the rage for psychological therapy and spiritual healing. Under scrutiny, these matters, the topic of the next chapter, prove to be an integral part of the age of paranoia.

CHAPTER THREE

Brought to Heal

IN 1996 a conference was held at the Omni Shoreham Hotel in Washington, D.C. Attended by close to 2,000 people, it was called the National Summit on Ethics and Meaning. Sounds innocuous enough. Yet despite its rather bland title this conference mirrored the millenarian paranoia that has infiltrated even middle-class liberalism. It was organized by the left-wing Jewish magazine *Tikkun*, founded and edited by Michael Lerner, a rabbi and practising psychotherapist. Lerner began as a theology student at Columbia in the 1960s. The trajectory of his life since then confirms that much of today's paranoia began amidst the turbulent counter-cultural politics of the 1960s. Indeed, Lerner's life and career form a kind of bridge between the paranoia of those years and the more subtly paranoid ideologies of the 1990s. The National Summit on Ethics and Meaning showed how good intentions and a sincere desire to explore human spirituality have been hijacked in recent years by unreflective paranoia.

Back in the 1960s, Michael Lerner was on the West Coast at Berkeley, positioned squarely within the paranoid maelstrom. His life as a student radical is an uncomfortable reminder of just how campus activism, the sixties drug culture, and political paranoia went hand in hand. As he told David Horowitz, a fellow radical at the time: "You *have* to take LSD. Until you've dropped acid, you don't know what socialism is." Lerner founded the Seattle Liberation Front, an organization dedicated to insurrection and the overthrow of what he called the "hopelessly imperialist" American state. When his sister married, the guests included the California governor and the state's senior senator. Lerner disrupted the wedding ceremony with a speech accusing the guests of murder because they had failed to prevent the Vietnam War. He then turned around and married the daughter of a military man. At *his* wedding the bride and groom exchanged rings made from the fuselage of a downed U.S. aircraft and on the wedding cake was the inscription "Smash monogamy." The marriage was over in a year.

Lerner, however, didn't disappear like so many of the political activists of the 1960s. He just changed the key to his political tune. After marrying a Safeway heiress he used much of her fortune to found *Tikkun*, its name a Hebrew word meaning "to heal and repair the world." In 1992 he enjoyed brief fame when Hillary Rodham Clinton used his phrase "the politics of meaning" in a speech. Lerner had urged the Democratic Party to recapture its old electoral support by combining politics and spirituality. The Clintons, when justifiably lampooned by the press for trumpeting such an amorphous term, abruptly dropped "the politics of meaning." Undaunted, Lerner condemned them for their "betrayal." He has since tried to remain at the center of political life by organizing meetings such as the National Summit on Ethics and Meaning. The impressive turnout at the conference shows that his message touches many Americans.

The trail leading back from "the politics of meaning" to Lerner's participation in the political paranoia of the sixties is a lot more trodden than some might think. Lerner remains convinced of the central tenets of radical leftism. He still promotes the view that America and Nazi Germany have an "uncanny resemblance." Like a good Marxist, he still blames capitalism – or what he now calls the "market system" – for America's problems. America, he claims, is no less in crisis in the 1990s than it was in the 1960s.

But his current philosophy is a classic case of old wine in a new bottle. Whereas in the sixties he emphasized politics and economics, in the 1990s it's psychology. As his critics note, in his transition from New Left, neo-Marxist activist of the sixties to New Age psychobabble therapist of the nineties he has replaced economic determinism with a psychological-spiritual determinism every bit as rigid and simplistic. Lerner's new twist is that Americans must first address the spiritual side of the country's malaise. Spiritual values are in steep decline and human relationships in tatters. The "legacy of patriarchy" weighs heavily on us all. All Americans, he claims, are in terrible emotional pain because of the global market. Each one of us harbors a "wounded inner child" who acts out the pain inflicted on us by a hostile, uncaring, and "militantly anti-meaning" world. As one participant at Lerner's conference said, America is "a dysfunctional family in denial." America is a nation of victims.

What Lerner proposes for making America more "functional" is never made clear. In the politics of meaning there is a lot of vague talk about "honoring loving behavior" and communities "re-assuming moral responsibility." But mostly what he and his associates serve up is New Age therapeutic ideas mixed with the kind of liberal reforms that tempt with anodyne superficiality, such as thirty-hour workweeks and a year's paid leave for all new parents. His therapeutic politics attracts countless men and women who think that "healing" will solve political problems. According to Lerner, if there had been a "politics of meaning" in Nazi Germany, there never would have been a Holocaust. All Germans needed was a good therapist (presumably like Lerner), and we could have avoided World War II and the Final Solution.

To Peter Marin in *Harper's* magazine the summit featured "some of the worst nonsense I have come across in more than forty years of listening to people in public places butcher truth and sell themselves to others." But that of course isn't the point. Lerner may be in the grip of delusions of grandeur. In their haste to self-promote, he and his ilk may lapse into unintentional self-parody. They may in fact marginalize themselves eventually. The deeper condition remains, however. All over Canada and the United States otherwise sensible people are responding to the same basic messages, as any trip to a bookstore these days would prove. New Age ideas are flourishing on both sides of the border, from one coast to another. What was once chiefly associated with the West Coast has now become as American as apple pie, as Canadian as back bacon. New Age ideas don't attract just the uneducated and the poor. Their followers are often educated and affluent men and women. One New Age bookstore manager in Toronto claims that the movement blossomed in the 1990s largely because the baby-boomer generation realized the materialism of the 1980s wasn't enough. When baby-boomers realized that accumulating material products made them feel that something was missing, they acknowledged that personal and spiritual growth was more important to them. As a result the New Age industry is thriving. Sales of amulets, crystals, tarot cards, and talismans have never been better.

New Age trends span a broad range of seemingly different beliefs, including astrology, numerology, "magick," hypnosis, witchcraft, and energy fields, but they are united by a belief in the paranormal and supernaturalism. New Agers buy books about levitation, teleportation, star-walking, and alien encounters. Reincarnation is also a hot topic. "Channelers" tell their clientele about past lives, some lived in other planetary systems. Other psychics confide they are being guided by races of aliens. According to leading figures in the New Age movement, like Dr. Deepak Chopra (an MD who doesn't possess a license to practice medicine in California, his home state), external reality is an illusion. Physical, material things like the body and money are subject to the power of positive thinking. Drawing heavily on Eastern religions and philosophies, people like Chopra promote the view that the only reality is spiritual or metaphysical. The material world is an obstacle to our happiness and prosperity and needs to be surmounted.

New Agers, obsessed with health, have imbibed Chopra's message. Many are baby-boomers reaching middle age, a time when afflictions arise to remind them of their mortality. The jogger who develops bad knees, the sunbather who begins to discover suspicious-looking moles, the fashion-conscious woman who can never be thin enough, the former ladies' man who becomes impotent, the bathhouse habitué who one day finds out he has AIDS: these and other stories help to explain why so many are paranoid about their own bodies. Once upon a time we were taught that our bodies were part of the created and hence sacred world, something awesome and mysterious. In a cosmic sense they really belonged to our Creator. Then we were taught by sexologists that our bodies were special because they belonged only to ourselves, there for our pleasure. Now we are being taught the need to "strategize" the management of our bodies through medication, therapy, support groups, and the like. Otherwise they will turn on us. The media reflect this theme by bombarding their audiences with countless "personal interest," health-related stories. Whether it's the politics of breast cancer, AIDS, or chronic fatigue syndrome, the subliminal messages are conspiratorial: something or someone is to blame. It's either advertising or organized medicine or toxic environments or social attitudes that harm us. Our bodies have been transformed into foes to be conquered through technocratic means, such as genetic engineering, physician-assisted suicide, cosmetic surgery, or drugs like Viagra. Or our bodies have become obstacles to spiritual perfection from which we must escape by literal or figurative neutering. Either way, there's been a swing away from the blissful unconcern about our bodies of only a few years ago to paranoid distrust and loathing of our "temporal vessels." Society has gone from the Kinsey Report and Masters and Johnson to the bizarre sexlessness of Heaven's Gate.

New Age claims address this fear of the body with often bizarre and extreme claims. Trading on the well-documented placebo effect, which says the mind can influence physical healing, New Agers contend that HIV and cancer can be cured through meditation and blind faith. One Website actually claims that electronic data about homeopathic remedies stored in a computer can somehow be transferred into containers that normally hold pills or liquids. Psychic healers teach their followers that by recovering the histories of their past lives they can end cycles of abuse and patterns of dysfunctional behavior. Like Michael Lerner, they hold out the hope that war, poverty, and injustice can be eradicated if only people heed their inner children. New Age psychology emphasizes "recovery," "healing," "addiction," and "self-esteem." People respond to the sermon that we are all damaged emotionally by others, that our pain is never due to our own weaknesses, mistakes, cruelties, or insensitivity. If we have a fault, it's that we can't say no to others. The task lies in learning to say no, to love ourselves and destroy the co-dependency that threatens to devastate us emotionally. We are enjoined to turn inward and rediscover the spiritual spark within us, the happy, innocent "inner child." Journeying into our souls will make us god-like and give us the power to cure our troubled souls. If nothing else, it will put meaning back into our humdrum lives. It will remind us of our childhood fantasies of power and encourage us to believe we can recapture them from those who stole them from us long ago. To critics like the Canadian journalist Donna Laframboise, New Age holistic philosophy is for "the individual finding easy gratification, rather than sacrificing and selflessly labouring for a better world." It is "the perfect self-delusion for the spoiled brat of any age, all decked out in the latest fashion, who loves to talk about solving the problems of the world but has no intention of sweating a drop in achieving this noble goal." Such a criticism is too broad, of course, for it demeans many in the movement who work hard for worthwhile objectives. But it applies to enough in the movement to make it an apt description.

Beneath almost every variation of New Age psychology is, first, the delusion that we are all persecuted remorselessly, that others work to make us unhappy; and, second, the delusion of grandeur that marks so many cases of genuine paranoia. New Agers like Lerner mimic what clinical paranoids do. They create in their imaginations what the psychiatrist Norman Cameron calls a "pseudo-community." A pseudo-community is "an imaginary organization, composed of real and imagined persons, whom the patient represents as united for the purpose of carrying out some action against him." The notion of a pseudo-community engaged in malevolent activities actually flatters the paranoid's feeling of centrality, the sense that he or she is a reference point, the object of compelling interest to others. With the creation of the pseudo-community the paranoid experiences a moment of epiphany. He or she sees how everything fits into place, how everything "clicks," how otherwise innocuous things, such as a stranger's glance or a wrong number on the telephone, become immediately charged with significance. In the paranoid's worldview there are no accidents. For the paranoid the personal is emphatically the political. In Lerner's politics of meaning, our paranoid tendencies aren't just reinforced, they're celebrated. We are told we are indeed special, worth the attention of others, worth the trouble of persecuting.

Nothing flatters the paranoid mentality and its taste for indulgent self-vindication like the "self-esteem" movement in education. Before the 1990s researchers noticed that those who succeeded in life tended to feel good about themselves. Convinced of the link between achievement and self-esteem, educators imagined the process could be reversed. They thought that if self-esteem became a goal in itself, high-level performance would follow. Armed with self-esteem, students would do better, employees would work harder, and women who felt inferior because of poor body image or substandard math scores would conquer their phobias. In her 1992 book *Revolution From Within* the feminist Gloria Steinem gave the whole movement a plug when she extolled the virtues of self-esteem, claiming it determined not only academic and occupational performance but the rise and fall of nations as well. Before long library and bookstore shelves were groaning from the weight of self-esteem books. As the American psychologist Joseph Adelson remarked in 1996, when he dropped in at his local library to see if they had a few titles on self-esteem, he discovered forty-one. When he went to a mega-bookstore for the same purpose he found forty-nine *shelves*, "each three feet long, holding altogether at least 1,000 separate titles. Almost all were less than five years old, and almost all offered practical help: how to protect your self-esteem, improve your self-esteem, repair your self-esteem; seven steps, ten steps, twelve steps to a better view of yourself; self-esteem through physical fitness or a more balanced diet; how women should deal with men who damage their self-esteem; how to guarantee the self-esteem of your children; how to recover self-esteem after losing your job, or your fiancée, or your spouse." For all the opportunism that accompanied and sustained this trend, somebody was reading these books. And whoever was reading them was attuned to their paranoid message that the only thing that stood between them and unbridled success was the failure of others to recognize their brilliance.

The sorry history of self-esteem programs since the movement's heyday in the 1980s proves that most of self-esteem theory was founded on a pipe dream. Standardized educational test results continued to plummet and student behavior remained as unruly as ever. The anxious efforts of educators to instill an uncritical self-esteem in students only emboldened those with paranoid tendencies to think more highly of themselves. Instead of self-confidence we got self-congratulation, undue estimations of self, delusions of grandeur. As befits an enterprise that tries to put paranoia into practice, the entire self-esteem movement is tottering as the 1990s come to a close. Despite its many good intentions, the self-esteem movement stands as a perverse monument to the acceptance of paranoia among professional groups whose experience and expertise should have told them otherwise. Trying to shore up self-esteem plays right into the hands of the paranoid, who has self-esteem to burn. Any glance at the parade of "self-esteeming" people on a typical daytime talk show will tell us that.

Central to the doctrine of self-esteem and all New Age psychology is the therapeutic sensibility, the emotional hunger for healing and its seeming power to deliver us psychic, personal well-being. Most therapy tends to do nothing to disabuse paranoids of their delusions; instead it congratulates paranoids on their special insights. In therapy the paranoid finally realizes that each one of us has been abused. Each one of us is a victim. Therapy is intended to accept this version of things as a literal fact. Therapy becomes merely another stage in the paranoid's process of erecting a delusional system of thought. Self-glorification follows as day follows night. It is no coincidence that New Age psychology engenders in many people a belief in the supernatural, in out-of-body experiences, near-death experiences, and alien abductions.

Under the therapeutic guise of restoring esteem we are taught to be ever vigilant about the people and things around us, to suspect something is going on out of sight, to smell conspiracy everywhere, to covet what our putative enemies possess, to deny our own foibles and mistakes, and to project our own guilt and self-doubt onto others. It's the ultimate exercise in scapegoating. In our manic efforts to stop blaming ourselves we blame everyone else. We lose the critical ability to recognize when the personal is *not* the political, when our own pain and dissatisfactions aren't anyone else's fault. When we lose this ability, clinical psychiatry reminds us, the paranoid himself turns into the persecutor. Perhaps the greatest tragedy of contemporary New Age psychology is that it accelerates this process, laying the groundwork for that favorite pastime of the inquisitorially minded: witch-hunting.

The paranoid slope of New Age psychology is indeed slippery. It takes us past 1990s phenomena that range from the mildly amusing, through to the quirky and bizarre, and ultimately to the tragic and downright lethal.

It's a ride that gives us glimpses at the UFO craze, the recovered memory movement, multiple personality syndrome, cults like Heaven's Gate and the Solar Temple, and court cases involving alleged satanic abuse. Each of these movements has a distinctive quality, but all are united by some basic characteristics. All start with the entrenched assumption that we are a society of victims. All mirror the self-pitying, world-denying, recovery-seeking craze that has swept North America in recent years. Books like Charles Sykes's *A Nation of Victims* (1992), Wendy Kaminer's *I'm Dysfunctional, You're Dysfunctional* (1992), and Robert Hughes's *Culture of Complaint* (1993) have all blown the whistle on this trend, but that hasn't yet stopped it.

The thirst for recovery, for example, has hit the airwaves in a big way. On April 23, 1997, the Recovery Network went national on cable television in the United States. "The plan is to be a twenty-four-hour-a-day, seven-day-a-week lifeline into the community," proclaimed the network's chief executive officer. The network is designed to appeal to the millions of Americans convinced they are addicted to something and to persuade all the others they are in denial. "The size of the problem is so staggering, it clearly deserves its own bandwidth," said the CEO. Indeed, it's hard not to share its executives' enthusiasm when one reads down the list of problems the network will cover: drugs, alcohol, sex, depression, obsession, eating disorders, compulsive gambling, family violence. And the network practices what it preaches: some 60 percent of its employees are themselves in recovery. Ruth Shalit, writing in *The New Republic*, says the network's slogan should be "All recovery, all the time."

The Recovery Network, of course, wasn't the first medium for the victimization movement. TV talk shows preceded it, providing viewers with a cavalcade of guests claiming to be victims of a seemingly endless list of disorders. The syndromes of victimization include marital rape, acquaintance rape, date rape, gay-bashing, elder abuse, sibling abuse, peer abuse, emotional abuse, telephone abuse, clergy abuse, satanic ritual abuse, sexual abuse, sexual harassment, sexual addiction, eating disorders, post-traumatic stress syndrome, multiple personality disorder, chronic fatigue syndrome, credit-card dependency, co-dependency, dysfunctional families, hate crimes, battering, stalking, drunk driving, and UFO abductions. Singly, each of these syndromes causes emotional or physical pain to someone. Taken together, they underscore the propensity of people today to designate themselves as victims.

TV talk shows provide journalists, academics, actors, victims' advocates, and health care personnel with a forum to discuss victimization. An entire industry has grown up around the idea of victimization. Victimology has emerged as a specialty within the social and medical sciences, with its own professional societies, textbooks, and journals. Not the least guilty party in the creation of a victimization industry is the psychiatric profession. The 1994 edition of the American Psychiatric Association's *Diagnostic and Statistical Manual* is the fourth one, known as the *DSM-IV*. The first *DSM*, published in 1952, included 106 possible diagnoses. The *DSM-IV* describes roughly 330 official nervous and mental disorders. It features categories such as sexual aversion disorder, binge-eating disorder, dependent personality disorder, partner relational problem, and post-traumatic stress disorder. This expansion in the number of psychiatric disorders has imposed a scientific patina on the recovery movement and much of the victimization ideology. It has encouraged those laying claim to victim status to believe there is indeed a medical label somewhere out there for each of their complaints. Perhaps more important, it has legitimized the growth of a mental health profession that, besides psychiatrists, includes psychologists, nurses, counselors, and social workers. All benefit from the medicalization of victimology. Treating the disorders of victimization means they are eligible to receive compensation from either government or private insurers.

Like most of today's paranoid movements, victimology enjoys support from both ends of the political spectrum. Political conservatives have long and loudly deplored the courts' defense of criminals' rights. They've advocated victims' rights, demanding reforms such as victim compensation, victim impact statements, and victim allocution at sentencing and parole hearings. But victimology's main roots date back to the 1960s movements demanding equal rights for blacks, women, homosexuals, the disabled, the elderly, and so on. Activists argued that a variety of groups both big and small in society had suffered from prejudice, discrimination, and exploitation. In fact, the phrase "blaming the victim" was coined in 1971 by William Ryan, a psychologist and civil rights activist. Ryan maintained that debates surrounding crime and welfare usually held the black underclass accountable for its own misfortunes. Protesting that this was grossly unfair, he tried to shift attention to the social causes of such conditions. In short order the phrase became serviceable for describing *any* group's problems. The number of victims and victims' groups escalated. Armed with the theory of victimization, they were able to swing the pendulum in the other direction, translating any misfortune into a proud badge of faultless suffering. But if it became ever easier to multiply the categories of victims, it was rarely made clear who specifically was doing the actual victimizing. Multiplying the categories of victims also inflated the meaning of victimhood, so that the pain of sufferers who truly deserved sympathy and compensation – like the innocent victims of tainted blood – was devalued.

In their pursuit of targets for blame, some elements of the victimization movement have gone so far as to blame aliens. The UFO craze has been fed by both victimology and conspiracy theories. A June 1997 poll for *Time* magazine discovered that 80 percent of Americans believe the U.S. government knows more about extraterrestrials than it lets on. Sixty-five percent believe that a UFO crash-landed in 1947 near Roswell, New Mexico, despite persistent denials by the U.S. military. Feeding on widespread suspicions, "ufologists" contend that a conspiracy exists in Washington to keep information from the public about alien visits to Earth.

Recognizing a good thing when it sees it, the 1990s entertainment industry has repeatedly exploited this paranoid theory. As the founder of the Roswell UFO Enigma Museum in New Mexico has said, the producers of *The X-Files* call him up once in a while for "information." The blockbuster 1997 movie hits *Men in Black* and *Independence Day* depict secret agencies within the U.S. government hiding startling evidence about aliens. In *Independence Day* even the president isn't in on the secret. It's a sign of our paranoid times that in this film the heroes who save the planet from alien invasion include people out of the loop of the clandestine bureaucracy: the president himself; a wisecracking, recently divorced computer whiz; a swashbuckling jet fighter pilot married to a nightclub stripper. Yet another hero is an alcoholic who was a pilot in the Vietnam War and who claims to have been abducted by aliens himself. It's clear what *Independence Day* is trying to say: ignore the ufologists at your peril. Never trust government.

In recent years belief in alien abduction has grown in both the U.S. and Canada. Surprisingly large numbers of people accept that human beings have been victimized by peripatetic aliens. The same 1997 *Time* poll found that 22 percent of Americans believe intelligent beings from other planets have been in contact with human beings. Seventeen percent believe that intelligent beings from other planets have abducted human beings to observe or experiment on them. How many think they themselves were abduction victims is less easy to determine, but as early as the 1970s there were enough self-professed abductees to hold conventions and publish magazines about their experiences.

Despite its numerous adherents, alien abduction theory still strikes a great many people as silly and harmless. But the extraterrestrial fantasies of the alien abduction crowd have led to some tragic results. Two cases in point are the Heaven's Gate and Solar Temple cults. Between October 1994 and March 1997, seventy-four Swiss, French, and Canadian people associated with the Solar Temple cult died violent deaths. The carnage began in Morin Heights, Quebec, and ended in St. Casimir, Quebec, when five members drugged themselves and set fire to their house. The disciples of the Solar Temple had sought a better afterlife on the star Sirius.

Also in March 1997, across the continent in California, police made an equally grisly discovery. At an isolated mansion owned by the Heaven's Gate cult outside San Diego twenty women and nineteen men were laid out in orderly rows throughout the house. All were dressed in black and wearing new Nike running shoes. At their feet were athletic bags. Their pockets were stuffed with five-dollar bills and their heads were covered with purple silk shrouds. Twelve of the nineteen men were surgically castrated. All had ingested phenobarbital-laced applesauce, washed down with vodka. Most had died from suffocation from the plastic bags over their heads. All the deaths had been voluntary.

The Heaven's Gate group had killed themselves in expectation of joining an alien spaceship. Cult co-founder Marshall Applewhite, having recently changed his name from "Bo" to "Do," had been struck by the appearance of the Hale-Bopp comet in 1996. Using the cult's Website, called "Higher Source," Do announced that there was a spaceship hiding behind the comet. Inside the spaceship was "Peep," the other Heaven's Gate founder, who had died in 1985. Since she had allegedly shed her bodily "container" to travel into space, cult members were encouraged to do the same. They, like the Solar Temple group, sought transportation to the stars through suicide. For their sakes we can only hope that's what they got.

It's tempting to dismiss the Heaven's Gate and Solar Temple members as kooks on the lunatic fringes of North American society. But they were far more mainstream than that. "By pretending that the victims of Heaven's Gate were half-alien freaks, we conveniently sidestep our own privileged retreats from the world," writes Chris Lehmann in *Harper's* magazine. Cult members were fans of *The X-Files*, *Star Trek*, and *Star Wars*. They were at home on the Internet. Their theories were straight out of the ancient teachings of Gnosticism. Gnosticism forms a large part of today's New Age psychology, informing the views of respected, best-selling authors like Bill Moyers, Joseph Campbell, and Elaine Pagels. Carl Jung, whose books are widely read today by New Agers, was also a keen follower of the Gnostics. The original Gnostics taught that the created world was actually the work of a sinister supernatural entity. The true God had retreated to another realm that could be reached only through "gnosis," a secret knowledge divulged to a select few. Lehmann writes that the Gnostic "cosmology had no room for politics and history: the individual's salvation and rapid, fastidious retreat from the world were its sole aim, and gnostics saw themselves, quite unapologetically, as a tiny, elect spiritual aristocracy. The rest of the world, quite literally, could be damned."

Such a description fits the Heaven's Gate bunch to a T. They referred to their own bodies as "containers" or "vehicles" to be discarded like yesterday's milk cartons. They blamed the world's corruption on space aliens called "luciferians," who supposedly founded our organized religions and political institutions. Affluent and well educated, they were witnesses to the power of paranoid collective delusions at all levels of society.

A common thread that runs through cults like these is a pattern of insulation, isolation, paranoia, and utter contempt for those outside. Cults, like paranoids, shun society. They renounce physical, material nature as a veil shrouding the true order of the universe. They reject virtually all of modern science because of its dedication to discovering the laws of the physical world. What counts for paranoids and cultists, as for the ancient Gnostics, is the *unseen* realm hidden behind the world of the senses. But unlike monks, who are taught the virtues of humility and obedience, paranoids fantasize about their own superiority, their unique capacity to see what other mortals cannot. In some cases, like the Heaven's Gate group, they believe they can suspend the ordinary laws of nature.

Cultic paranoia has become so mundane that we hardly notice it any more. We hear about it when the suicide headlines hit the streets. But when we see or hear the same delusions peddled on talk radio or daytime TV we tend not to make the connection. As we ease ever more gradually toward what Lehmann calls "a culture-wide posture of civic disengagement" with its veneration of the individual soul and its quest for "authenticity," it's clear how cultish we all are becoming.

Extraterrestrial-like features also adorn the repressed memory movement, with its fixation on the epidemic of sexual abuse. As Elaine Showalter has shown in *Hystories* (1997), the stories told by abductees, often women, are eerily similar to those told by victims of sexual abuse. Both narratives are tinged with sexual references to touching, probing, and violation. Both stress the necessity of reaffirming the victim's narrative, of taking it seriously in defiance of all evidence to the contrary. The tracks running back and forth between the two currents are well traveled, though some in the abuse or recovered memory movement would deny it vehemently. The rails have been forged in the white heat of paranoia.

If the recovered memory crusade has any advantage over the alien abduction craze, it is that it can lay claim to more credible support from Hollywood and the networks. Victim-celebrities abound, immediately assuming the unctuous mantle conferred by such status. The comedian and talk-show host Roseanne Barr is perhaps the best example of Hollywood's and TV's capitulation to this trend. Even more famous is Oprah Winfrey, the ultimate victim who made good. Born out of wedlock and deserted by her father, she grew up poor in Mississippi, sexually molested by her family. She had an illegitimate child at fourteen and a cocaine habit in her twenties. Even her battle with her weight has become the stuff of legend. Whether chubby or thin and dieting, in the eyes of her innumerable fans she is both a guru and a crusading icon for all Americans struggling with their own bodies and other demons. That she can afford her personal weight and fitness consultant does little to dull her populist luster. Despite her immense wealth, she's a victim just like the rest of us.

Examples from the entertainment industry may make us think that the paranoia of victimology is as easy to escape as turning off our TV sets. If paranoia were confined to TV or the tabloids it might be harmless enough, a source of amusement for cynics, skeptics, and stand-up comedians. But it has a far more serious and tragic edge. The more the victimology movement is indulged, the more people feel entitled to grieve formally. The result has been that human rights commissions are clogged with cases and the interests of real victims are sometimes lost in the deluge. In Ontario, for example, site of Canada's first provincial human rights commission, founded in 1962, a huge backlog had developed by 1997. People with legitimate grievances were being pressured to drop their complaints. In the meantime the system was inundated with complaints of sexual harassment and other charges devilishly difficult to litigate.

The paranoid thinking behind the victimology movement can devastate lives in other, more catastrophic ways. Since the 1970s North America has been swamped by a psychological epidemic whose effects have touched families, clinics, hospitals, and courts of law. It is a psychological contagion, a hysterical plague, circulating and multiplying through society. But its guiding beliefs are drenched in paranoia, delusional fears that at some time in the past terrible wrongs were committed against perfectly innocent people, usually children. Its poignancy stems from the widely held notion that *we* may once have been these innocent children. This epidemic has all the ingredients of a paranoid fantasy tale, complete with wild, Gothic horror stories about conspirators who lurk menacingly in dark corners. It has spawned poetry, novels, self-help manuals, and Hollywood and made-for-TV movies, most of them dreadful but drearily earnest. It plays on the alarmism, victimization, and survivalist sentiments so many feel today.

The principal battleground for this contagion is the highly contested terrain of memory, the place where fact and fiction often blend imperceptibly. Without memory, its cardinal myths would evaporate like a morning fog on a sunny day. Belief in recovered (or repressed) memory syndrome (RMS), satanic ritual abuse (SRA), and multiple personality disorder (MPD) rests on the theory that the mind forgets or represses painful, traumatic events in a person's distant past. The consensus among therapists who accept this theory is that the traumatic events in question usually have to do with sexual abuse, frequently incest, often at the hands of satanic cults. Numerous celebrities have come forward as victims of abuse, such as Oprah, Roseanne, and La Toya Jackson. The process of repression, goes the theory, produces a host of emotional and physical symptoms. For Roseanne, molestation by her father was the cause of her eating disorders, self-mutilation, teenage pregnancy, juvenile delinquency, and prostitution. She contends that she repressed this memory until middle age when it surfaced in therapy.

It's the challenge of talk-oriented treatment or psychotherapy to recover these memories. Ellen Bass and Laura Davis, authors of the enormously influential *The Courage to Heal* (1988), the bible of the recovered memory movement, have risen to this challenge. Clear memories of sexual abuse aren't necessary to prove someone has been victimized. You don't even have to suspect you were abused. If you have some of the many symptoms Bass and Davis link to abuse, it's more than likely that you were. To determine whether someone has these symptoms, Bass and Davis provide a checklist of seventy-eight questions. Questions include the following: "Do you feel you have to be perfect?" "Do you have trouble expressing your feelings?" "Are you prone to depression?" "Do you feel alienated and lonely?" "Can you say no?" These questions are leading enough. Others – "Are you satisfied with your family relationships?" – are downright disingenuous. How many could truthfully answer yes to that one?

Enlightened by her responses to these questions, the victim of abuse is advised to seek out a therapist. Once therapy begins, the therapist is entrusted with the task of uncovering the traumatic memories. When the patient remembers traumatic sexual events, a healing process supposedly ensues.

The patient gains a new and more respectful awareness of self, a greater confidence and insight into the problems of life.

Such, at least, is the theory. A historical perspective teaches us that the reality is often decidedly different. The origins of this cultural shock wave date back to the sixties and seventies, according to the University of Toronto professor Ian Hacking. At that time there was a massive upsurge of interest in MPD, now called dissociative identity disorder by the American Psychiatric Association. MPD is the name doctors gave to a mental process characterized by psychological dissociation, a sort of splitting of consciousness from the world. "Multiples" are people who on certain occasions seemingly split into different personalities, or "alters."

Before the seventies "multiples" had been known to physicians under various names, though actual case histories recorded in the medical litera-ture have not been numerous. For much of the twentieth century Robert Louis Stevenson's story of Dr. Jekyll and Mr. Hyde was arguably the most famous example of a personality being split into different selves. But the idea of MPD can be traced back to the New Testament's Gospel of St. Mark, where Jesus is said to have cured a man possessed by demons. When Jesus asked him who he was, the reply was, "My name is Legion; for we are many."

In the 1970s, many more cases of MPD began to emerge. By 1990 more than 22,000 cases had been recorded in the U.S. As of 1997 over 6,000 new cases were being reported annually, 90 percent of them in women. A leading MPD booster recently announced that one percent of Americans – or about two million people – are multiples. These statements quickly found their way into newspapers and magazines, especially women's publications. Television talk shows kept pace. Phil Donahue, Sally Jessy Raphael, Larry King, Leeza Gibbons, and Oprah Winfrey presented programs on MPD. Roseanne Barr came forward to declare she had unearthed twenty-one per-sonalities living under her skin, including Piggy, Bambi, and Fucker. Virtually all these celebrities told their viewers that MPD was not rare.

"This could be someone you know," Sally Jessy Raphael warned.

A specific theory of what causes MPD has crystalized around the issue of child sexual abuse. Because of the pain, fear, and shock of a past severe trauma, almost always sexual in nature, MPD therapists argue, the mind's normal defenses break down and a splitting of consciousness occurs. With the integration of the mind impaired, alternative personalities take shape. They lurk and co-exist in the patient's psyche until they are beckoned forth by a trained therapist. The linchpin of the MPD theory is the conviction that the incidence of child abuse is far larger than many realize, and that child sexual abuse is the primary cause of personality dissociation in MPD.

MPD theory oozes paranoia. It neatly divides the world into two simplistic classes: abusers and abused. The MPD sufferer is truly ill; all guilt and responsibility is assigned to the abuser. The insistent emphasis on the absolute innocence of the abused assumes the trappings of a delusion of grandeur, excusing patient and therapist of any possibility of wrongdoing. It transforms them into intrepid, blameless pursuers of a hidden truth the rest of society wants to cover up. Heated exaggeration is the order of the day. The 1993 annual conference on MPD declared child abuse to be "the cancer of our society," metastasizing across families and generations. Like the entire child abuse movement, MPD proponents repeatedly chant the "conspiracy of silence" mantra to account for society's admittedly regrettable early resistance to the seriousness of child sexual abuse. But using the term "conspiracy" merely conjures up visions of people meeting *in camera* to plot mischief against guiltless individuals, a gross distortion of the real situation.

Conspiracy thinking goes even further among MPD supporters. The tactics of therapists to root out "alters" often sound suspiciously like those of KGB or Maoist Red Guard interrogators, to say nothing of witch-hunt inquisitors of old. MPD therapists talk about uncovering enormous numbers of hidden personalities and forcing them into revealing their hidden secrets. Until this is achieved, therapists contend, these alters persist within the unconscious, in the process destroying the lives of largely unsuspecting women and men. MPD advocates mimic the proverbial paranoid Cold Warriors who looked for Communists behind every tree. The message of the MPD movement is even more alarmist: alters can be lurking in your own mind.

There is yet a third level of conspiracy mania that haunts the MPD movement. Colin Ross, former president of the International Society for the Study of Multiple Personality and Dissociation (ISSMP&D) and a Canadian now residing in Texas, is convinced he and his patients are targets of the CIA. In 1993 he told the Canadian television show *The Fifth Estate* that by investigating MPD he was actually uncovering a huge government plot. Following the example of techniques used in the 1962 movie *The Manchurian Candidate*, the CIA, Ross alleges, brainwashed countless men and women to be assassins. Ross includes Sirhan Sirhan, the assassin of Robert Kennedy, in this category. The alters a therapist encounters are for Ross merely personalities created by CIA operatives. Attacks against MPD must therefore be part of a covert attempt to silence him for blowing the whistle on the CIA.

Ross's mind is triply paranoid. Because he sees himself exposing the conspiracy of child abuse and the conspiracy against the psyche represented by multiple personalities, he imagines himself to be the victim of a conspiracy for divulging such inflammatory information. Nor is he alone in the MPD movement. Another past president of the ISSMP&D also charges that the FBI is trying to kill him for basically the same reasons. The MPD movement is a striking illustration of how paranoia feeds voraciously on paranoia.

The truly catalytic event that launched the MPD movement was the 1973 publication of the bestseller *Sybil*. Written by the journalist and professor Flora Rheta Schreiber, *Sybil* is the account of a young woman who during the course of 2,354 office sessions over eleven years with her psychiatrist, Cornelia Wilbur, developed no fewer than sixteen separate personalities. In therapy Sybil, an intelligent and artistic woman whose exact whereabouts no one knows today, remembered being the target of repeated and ritualistic abuse administered by her mother, including cold water enemas and the insertion of sharp objects into Sybil's anus and vagina.

Sybil was a book whose time had come. It swiftly vaulted to the *New York Times* bestseller list. A movie was released with Sally Field playing Sybil and Joanne Woodward, who also appeared in *The Three Faces of Eve*, a 1957 film about MPD, playing Cornelia Wilbur. Since then Sybil has assumed cultish and mythic proportions. She is a sort of patron saint within the MPD movement.

Yet in 1994 the news broke that Sybil was probably a fraud. According to another psychiatrist who knew both Sybil and Wilbur, and who treated Sybil for a time, the Sybil story was cooked up by them in collaboration with Schreiber. The three of them ended up living together for a while. They were also under pressure from a publisher who wanted a book about multiple personality with a happy ending. Sybil probably read *The Three Faces of Eve* at a critical point in her treatment, learning by imitation how to express her unhappiness through her multiple personalities, especially if they were encouraged by the therapist. Sybil even recanted her alters at one point in her treatment. Nor is there proof that she suffered the abuse she cited. The one unassailable truth that emerges from a close examination of the facts surrounding the Sybil case is that she was indeed a victim. She suffered from a genuine emotional disorder, though its true nature remains unclear. She was also a "grade five," one of the five percent of the population who are "fantasy-prone" and highly hypnotizable, extremely open to suggestion and able to internalize the craziest of beliefs. Her true victimhood stems from the mischievously botched therapy she received from Wilbur, who was either tremendously gullible or uncommonly unscrupulous.

MPD enthusiasts might be able to live with these revelations about Sybil if it weren't for the fact that they apply equally to countless other alleged MPD cases. They follow a drearily typical script. A young woman sees a therapist complaining of depression and vague demoralization. Her relationships with other people are unsatisfying. She thinks herself unloved and incapable of loving in return. After months of intense treatment and under blatant encouragement from a therapist, accusations of sexual abuse are leveled against her mother, her father, or a familiar male figure from childhood. Usually these accusations are based on misty recollections of imagined events, such as sex forced on the patient as a child. Refuting testimony is discounted. Memories alone are deemed sufficient proof.

The Johns Hopkins University psychiatrist Paul McHugh has recounted one case that shows how unshakable faith in MPD can become. A woman in therapy phoned her mother one day to tell her that when she was young she had been molested repeatedly by her uncle, the mother's brother. Skeptical, the mother obtained the dates and times of the alleged incidents. She then discovered that her brother had been in Korea at the times of the putative abuse. When the daughter was informed of this she hesitated, then replied: "I see, Mother. Yes. Well, let me think. If your dates are right, I suppose it must have been Dad." As critics have said, science and the normal rules of verification are firmly assigned to the back seat when it comes to MPD.

McHugh's example and the Sybil case indicate that much of the psychotherapy sustaining MPD and RMS is itself an exercise in clinical paranoia. For years psychiatrists have observed that paranoia can be contagious. Delusions can actually be shared. This phenomenon, first documented by nineteenth-century French psychiatrists, has often been called folie à deux, the transference of delusional ideas from one person to another. It occurs when two or sometimes more people, often but not necessarily women and family members, enter into a prolonged and intense emotional association. Those involved are usually isolated from counterbalancing forces. Folie à deux relationships are frequently characterized by dominant and passive roles. Over time the dominant person assumes the role of rescuer. Using constant repetition of a particular theme the dominant person ultimately manages to convince the submissive individual of the delusional idea.

This description of folie à deux has an uncanny resemblance to what transpires in much MPD or repressed memory therapy. Immersed for lengthy periods in a private and highly charged atmosphere, the unhappy and emotionally vulnerable patient grows increasingly dependent on the therapist. In turn the therapist, ideologically riveted to the theory that MPD is caused by child sexual abuse, tries to get the patient to admit that somewhere, sometime in her past, she was the victim of such an incident. Eventually the patient, psychologically unstable and lacking in self-esteem to begin with, begins to accept the therapist's teaching. As she does, she also starts to trust her therapist to the exclusion of anyone else – spouse, siblings, parents, and so on. The therapist ceases to be an objective, scientific searcher after truth and becomes a guru who seeks to implant a fixed idea in the patient's mind. Even with the best of intentions – and most therapists do have good intentions, of course – this is not very different from brainwashing.

A patient doesn't have to be paranoid to begin with to play the submissive role in a folie à deux. Clinical paranoids, in fact, make extremely bad patients in psychotherapy. They suspect their therapists inordinately. They are normally resistant to forming any bond of trust between themselves and their therapists. But paranoids make resourceful and mesmerizing MPD therapists. With a diploma on the wall and the powers of persuasion they can marshal, paranoids are well suited for the active role demanded by psychotherapy. They can transform merely unhappy individuals into paranoids.

The Sybil tale confirms that the abuser needn't be male. Nor does the patient have to be a woman for such a volatile and paranoid situation to get out of hand. The story of Paul Lozano is a good example of this form of psychiatric malpractice that transcends gender. Lozano, a Mexican American from El Paso, Texas, was a promising MD-PhD student at Harvard Medical School in 1986 when he sought treatment for depression. His doctor was Margaret Bean-Bayog, a school-affiliated psychiatrist. On April 2, 1991, after several years of treatment at the hands of Bean-Bayog, Lozano died by injecting himself dozens of times with cocaine. The investigation into Lozano's at times erotic relationship with his psychiatrist teaches us a great deal about the potentially lethal mischief in modern psychotherapy. It also teaches us that its zealots blindly refuse to see the error of their ways.

From the beginning of his treatment, Bean-Bayog drove home the message that Lozano's depression was due to years of sexual abuse by his mother. As usual in these kinds of settings, the patient initially denied such events. Delegating Lozano's drug therapy to another physician, Bean-Bayog proceeded to try to break down her patient's defenses with psychological therapy. Her therapeutic strategy, mixed liberally with her own erotic feelings, was intended to duplicate what she imagined had been Lozano's highly sexual relationship with his mother. Besides the hanky-panky that went on during therapy sessions, she barraged Lozano with notes and letters that recorded her own pornographic fantasies. She allowed Lozano to take provocative pictures of her. She conveyed to Lozano in no uncertain terms the impression that she was both his mother and his sexual object.

Then in the spring of 1990 she broke off relations with Lozano. Naturally he was distraught. His new physicians, supplied with the more than thirty pages of Bean-Bayog's handwritten sexual fantasies, reported her to the Massachusetts Board of Registration in Medicine. Lozano committed suicide the next year, amid sensationalist press coverage of the investigation. Before any verdict was rendered, however, Bean-Bayog relinquished her medical license for life. The fallout from the whole episode? In Paul McHugh's words, "A talented young student-scientist at the Harvard Medical School is dead. His family, and particularly his mother, remains to this day besmirched by the accusations. A physician with a national reputation is disgraced, her medical career snuffed out."

Who or what is to blame for this fiasco? Clearly, the whole incident would never have occurred without the folie à deux style of psychotherapy

Bean-Bayog practised. Utterly wedded to the theme of incest as the cause of emotional disorders, she never tried to verify the alleged events of abuse. She employed a therapeutically irresponsible technique to convince Lozano of the same theory. Lozano confided in another therapist that he went along with the stories of abuse only to retain Bean-Bayog's affection and interest. In the end she failed miserably.

Indicative of the paranoia underlying this variety of psychotherapy was the response of other psychiatrists. Some actually rallied to Bean-Bayog's defense in a vicious example of blaming the victim. Bean-Bayog was depicted as an innocent and humane therapist who had resorted to any tactic to save her patient from self-destruction. Her bad press was blamed on the nature of Lozano's illness, a deft way of shifting attention from her abject professional failure to his damaged psyche. Others even said that *she* was the victim in the whole tragedy, a martyr to the "backlash" against women, a convenient scapegoat for a misogynist society.

Like so much of the MPD and RMS movement, "nothing in the Lozano case was seen for what it was, to be judged for itself," according to McHugh. Just as paranoid logic teaches that appearances inevitably deceive, so much of the psychotherapy industry urges us to suspend our rational judgment on command. In defiance of all conventional rules of thought, the tables are being turned perpetually in this paranoid mindset. Up becomes down, left becomes right in their topsy-turvy wonderland. In a twisted version of canonization, victimhood is conferred on the abusers. The Paul Lozanos of this world become the persecutors, the conspirators.

Much if not most of the paranoia underlying the repressed memory movement can be traced to bread-and-butter factors. Beneath the catchy rhetoric about "recovery," "healing," and "empowerment" is the banal fact that therapists have to make a living. It's no coincidence that many MPD and abuse patients have rich insurance plans that until recently were willing to pay for their treatment. As the psychiatrist Herbert Spiegel said recently, "all of this multiple personality business rarely takes place when financial resources are not available or when the patient has no legal or social reason to evade responsibility. It seems to be related to the amount of money the patients have to indulge in this kind of invalidism of histrionic display ... That is a sad commentary on the motivation of some therapists."

A treatment that lasts years might not help the patient much but it can make a therapist rich. There are also workshops to be hosted and fees to collect for expert testimony in custody litigation. Publishers pay substantial advances for self-help recovery manuals. Still, money alone cannot explain the MPD and repressed memory movement. It had to start somehow and somewhere. What was needed was a theory that addressed and justified the desperate need some people feel to escape normal human obligations and challenges. What was needed was a theory that enabled these men and women to retreat emotionally into a psychological realm ruled by delusions of persecution and grandeur.

The entire movement might be exonerated if there were any data showing that this kind of therapy worked. After all, who cares how flawed the theory is as long as men and women are helped? But Paul Lozano was not exceptional. For the vast majority of patients who manage to see their way through to the end of marathon treatment there is no real closure. Even therapists admit as much. Anxiety, depression, and suicidal thoughts frequently accompany the unpalatable process of dredging memory's bottom layers. Therapists acknowledge that the patient's real suffering actually *begins* with this stage of treatment. Like chemotherapy and radiation treatment for cancer, psychotherapy makes you sick. But at least many cancer patients see their symptoms go into remission. Psychotherapy's patients aren't so lucky. Unhappiness governs their lives. Often they find themselves stripped of family life. They learn to chronically suspect that their fondest recollections of childhood are simply screen memories of familial abuse. "The result is a lasting sacrifice of resilience, security of identity, humour, [and] capacity to show affection," the critic Frederick Crews has written. No wonder that some survivors of this type of therapy have started suing their therapists for the considerable damage done to their lives.

Another side of the therapy used in MPD cases is revealed in the 1993 documentary film *MPD: The Search for Deadly Memories*, narrated by the iconic feminist Gloria Steinem. In a scene reminiscent of witch-hunting of old, a young woman patient is strapped to a bed with thick restraints fastened to her wrist, ankles, and waist. She receives injections of the barbiturate sodium amytal, the so-called truth serum. While the therapist tries to get the patient to recover repressed memories of childhood sexual abuse, she struggles against her restraints so vigorously that four people have to seize her limbs and hold her down. This form of genuine abuse didn't take place in some quack hypnotist's private office; it happened on a hospital psychiatric ward.

Another paranoid trait of the MPD-RMS movement is its reaction to criticism. Paranoids avoid open debate. They don't like to discuss their delusions, not because they fear seeing their views disproved – they don't – but because they believe that free and public debate is itself a sham orchestrated by a conspiracy. The paranoid's preferred tactics include threats, name-calling, defamation of character, refusal to debate, shouting down opponents, and occasionally violence. The object is to censor and silence, not engage different opinions. Elizabeth Loftus, who has lectured that repressed memory is a myth, has been the recipient of boos and hisses at public appearances. She has been denounced and told she is disloyal to women. Another courageous woman with similar views was informed that she was "on the side of the molesters, rapists, pedophiles and other misogynists." When the noted scholar Elaine Showalter began questioning chronic fatigue syndrome she received comparable treatment. One Website called "Handling Showalter" dispensed information on how and where activists could confront her while on her *Hystories* book tour. When she showed up for book signings or appearances on TV talk shows she was greeted by all kinds of verbal abuse including shouts of "Bullets are too good for you." Stalkers pestered her. Conspiracy theorists badgered her night and day, charging that she was being funded by "U.S. chemical mega-corporations." Avengers wrote Princeton University, her employer, trying to get her fired. Some threatened legal or physical retaliation. Showalter learned that to paranoids, one is either for them or against them. If against, prepare to be demonized.

Unsurprisingly, the conspiracy thinking of the MPD movement is closely tied to a belief in the reality of satanic cult abuse. Indeed, by the mid-1980s an increasing number of MPD women patients were recounting abuse stories featuring satanic cults. Their tales – what Showalter calls their "hystories" – were remarkably alike, regardless of their ethnic, religious, economic, or linguistic background. Patients complained about being forced to attend satanic rituals, to kill and eat babies, to witness children being drugged, tortured, dismembered, burned, raped with crucifixes, and buried in coffins with live snakes. There were also reports about child pornography satanists who organized huge child prostitution rings.

What brought the matter to media and public attention was the fact that their therapists believed them. Having deserted the reliable terrain of hard evidence, and having banked their careers and reputations on the notion that patients with the proper suggestive encouragement never lie, they could hardly do otherwise. MPD and RMS therapists dutifully began to speak about huge satanic conspiracies. In 1988 the talk-show celebrity Geraldo Rivera hosted a prime-time TV special titled *Devil Worship: Exposing Satan's Underground*. In Canada the province of Manitoba, on the advice of the now discredited MPD promoter Colin Ross and others, struck a committee that between 1990 and 1994 trained some 3,000 Manitobans on how to handle survivors of cult abuse. Ellen Bass and Laura Davis have admitted that gruesome tales of satanic abuse are hard to believe, but they operate on the truly paranoid premise that the more incredible the idea, the more plausible it is. They declared in their 1994 edition of *The Courage to Heal* that those who questioned satanic ritual abuse were themselves in "collective denial." Other therapists have taken the hint. One badgered a patient over the course of a seventy-two-day stay in hospital, telling her she had been abused by a cult and its members were after her. So with the help of "experts" like Bass, Davis, and Ross, Americans and Canadians in the early 1990s were seeing covens everywhere.

The trouble was that there was nothing but patients' testimony to back up such claims. In court case after court case, charges of satanic abuse had to be thrown out for lack of independent evidence. In 1994 the British government issued a report based on a three-year investigation of eighty-three satanic abuse charges. Not one case could be corroborated. In early 1998 Britain's Royal College of Psychiatrists announced that "no empirical evidence exists to support either repression [of memories of child sexual abuse] or dissociation," a severe blow to the SRA industry.

In the U.S., the FBI has likewise been unable to verify a single case of satanic ritual abuse. Courageous individuals like Mark Pendergrast, himself wrongly accused of abusing his daughters, have patiently documented the facts and blown the whistle on the entire SRA movement. Despite the painstaking inquiries of countless law enforcement officials on both sides of the Atlantic, in other words, not a shred of evidence has been produced to substantiate satanic ritual abuse. Is that because it exists only in the minds of therapists, their emotionally damaged patients, and those predisposed to believe in it in the first place?

Two court cases, one in the United States and one in Canada, have subjected satanic ritual abuse to intense media scrutiny. In both cases the theory has been thoroughly discredited. In 1990 the longest criminal prosecution in U.S. history came to an end in Los Angeles after the state of California had spent $15 million trying to convict Raymond Buckley and his mother, Peggy McMartin Buckley, on fifty-two charges of child molestation. Buckley, his mother, and other family members had taught at the Virginia McMartin Pre-School in upscale Manhattan Beach, California. In 1983 the mother of a child at the school told a policeman that her son had been sodomized by a man named Ray. This woman, later diagnosed as a paranoid schizophrenic, died in 1986 of an alcohol-related illness, but before she did she also accused her ex-husband of sodomizing the family dog. Once the original accusation had been made, literally hundreds more incidents of child abuse at the nursery were alleged. Children were said to have witnessed satanic rituals in underground tunnels, been forced to watch animals being slaughtered, and been made to take part in child pornography. Buckley and his mother had to endure two trials. He spent three years in court and five years in jail. Their ordeal finally ceased in 1990 when the prosecution decided not to seek a third trial, after juries had refused to convict on any count.

In Canada a similar paranoia-soaked drama quickly came to be known as the Martensville Horror, one of the most shocking trials for child sex abuse in the country's history. Martensville, Saskatchewan, a Mennonite community with a sprinkling of Alliance and Pentecostal churches, is a town 10 kilometres north of Saskatoon with a population of about 3,000. In early June 1992 Martensville's residents were amazed to learn that nine of the town's most prominent citizens had been arrested. Those charged included Ronald Sterling, his wife, Linda, and their son, Travis. They pleaded not guilty to forty-five charges of abusing seven children in their unlicensed home while babysitting between 1988 and 1991. Also charged were two former police chiefs, three police officers, and a nineteen-year-old woman who was tried as a young offender. The Crown charged that the accused had operated a child abuse cult. The allegations were horrific. Little children were said to have been sodomized, thrown into cages, forced to eat feces. "There were hints and whispers of ritual abuse, covens, something called The Devil's Church," wrote David Roberts of the *Globe and Mail*. Thanks to a court-ordered ban on publication, few facts reached public notice.

In June 1993 one of the police officers was cleared. Ultimately in February 1994 a jury found Ron and Linda Sterling innocent on all counts. A week later the Crown stayed all charges against four of the other defendants. In May 1995 the Saskatchewan Court of Appeal overturned the 1992 conviction of the young offender on ten counts of sexual abuse. Travis Sterling was convicted on two counts of sexual touching, but the eight others originally arrested on 180 criminal charges in 1992 were free.

The police investigation and the trial of the "Martensville Nine" serve as a classic example of how the justice system by the early 1990s was getting the issues of child and satanic ritual abuse wrong. They also illustrate two things about epidemic paranoia: it often starts through the efforts of one person; and, once contracted, it spreads like wildfire. The person in question in the Martensville case was a police officer, Claudia Bryden. She joined the Martensville police department in September 1991 with less than one year's policing experience. She was young and energetic with a seemingly promising future. She also firmly believed that she herself had been sexually abused as a child. Another Martensville officer who encountered Bryden at that time described her later as "terribly paranoid." Barely a week after joining the Martensville force she was assigned by another constable, who in a spooky twist of fate later became one of the defendants, the job of investigating a complaint lodged by the parents of a two-year-old child against Travis Sterling. Bryden then discovered that a similar 1988 complaint had been laid against Travis Sterling by a ten-year-old girl. Since the Sterlings had links with the town police, Bryden smelled a cover-up. Within seventy-two hours of the start of her investigation, Bryden had Travis Sterling charged on three counts of sexual assault.

She then began to tell the parents of other children the Sterlings babysat that sexual abuse had occurred at the Sterlings' home. Alarmed parents panicked, interrogating their own children. The children said nothing incriminating. Then Bryden and a Saskatoon officer, Rod Moor, took over.

They subjected children to intense and repeated interviews, grilling some children sixty times. When children answered that they hadn't been touched inappropriately by anyone at the Sterlings', Bryden and Moor persevered. One boy was asked nineteen times "where else" he had been touched. Gradually the children wilted. Allegations of orgiastic sexual abuse and satanic worship surfaced and then snowballed. Although there was no physical evidence whatsoever, the defendants were accused of ritual abuse in both their home and a storage building outside Martensville.

Bryden, fearing for her life, took to carrying a pistol off-duty. She wasn't alone in assuming the existence of a cult-like conspiracy; from the beginning, public officials behaved as if the allegations of abuse were true and the Sterlings were guilty. The mayor of Martensville compared the residents of the town to the families of victims of the Westray, Nova Scotia, mine disaster, though in Martensville there was no proof anyone had been molested, much less killed. Premier Roy Romanow and the social services minister, Janice MacKinnon, went to Martensville themselves to tell its citizens that everything possible would be done to help them in their time of crisis. A task force of psychologists, social workers, and RCMP officers descended on Martensville shortly after the charges were laid to counsel the roughly thirty children, aged two to thirteen. Everyone acted as if the children had in fact been victims of a crime. No one, not even the media, appeared willing to assume the defendants' innocence. It was only once the trials were well under way that journalists began to raise questions about the obvious absurdity of the Crown's case.

The press have often noted that the Martensville and McMartin trials bear an uncanny, eerie resemblance to the witch hunts of old. Of course, one should never forget that Travis Sterling was convicted, so sexual abuse does occur, unlike the fanciful crimes of witches in a bygone era. Similarly, the punishment meted out to those falsely accused of abuse today doesn't measure up to the torture, burnings, hangings, and drownings of yesteryear.

But the huge legal costs of fighting these charges and the stigma of being charged with child abuse can ruin lives. In the eyes of a society in the grip of sex abuse paranoia, the stigma is not washed away by a verdict of not guilty. In the case of the young Martensville woman found guilty in 1992 and then exonerated, a life has been changed irrevocably for the worse. Freed on bail while her case was being appealed, she was ordered to leave Martensville because one of the boys interrogated said he was too frightened to have her in town. Even away from Martensville she finds it hard to find a job. She certainly will never work with children again, though it's what she would enjoy most. "You know there's a percentage of people who think you did it," she said in 1995. "In their eyes you are scum. That's the hardest part."

Ironically, in its frantically persistent search for satanic cults, the RMS and SRA movement in recent years has itself assumed the trappings of a paranoid cult. One therapist, George Ganaway, saw this possibility as early as 1989. He warned, "Unless scientifically documented proof is forthcoming, patients and therapists who validate and publicly defend the unsubstantiated veracity of these reports may find themselves developing into a cult of their own, validating each other's beliefs while ignoring (and being ignored by) the scientific and psychotherapeutic community at large." By the late 1990s this appears to have come true. The movement's members rally around one another, closing ranks like settlers circling their wagons. With insulation comes the isolation, world-denying, and contempt for other human beings characteristic of cults like Heaven's Gate and the Solar Temple. The members imagine themselves a tiny, exalted, self-righteous elite able to see things others cannot. The more criticism they face, the more they view themselves wrestling with demonic currents out to destroy them. In typical paranoid fashion they reduce all objections to "denial," a shorthand term meant to say, "You only oppose us because you yourself are sick." This favorite tactic of the psychoanalytic establishment seems to have gained acceptance in society at large. But the demons are almost entirely self-made.

The RMS movement, like Freud's own legacy, is under attack as the nineties come to a close because of the terrible wrongs committed by the movement itself, the terrible hardships imposed on literally thousands of families. The backlash was necessary to reintroduce some reason into a searingly controversial matter.

Perhaps the greatest tragedy about the RMS and victimization movements is that in going to such extremes they have tempted people to think that sexual abuse does not exist at all. Revelations about abuse in denominational or state reformatories, in minor-league hockey, or in native residential schools confirm that abuse happens. Currently there are many clearheaded and dedicated men and women working to mitigate the devastating effects of abuse on victims' lives. Professionals and the public have learned a great deal from airing the issue. They have learned, for example, that there are different kinds of abuse. Like most sensitive matters, however, the issue of abuse is volatile. The potential exists for minds to reject reason and search for scapegoats. Scapegoating, as history tells us, inevitably targets the innocent. Common sense, therefore, tells us that on such issues society should proceed cautiously. When nothing of the sort occurs, when people – acting because of opportunism, malice, ignorance, or hysteria – turn the investigation of a grave social problem into a witch hunt, their approach is symptomatic of a deeper, underlying condition.

Is this current of paranoid contagion finally receding? Psychologists, psychiatrists, and other mental health professionals themselves are increasingly questioning the whole repressed memory movement. The mounting empirical evidence, growing numbers of lawsuits, and the escalating reluctance of insurers to pay for this type of therapy make it tempting to predict that we are seeing the last of this modern-day witch hunt. But much of the repressed memory movement stemmed from the growth of gender feminism starting in the 1970s. As the next chapter will argue, gender feminism in the late 1990s is alive and well.

Sex, Lies,
and Videotaped
Testimony

O N TUESDAY MORNING, January 27, 1998, Hillary Rodham Clinton, the first lady of the United States, appeared on network television. That evening her husband, the president of the United States, was scheduled to give his State of the Union address. The occasion ought to have been a happy one for the Clintons. A year into his second term of office, Bill Clinton was a popular president, with an approval rating of over 60 percent. Unemployment, inflation, and interest rates were low. America was still the undisputed policeman of the world, its global leadership "unrivaled," in Clinton's own description. He was preparing to bring down a balanced budget, with hope for a surplus the following year. Despite resistance from a fiscally conservative, Republican-dominated Congress, Clinton could realistically hope to use this surplus to protect Social Security.

But Mrs. Clinton's mood that morning on NBC was far from upbeat. In her interview, she charged that a "vast right-wing conspiracy" had "been conspiring against my husband since the day he announced for president."

Her husband's "right-wing opponents," she continued, had been "looking at every telephone call we've made, every check we've ever written, scratching for dirt, intimidating witnesses, doing everything possible to try to make some kind of accusation against my husband." Their aim? "To undo the results of two elections," Mrs. Clinton stated without missing a beat. The next morning on ABC Television's *Good Morning America*, she refused to back down from these comments. Why was Hillary Clinton talking like a militiaman? Why did she sound suspiciously like the longtime Clinton foes Pat Robertson and Pat Buchanan, well known for their own conspiracy theories? Or Johnnie Cochran, the star of O.J. Simpson's "dream team" of lawyers?

The cause of Hillary Clinton's paranoid outburst was the snowballing scandal that was threatening her husband's presidency by the end of January 1998. Rumors were circulating that during his presidency Clinton had had a sexual relationship with Monica Lewinsky, a former White House intern. Far more seriously, Clinton and his close friend Vernon Jordan were alleged to have encouraged Lewinsky to lie in a sworn affidavit in connection with a sexual harassment lawsuit brought against the president by Paula Jones. If these allegations were true, Clinton could be charged with advising someone to lie under oath, a criminal offense. Little wonder that Mrs. Clinton uttered her accusations of conspiracy at a time when many in the media were discussing the possibility that President Clinton might resign or face impeachment.

The key figure in Mrs. Clinton's charges of conspiracy was Kenneth Starr, appointed in August 1994 as independent counsel and special prosecutor in the investigation into the Clintons' alleged financial improprieties in the Whitewater land deal in Arkansas. When informed of the new allegations against Clinton and Jordan, Starr sought and received the go-ahead from Clinton's attorney general, Janet Reno, and the Special Division of the D.C. Circuit Court to open a grand jury investigation. Mrs. Clinton's comments came the day that Starr began to hear testimony from subpoenaed witnesses. If there was a conspiracy, it included the president's own attorney general.

In a terse reply to Mrs. Clinton's accusations, Starr dismissed them as nonsense. Not that there aren't links among Starr, Paula Jones, key witnesses ranged against the president, and various conservative publications and think tanks. For example, Jones's case was financed by the conservative Rutherford Institute, and much of the funding behind the attacks on the president came from the Clinton-hater Richard Mellon Scaife, an heir to the Mellon banking fortune.

Yet that doesn't add up to a conspiracy. Simply demonstrating that Clinton's opponents are from one end of the political spectrum doesn't prove that they constitute an organized and unified campaign to discredit the president. Private individuals often have to turn to wealthy backers for the huge sums needed to fight legal battles, especially when the tussle is with an institution as powerful as the White House. Mrs. Clinton's use of the term "conspiracy" to describe her husband's opponents simply doesn't accord with the facts. If there's some veracity to the allegations, as appears likely, couldn't one just as easily describe the president's enemies as dogged pursuers of the truth? And can Mrs. Clinton seriously believe the *Washington Post*, the *Los Angeles Times*, the *New York Times*, *Newsweek*, *Time*, *U.S. News and World Report*, ABC, NBC, CBS, CNN, PBS, and National Public Radio are part of a right-wing conspiracy just because they covered the Lewinsky story? Exactly how did the Reverend Jerry Falwell and other Clinton-haters plant a twenty-one-year-old daughter of a rich Democratic Party contributor in the White House late at night? Were they also behind Kathleen Willey, the former White House volunteer who went on CBS's *60 Minutes* to claim she had been sexually assaulted by the president in 1993 right in the Oval Office?

Opinion over Mrs. Clinton's remarks was divided at the time. The White House had obviously approved of them, calculating that going on the offensive was the best way to deal with the situation. In fact, Mrs.

Clinton had earlier formed and was heading at the time of her interview a special crisis team of advisors to try to forestall the media "feeding frenzy," as she herself called it. The American public itself was unsure about the whole matter. Although the president's approval rating dropped briefly, a majority of Americans did not want him to resign or be impeached, a statistic that had hardly budged a year later when the Senate voted not to remove him from office.

Mrs. Clinton's charges of conspiracy warrant particular attention. Back in Arkansas, she had consistently blamed the media for her husband's troubles when he was governor. Her 1998 statement, coming from virtually the highest office in the land, reveals the extent to which paranoia has become common currency in today's politics. At a time when countless viewers of *The X-Files* believe the show's plots aren't fanciful, Mrs. Clinton's comments are hardly accidental. Her reliance on paranoid rhetoric indicates that it appeals not just to wild-eyed militiamen holed up in ranches in Montana. It works for the millions of middle-class, well-educated men and women who support the Democratic Party. It probably works for the Clintons themselves. It works for the many men and women who approve of Mrs. Clinton's pro-feminist stance. In other words, it shows how much of 1990s feminism has been co-opted by the politics of paranoia.

Mrs. Clinton's paranoia is in some ways reminiscent of a prior presidency, one headed by arguably the most paranoid of all presidents, Richard M. Nixon. When Nixon was running for and occupying the presidency, his loathing of the press was pronounced to the point of paranoia. The press returned the favor in spades. After his landslide victory in the 1972 election, at least one editor vowed to reverse the electoral verdict through a "bloodletting." Then revelations began to surface about the illegal break-in at the Democratic Party's headquarters in the Watergate complex in June 1972. The story gathered momentum as the press doggedly pursued it. Finally, in August 1974, Nixon resigned rather than face impeachment at the hands of the Democrat-dominated Congress. Robert S. Robins, co-author of *Political Paranoia*, who was living in England at the time of Nixon's resignation, remembered a news reader on British television "literally bouncing up and down on his chair in glee as he announced the event." Such was the animosity that Nixon sparked in the media.

If anyone in American history was temperamentally unsuited to occupy an executive position in government it was Richard Nixon, a loner with a "warfare personality," "adversarial suspiciousness," and a chronic inability to trust, according to Robins and his co-author, Jerrold M. Post. Nixon was so solitary in his relations with the world that even his wife, Pat, was never his confidante. The Clintons, on the other hand, are often referred to as running a "co-presidency." Together they have a tremendous upside but also a steep downside, horrendous risks balancing spectacular gains. Sources like the novel *Primary Colors* create the impression that the Clintons are very much a political team, she the women's role model supplying focus and discipline, he the affable, backslapping vote-getter. Hillary wants political power but knows her talents are not great enough to get her to a governor's mansion, much less the White House. By marrying Bill she could hope to get this power. The catch has been Bill's extramarital sexual appetite, which has threatened his political victories and her status as an independent career woman with impeccable feminist credentials. Where Nixon was a lone character combining individual skills and weaknesses, the Clintons are really two sides of a single persona. Each needs the other's talents desperately.

Having been schooled in a post-Watergate world of politics where public relations are far more important than during Nixon's day, Mrs. Clinton is also much smoother and slicker than Nixon ever was. If nothing else Hillary Clinton is a lot more photogenic than Nixon, who looked as if he never met a camera he liked. Nixon was all arms and head, while Mrs. Clinton projects a cool, firm, and urbane image.

But in their paranoid outlooks, however, Nixon and Hillary Clinton aren't very far apart. Neither Hillary nor her husband could have had any illusions about national politics when Bill ran for president in 1992 and 1996. Neither could plead ignorance of the internecine nature of politics inside the Beltway. She can hardly be surprised that the Republicans who enjoy such power in Congress are trying to make life miserable for her and her husband. If the Republicans are up to these kinds of shenanigans she has only to remind herself how the Democrats have used the Office of the Independent Counsel to badger Republican presidents over the last few decades when they had the majority on Capitol Hill. She might also remind herself of how she had served as a young staffer on the House Judiciary Committee that investigated the Watergate scandal and helped to create the position of the independent counsel in the first place in the late 1970s. The office was created to enable prosecutors outside the attorney general's office to investigate things like White House hanky-panky.

Saying she and her husband have political enemies in Washington, then, is about as surprising as saying the sun will set in the west. But it's quite another matter to allege that these enemies are the cause of all the Clintons' woes, a distinction Hillary and her husband doubtless know. Wasn't Mrs. Clinton being a tad disingenuous, then, when she accused her opponents of plotting against her husband? If the president thought a right-wing conspiracy was out to get him, why didn't he watch his back and just behave? The likelihood is that when Mrs. Clinton spoke out about a conspiracy she did so as much for tactical reasons as out of conviction. Whereas Nixon truly believed himself a victim of persecution, Mrs. Clinton probably doesn't.

But if Mrs. Clinton knows better, why her outburst? The answer is that the Clinton presidency wears the coat of paranoia comfortably. When not trying to smear opponents with charges of conspiracy, it does things that cry out for a conspiracist interpretation. It is the ideal administration for the age of paranoia. Mrs. Clinton may console herself with the thought that just because she has paranoid fears doesn't mean they're not out to get you; she should also remember that just because you have enemies doesn't mean you have to act paranoid. Since her charges of conspiracy probably weren't an inadvertent slip of the tongue, she was probably indulging in a little tactical paranoia of her own. The question is: What is more reprehensible, Mrs. Clinton's playing with paranoia or true believers like Bob Fletcher?

In one respect, though, Mrs. Clinton is right to feel paranoid. If the Clintons are drawing media heat, it's partly because of the role of the Internet in the Lewinsky affair. The Internet, as we've seen, is a favorite breeding place for paranoia. Naturally White House sex scandals are big news on the Net, with cybersurfing news junkies exchanging gossip ranging from the humorous to the absolutely paranoid. Sex scandal jokes abound. One goes: "In a survey of American women, when asked, 'Would you sleep with President Clinton?' 86 percent replied: 'Not again.'" Other material is less comedic. Some deals with the evidence for a right-wing conspiracy. Some suggests that the Lewinsky scandal was a Communist plot to achieve world domination. Either way the World Wide Web gives those who like Mrs. Clinton's paranoia a place to indulge their delusions.

The Internet's influence on the scandal may have signaled a new era in news reporting. The original story of the president's dalliance with Lewinsky broke not in the mainstream media but on the muckraking journalist Matt Drudge's Website. This compelled America's major news organizations to put the Lewinsky accusations on their own Websites, in some cases even *before* they announced them on their networks or in their publications. "The Web will turn every daily newspaper into a wire service," says one journalist. "We have revived a dead institution," the breaking news story, says another. Such a result can cut two ways. Either investigative journalism that didn't have any chance of seeing the light of day prior to the Net will enjoy a new life, or the worst kind of conspiracist rumormongering will flourish. Either way, news will travel exceedingly fast, making it hard for anyone to control a media feeding frenzy.

If Mrs. Clinton's paranoia wasn't the most surprising feature of the Lewinsky scandal, then perhaps it was the uncanny way paranoid politics was beginning to imitate art. Mere weeks before the Lewinsky story hit the headlines Hollywood released *Wag the Dog*, a political satire produced by some of the highest-paid talent in the movie business. The movie depicts a political media advisor, played by Robert DeNiro, who engages a colorful Hollywood producer, played by Dustin Hoffman, to fake a war with tiny Albania in an effort to divert national attention from a presidential sex scandal. In the end the trickery works and the president, never seen on screen, is elected.

Wag the Dog's popularity was largely due to the widespread belief that politicians are forever trying to hoodwink the electorate. It's become conventional wisdom in Hollywood that conspiracy extends right into the White House. The 1997 film *Absolute Power* featured a president, played by Gene Hackman, who shares complicity in a plot to cover up a woman's gruesome murder. *Wag the Dog* did nothing to dispel paranoid suspicions. The film gained credibility when, in a move that pundits saw as linked to President Clinton's sex-scandal difficulties, the White House began to threaten Iraqi leader Saddam Hussein with military retaliation for refusing United Nations arms inspectors access to Iraqi weapons installations. In his State of the Union address, amid the swirling rumors of possible impeachment, Clinton referred to the "crisis" with Iraq and warned Saddam Hussein of America's determination to bomb if his "defiance" of world opinion continued. Was it just a coincidence that Clinton's saber-rattling occurred during one of his worst weeks as president? The Iraqi situation had been ongoing for weeks. "Why must we bomb now, rather than three weeks ago or three weeks hence?" asked the publisher of *Harper's* magazine. Why did Clinton choose this particular time to heighten the tension surrounding the inspection of Iraqi weapons systems?

White House paranoia isn't restricted to the Clintons either. Just a heartbeat away from the presidency is environmentally correct Vice-President Al Gore. Gore has positioned himself as the next Democratic candidate for the presidency, in part by promoting the environmentalist cause. But Gore's environmentalism, revealed in his popular book *Earth in the Balance* (1992), displays the same symptoms of New Age psychology evident in Michael Lerner's "politics of meaning." Exploiting the kinds of anxieties bred by the erratic climate of the winter of 1997–98, Gore has managed to turn interest in the weather into a paranoid obsession. To Gore, and many in the environmentalist movement, we are headed for environmental hell in a hand-basket. Why? Because of our destructive crimes against the environment.

Gore doesn't really mean "our" – meaning the little guy's – crimes. The enemy he has in mind is big business. Identifying his cause with the very existence of the nation, he depicts himself and others inclined to push the environmentalist panic button as the "Paul Reveres" of the revolutionary movement to save the planet. "We too are working as a team," Gore tells environmentalists. "The enemy is more subtle than a British fleet," he cautions. In fact, Gore isn't satisfied with dubbing himself a Paul Revere–like hero. Like the paranoids of New Age psychology, he feels the mantle of heroism isn't complete without the thread of persecution too. So he imagines himself and other environmentalist Paul Reveres as the modern-day equivalents of Galileo, the seventeenth-century physicist browbeaten into silence by the Vatican. Naturally, those who question Gore's warnings about global warming are transformed into the equivalent of Galileo's Inquisitional tormentors. Here Gore flirts ominously with the paranoid's favorite debating tactic: demonize your opponent before he has a chance to marshal a counter-argument.

Of course, environmental degradation and pollution are issues of supreme importance. Public health is seriously affected by how we treat our natural environment, our air, trees, lakes, rivers, farmlands. Just as we should heed warnings from medical scientists about dangerous developments in the field of microbial research, so we should listen carefully to environmentalists who point out the very real consequences of ill-considered economic policies. But that hardly excuses Gore's alarmist preachings, his wild exaggerations. How different is Gore's environmentalism from Shirley MacLaine's crackpot theory that the eruption of Mount St. Helens was due to environmental destruction? It may be significant that the Unabomber, Theodore Kaczynski, avidly read Gore's *Earth in the Balance* while holed up in his Montana shack. Is it unfair to call the Unabomber "Al Gore with attitude," as the journalist Mark Steyn did?

Is Gore's expectation that human beings can actually keep climate from changing by recycling and planting trees realistic? Weather patterns have been shifting ever since human technology began to have an impact on nature. Meteorological instability has been a fact of life throughout recorded history. In blaming big business for mudslides in California, Gore sounds suspiciously like the "full-time militia staff researcher" Bob Fletcher, who says the U.S. government "has developed weather-tampering techniques to create drought and famine, so the New World Order can starve millions in America and control the rest." Who is more paranoid: he who blames oil companies' executives for bad weather, or he who blames the government?

The paranoia-mongering of the Clintonites doesn't stop there. Perhaps the least admirable of their strategies was the half-hearted attempt during the president's bleakest days to depict him as a victim not only of "right-wing conspiracies" but of what some psychologists call sexual addiction. According to this theory, the president couldn't control himself when it came to pretty women. As we have seen, victimology is the ideology of choice for many paranoids and paranoia-pushers. This was a tricky line of defense, since Clinton at the time was emphatically denying having an affair with Monica Lewinsky. Still, in a desperate effort to cover every base some admirers of the president were telling us that "libido and leadership are linked." More inventive sympathizers were saying that the president's admittedly voracious sexual appetite was determined by his more lusty than average hormones. This made him a superb candidate for victim status.

Thus, paranoia has become as natural as breathing in Washington, and the public does not appear to have any grave problems with that. Few blinked when Hillary Clinton cried "conspiracy"; to many she was stating the obvious. If anything her remarks may have helped restore some of the luster to the Clintons' popularity ratings. When her husband's difficulties mounted in later months amidst increasing threats of impeachment, her own approval ratings rose. As of summer 1999, she was so popular that she was considering running for a Senate seat in New York. Her steadfast willingness to ignore her husband's blatant womanizing and go on the offensive charging conspiracies seemed to tap a deep vein in the American public. American women especially appeared to admire her for her plucky combativeness in the service of paranoia. It's as if people were saying: "Well, Hillary, it's about time you woke up and smelled the coffee." People nowadays seem to have infinite patience with paranoia. Playing the paranoia card may have been a liability during the Nixon years; it may actually be an asset in today's politics.

Hillary Clinton's paranoia-mongering was not due solely to her being on the political defensive in 1998. It also derived from her close association with the radical feminist movement and its unswerving support for sexual harassment laws. For years Mrs. Clinton has been a symbol for countless women of what they can achieve through brains and determination. She has been hailed as "a first lady for the '90s" or "a new kind of first lady." A talented lawyer, a savvy and articulate politician in her own right, and a steadfast wife and mother, she has made her politics clear in speeches and books such as *It Takes a Village* (1996). She is pro-choice. She supports subsidized child care, affirmative action, extended maternity leave, national health insurance, zero tolerance of sexual harassment, ending domestic violence. Her vision of American family life is one calculated to appeal to the growing number of "soccer moms," the women who helped re-elect her husband in

1996. These women typically hold down jobs. They are often single mothers. Polling data tell us they are tired, overworked, overextended, unsure what the future holds for them and their kids. Mrs. Clinton's message looks crafted for their consumption. It is based on the overarching notion that the state should be poised to intervene at any time with all the force it can muster if children are at risk. Her theory of the American family reassures stressed-out parents that what they can't provide for their children, the government will.

But Hillary Clinton has also become a kind of feminist icon. As recently as the 1996 Democratic Party convention she was celebrated at a series of meetings organized and run by the party's women's caucus. Well concealed from the mainstream media, these events featured speeches in tribute to Mrs. Clinton. Some smacked of white-male-bashing. Gloria Steinem lamented that while Washington was lucky to have Hillary Clinton, in New York City "we have only white, warlike, testosterone-poisoned men." In the eyes of this constituency Mrs. Clinton's pre-1998 credentials were impeccable.

No issue is closer to the heart of the current feminist movement than sexual harassment. And one of the grand ironies of Clinton's troubles is that the Clintons remain firm on the issue. In 1994 the president himself signed the Violence Against Women Act, which restricted defendants' digging into the past of sexual harassment plaintiffs. If the Clintons want to blame anyone for their difficulties they can forget about "right-wing conspiracies" and look closer to home. They can thank the radical feminists within their own party who have in some cases transformed consensual sex into a crime.

The current status of sexual harassment is a stunning example of how something that a quarter-century ago was viewed as loopy can become a generally accepted legal concept. It wasn't until the late 1970s that a U.S. federal court of importance decreed that harassment violated the 1964 Civil Rights Act's provisions on gender equality. Momentum began gathering shortly thereafter. Anita Hill's charges during the 1991 confirmation hearings of the Supreme Court nominee Clarence Thomas probably did more than anything else to publicize sexual harassment. As of March 1998, in the words of *Time* magazine, sexual harassment was "embedded in multiple Supreme Court decisions (three more are expected before July), thousands of corporate policies and a host of lower-court cases that have spread like kudzu across the legal landscape. The result is a thicket of rulings. Since 1991, juries have returned well over 500 verdicts on sexual harassment – decisions that often contradict one another and send mixed signals about how we should behave anytime we meet a co-worker we'd like to see after five."

Sexual harassment cases have led in recent years to some huge court settlements. The number of sexual harassment cases being filed in America has leveled off since 1995. But that's probably because of the anxious efforts of employers to impose their own zero tolerance policies in the workplace and nip harassment cases in the bud before they result in litigation.

The common view is that sexual harassment occurs when (typically) a man tries to pressure an unwilling woman into giving him sexual favors. Often referred to as "quid pro quo harassment," this type of incident usually takes place in the workplace when a boss punishes an employee – for example, by docking pay or firing – for rebuffing a sexual advance. If that were the whole story of sexual harassment, there would be little debate over it. But in both Canada and the United States, there are now other grounds for sexual harassment. As of 1986 U.S. courts recognize that speech or conduct can create an offensive or "hostile" environment of unwelcome verbal or physical behavior. Such an environment can be discriminatory even when there is no quid pro quo.

Clearly some cases of recent hostile-environment harassment are legitimate and justify the existence of anti-harassment laws. One employee of Rockwell International Corp. in the 1980s complained in her lawsuit that over an eight-month period she was the target of sexually crude and violent acts, including an incident when a co-worker held a knife to her throat. But what is offensive is sometimes hard to pinpoint. Ultimately sexual harassment can happen, defenders of the concept argue, even when no one but the complainant perceives the environment to be offensive. In Canada, provincial human rights codes define sexual harassment as vexatious sexual conduct that the harasser knows or ought to know is offensive. Canadian human rights tribunals have ruled that even a single incident can be enough to create a hostile environment. The incident can be an abuse of authority, such as Bill Clinton's alleged invitation when he was governor of Arkansas to Paula Jones, then a state employee, to perform oral sex. Or it can be as tame as what a former Miller Brewing executive did. He was accused by a co-worker of telling her about a *Seinfeld* episode which centred on the word "clitoris," which happened to rhyme with Jerry's girlfriend's name. After being fired, the defendant sued his former employer and a jury awarded him US$26.6 million. What is crucial in cases of hostile environment is the difference in power between the two parties. And the harasser can be guilty without having any idea he is harassing someone. As legal observers have pointed out, Paula Jones's lawsuit against President Clinton would have had a much better chance if filed in Canada. The first grope may now be free in America, but not in its neighbor to the north.

Embarking on sexual harassment policies means striding onto slippery terrain. The customary paranoid, as we've seen, is a chronically offended person who possesses zero tolerance for anyone else's opinions when they don't coincide with his own. The paranoid is always searching beyond appearances for the slightest evidence to confirm his suspicions. He is constantly on the lookout for actions or comments that are unwelcome, unwanted, or hostile. He perpetually nurses grievances, real or imagined. He adores using the courts or other legal mechanisms to redress his grievances, especially when proceedings are conducted behind closed doors. In his eyes, what offends *him* is invariably of earthshaking significance and ought to be the obsessive interest of everyone else. The paranoid is convinced that in ending his persecution nothing less than extreme prejudice should be used. All the resources of the state need to be mobilized to ensure that he is never offended again. To the paranoid, it's impossible to exaggerate the seriousness of what he endures.

The Ontario Ministry of Education's zero tolerance guidelines, introduced by the NDP government in 1993, were virtually guaranteed to flush out every paranoid in the province's colleges and universities. This government document was intended to define what constituted harassment and discrimination in the province's post-secondary schools. The document is a paranoid's dream. Examples of harassment range from stalking and physical assault to jokes, cartoons, graffiti, "lookism," and other gestures most people would never think twice about. Even "shunning" is grounds for punishment. Ontario's policy doesn't require evidence that someone was genuinely harmed by the alleged harassment. The document also states that "a complainant does not have to be a direct target to be adversely affected by a negative environment." Since the paranoid thinks he is *always* the direct target of harassment and persecution, such a guideline is music to his ears.

Canadian guidelines on sexual harassment are closer to what its doctrinaire defenders have contended it ought to mean. These robust defenders are frequently referred to as "second-wave" or "gender" feminists. Entering the world of gender feminist theory is like entering the solipsistic, tendentious mentality of the paranoid. Gender feminism might be called either the historical successor or the direct opposite of "first-wave" or equity feminism. Equity feminism, as the dissident feminist Christina Hoff Sommers argues in *Who Stole Feminism? How Women Have Betrayed Women* (1994), wants the end of civil discrimination against women. It advocates the extension of equal rights to women in matters like property, marriage, divorce, custody. Its first great struggle was the campaign to win women the vote years ago.

Gender feminism, on the other hand, holds different assumptions. Gender feminists include figures like Marilyn French, Susan Faludi, Naomi

Wolf, Gloria Steinem, Andrea Dworkin, and Catharine MacKinnon. They argue that virtually all politics and social relations can be reduced to the subordination of women at the hands of men. They believe women are the victims of mass persecution at the hands of what they call "patriarchy," a male-dominated system that seeks at every turn to penalize them. French has actually written that men are waging a "war" against women, a "purposeful policy" of oppressing women through violent means that stretch from verbal subordination to outright murder. Faludi's thesis is somewhat different but equally paranoid. She maintains that women are suffering from a systemic "backlash" orchestrated by patriarchy and designed to roll back all the civil, social, and political gains made by women since the sixties. Dworkin and MacKinnon infamously contend that all heterosexual intercourse is rape, whether consensual or not. Gender feminists assert that women may be equal but they are also different; as a disadvantaged, historically persecuted social group, they deserve special protection under the law. To paraphrase George Orwell, they argue that all people are equal, but some are more equal than others. French's and Faludi's theories are based on data that have been shown to be faulty, yet their theories enjoy a surprising currency. These fanciful dimensions of gender feminism are yet another example of how paranoia has entered the everyday currents of life.

Like old-time Marxists who could never say exactly what "capitalism" was, gender feminists have trouble describing patriarchy in detail. Patriarchy in gender feminists' terms has a surreal, abstract quality that confounds attempts to quantify it. Gender feminists also have trouble convincing people that men are waging total war against women when the usual weaponry, conditions, and tactics of war are largely absent from today's social relations. That helps to explain their heavy reliance on French philosophers such as Jacques Derrida, Michel Foucault, and Jacques Lacan. While these figures are largely unknown to the average North American man or woman, in recent years they have exerted an influence on Canadian and American campuses out of all proportion to the merit of their writings. Identified today as "deconstructionists," all became momentary luminaries in the Paris intellectual scene in the 1960s and 1970s, succeeding the French literary giants Jean-Paul Sartre and Simone de Beauvoir. Their stardom was largely forged during the student rebellions of the late sixties, especially the May 1968 street riots in Paris. All three were part of a cohort of thinkers who helped launch the "me generation," the demographic group that came of age in the seventies and eighties and is notorious for its fondness for narcissistic navel-gazing. It's impossible to account for gender feminism in the 1990s without acknowledging the huge influence of these three ideologues and their followers on university campuses across this continent.

Though each had a somewhat different message, they were united by their paranoid visions of reality. All agreed that universal truth is a myth. Humanism, the belief in the capacity of individual human beings for self-realization through reason, is dead. There is no such thing as a "subject," an autonomous human being capable of making judgments about himself or about justice, beauty, and morality. The traditional view of the rugged individual, author of his own acts and ideas, is false. No definitive boundaries exist between self and society. Everything is contingent, socially constructed.

The three writers urge us to happily embrace marginality as a condition of our lives. We are enjoined to suspect everyone and everything around us, to uncover the conspiracies hatched by the powerful. Only then could we recognize how the world is arranged to oppress us, calculated to deny us pleasure and happiness at every turn. Each argues that we inhabit a universe in which human consciousness is confronted by gigantic and malevolent forces that have basically tricked us into making ourselves miserable. Rather than being oppressed by police forces, armed soldiers, or concentration camps, we have been hoodwinked into policing ourselves. We end up complying unwittingly with social systems that enslave us in myriad yet largely invisible ways. The only reality in such a world is power, sheer, brutal, and blind. It is constantly being reconfigured, always by agencies beyond our control and always to our disadvantage, continually rendering us victims.

If anything plays a leading role in such deployments of power, Derrida, Lacan, and Foucault argue, it is language. Language has us in perpetual bondage. Derrida contends that written texts are ultimately independent of their authors' intentions, lives, and historical contexts. When reading a text, the critic's responsibility is to discover its hidden linguistic laws. The author, Derrida says, is a kind of unconscious dupe of the very language in which he or she writes. Language, in other words, has a sort of life of its own. The writer who creates something is really a myth; he or she in many ways is incidental to the text and its language. Indeed, language's actual purpose is to serve as a disguised weapon for the manipulation of power and the eventual subordination of disadvantaged groups. Reading books, far from enjoyable, is an exercise in oppression. Thus, the reader's task is to unmask the text's clandestine purpose as a medium of subordination. But if there are no universal truths, if nothing is absolutely true, then everything becomes true. There are no facts, only interpretation. It is impossible to say exactly what a book like *Moby Dick* is about, but it's also impossible to say what it *isn't* about.

Countless academic critics have cashed Derrida's blank check. In dissecting fiction, no proof is necessary for making the most egregious statements about a book. What's baffling is that more writers themselves don't protest against Derrida and his theories of literary criticism. After all, his views call into question *every* writer's work, subjecting all literature to the same charge of complicity in projects of oppression. In Derrida's theory every writer is potentially a witless mouthpiece for one totalitarian agenda or another. If Derrida's ideas have had any effect it's to trigger a perverse literary scramble for the moral high ground, occupied by writers who though they continue to write books gnostically affirm with a wink and a nod that they do in fact know what writing's all about.

A leader in this self-congratulatory enterprise is the Nobel Prize–winning novelist Toni Morrison. Morrison has gratefully expressed her indebtedness to Derrida. Her tortured diction may put off a non-academic audience, but to professors of literature and other university departments it merely signals Morrison's brilliance, her oblique claim to the gnostic insights of the insider. In the delusional paradigm of the Derridean critic, the absence of something simply signifies its presence, just as the absence of any evidence that the L.A. Police Department conspired to frame O.J. Simpson becomes evidence that it did. The overwhelming evidence that Simpson was guilty merely proves his innocence, Morrison has written. According to her, works of American literature are all about race, even if African Americans or other minorities do not appear. From this highly dubious theory she goes on to ask: "How free can [I] be as an African-American woman in my genderized, sexualized, wholly racialized world?" How indeed?

Celebrated on the cover of *Time* magazine, the recipient of an international award worth close to a million dollars, occupant of a chair at Princeton University since 1989, repeatedly invited to lecture, read, be interviewed, attend conferences, serve on government commissions, Morrison appears to be doing all right for herself in her "genderized, sexualized, wholly racialized world." Far from being the victim she imagines herself, she even benefits from TV, that form of popular entertainment the paranoid academic class loves to despise. In a splendid example of one millionaire victim scratching the back of another, Oprah Winfrey selected Morrison's 1997 novel *Song of Solomon* as the second offering of the Oprah Book Club; it sold a million copies and sales of Morrison's other books leapt by about 25 percent. Morrison and her myriad acolytes in the media and literary worlds are living proof that the people we normally look to for intellectual guidance have lost their senses. Seduced by the superficially profound teachings of deconstructionism, they have turned to paranoia-mongering.

The psychologist Jacques Lacan was a somewhat different kettle of fish than Derrida. He wore his paranoia more visibly on his sleeve. Lacan preached paranoia, taught about paranoia, acted out paranoia, and bred paranoia among his closest followers. A womanizer, a plagiarist, an unabashed exhibitionist, a tyrant in his personal and professional relations, and a genuine celebrity, Lacan used to pack them in at his Paris lectures in the 1970s. Students and France's cultural stars flocked to hear what the master had to say. What he actually espoused will always remain a matter of debate if only because he published so little. And what he did say was perversely confusing. As the literary critic J.G. Merquior has said, when Lacan died in 1981 "there were only two persons in the world able really to understand the theories of Dr. Jacques Lacan: himself and God." That only made him more of a star, especially to North American academics bedazzled by exotic Continental figures. He was an excellent example of someone who managed to disguise the paranoid confusion of his thinking beneath exotic verbiage, banking heavily on the human tendency to think that the more prolix a person, the more profound. Lacan, perhaps more than anyone else, was a paranoia-broker, a member of the elite professional classes who helped make paranoia a respectable intellectual fashion in the late twentieth century.

Lacan became famous as the psychologist who did the most to introduce Freudian psychoanalysis to France. But his version of psychoanalysis would have made Dr. Freud turn over in his grave. Perhaps his best-known contribution to psychoanalysis was his indifference to the length of therapeutic sessions. Whereas Freud's orthodox followers had decreed a set time limit of one hour, Lacan often ended sessions abruptly after ten or fifteen minutes, leaving disoriented patients guessing what had happened. If Lacan had a consistent thesis, it was that our personal egos are paranoid. The ego is the creation of a civilization out to punish us relentlessly by deceiving us into thinking that we can somehow satisfy our desires. We are born into a preexisting world whose speech codes condition and organize our unconscious mind. These linguistic systems create our egos. The bad news is that the ego has been created to mystify and handicap us. The ego constantly struggles to seek satisfaction in the outside world, but the battle is hopeless. Our unconscious minds have been colonized by the discipline of language, so that we can never totally free ourselves from its power to deceive us. The ego is so enslaved by linguistic illusions that it is quite literally our enemy.

The worst thing we can do, Lacan asserts, is follow customary theories of psychology which supposedly teach us how to mobilize our egos to master the environment around us. To do that is to submit to the paranoid dominance of the ego. The object of Lacanian psychology is to emancipate the unconscious so it can speak, allow it to express itself through dreams and similar involuntary acts of omission or commission, like slips of the tongue. That's why late in his life his lectures degenerated into little more than a series of puns and wordplays. That people thought this meant he was deep speaks mainly to the kinds of followers he attracted.

When we desire someone, Lacan tells us, we are really desiring the recognition of that other person. But, he goes on, desire for that recognition becomes desire for the other's object of desire. So a child in the Lacanian scheme of things doesn't desire the mother but what the mother most wants and lacks: the phallus. Incredibly, this theory didn't seem to faze the many feminist followers Lacan could claim before he died in 1981. Little wonder that critics have accused him of the same antics as his friend the painter Salvador Dali, a skilful performer of fake paranoia. Like Dali's, Lacan's performances were presented as spectacle with a message.

But if gender feminism is indebted to any one thinker it is Michel Foucault. As Foucault's biographer James Miller points out in *The Passion of Michel Foucault* (1993), Foucault was committed to the view that a person defines himself through experience only, and the more intense the experience the better – any experience. Foucault was obsessed with death, suicide, sexuality, and violence, especially any combination thereof. His heroes included the deranged pornographer the Marquis de Sade; his favorite visions included the haunted, infernal images of the painter Goya. His preferred locales were the gay bathhouses of San Francisco and Toronto, where sex was anonymous and open to unmitigated fantasy. Foucault wrote the final chapter of his autobiography in 1983 as he was dying of AIDS, amid hot rumors that he had purposely frequented bathhouses even after he had learned he was HIV-positive.

Those who admire Foucault insist that such information is gratuitous, merely a way of trying to discredit him. But that ignores what he himself said. To Foucault, the connection between a writer's life and his literary output meant something. In flagrant violation of everything that decon-structionism stood for, he insisted biography mattered.

Foucault originally came to prominence in the 1960s with a book titled *Madness and Civilization*. He followed up this bestseller with other books like *Discipline and Punish* and *Birth of the Clinic*. Each demonstrated a wide if shallow reading. Each was filled with historical errors. Each added fiber to his overall thesis that as history has inched closer to the present day, social control has become increasingly methodical. Before the development of mass, highly technological society the enforcement of law and order was haphazard and unsystematic. With the arrival of the modern nation-state and industrial capitalism, Foucault argues, society became more complex, triggering the growth of new institutions and methods of discipline. Schools, factories, prisons, hospitals, and the like emerged, each primarily built and managed to control human beings by teaching them to internalize conven-tional morality and ethics. As citizens we have been trained from the minute we are born to be law-abiding and deferential to the forces of authority, par-ticularly the professions of medicine, education, and law. In other words, we are complicit in our own subservience.

But not consciously. The ultimate blame for our predicament lies else-where, in what Foucault calls the "disciplines of power" that regulate our everyday lives. Foucault's thesis is grim indeed, for he insists that history has grown more oppressive as time goes on, not less, as defenders of progress and the democratic state might contend. The very things we imagine will liberate us – education, medicine, law – are actually the culprits behind our misery. Life is getting worse – much worse – not better.

If Foucault's message is bleak to most thoughtful readers, it is music to paranoid ears. To Foucault, the personal was the political, and the political the personal. His vision of a society dominated by an intangible configuration of oppressive forces appeals to those who see themselves as perpetual victims but can't readily identify the faces and names of their victimizers. His belief that people are unconscious collaborators in their own subordination inspires those who have difficulty explaining away the fact that some of the most astute and vocal critics of gender feminism in the 1990s are women themselves. His neologisms, largely a product of attempts to translate his French into English, still haunt the anglophone academic world today. He was the supreme gnostic of the modern age, viewing himself as some hermetic, mystical seer who by secretly exploring the dark side of sadomasochistic eroticism could confront the most fundamental instincts. But like most gnostics, past or present, he fell prey to the paranoid notion that gifted human beings like himself were embattled by ubiquitous, infernal elements that sought to keep him from becoming the person he desired to be.

The aggregate effect of Derrida, Lacan, and Foucault is most evident in contemporary language. By undermining the notion of individual identity and personal independence, they have encouraged the use of terms that express the popular uneasiness about the relations among people, especially the sexes. Perfectly serviceable words such as "piety," "privacy," "stoicism," and "introspection" are going out of fashion. People no longer refer to "friendships." Instead they talk about "relationships," as if they have trouble imagining the bonds of normal affection that tie individuals together, as if we no longer believe these links to be natural. Is it coincidence that in the age of paranoia we see the growing use of awkward words and

136

phrases like "co-dependency," "personal space," "quality time," and "significant other"? The stilted, artificial nature of this non-traditional terminology captures the way in which people sense the social ground shifting beneath their feet, their acute vulnerability to other persons and things. It is the quintessential language for the state-of-siege mentality characteristic of paranoia.

Gender feminists' version of patriarchy borrows heavily from this and other aspects of Foucault's writings. Foucault showed how one could demonize something as complex and multidimensional as modern medicine. Gender feminists could cite his theories as precedent for demonizing patriarchy. In Foucault's world view, sweeping generalizations are not only possible but often true. Like Foucault, the gender feminists picture themselves as engaged in a momentous struggle. They seek to overthrow the Goliath of patriarchy. All the rules can be challenged, all boundaries transgressed, because the stakes are absolute power. Foucault was obsessed with power. Sex to him is really about power, not biology, and thus could be literally liberating. Accordingly, Foucault saw gay liberation as an avenue that led to concrete emancipation. But sex, being ultimately about power, could also be a means of subordination. To gender feminists heterosexuality was one of patriarchy's favorite techniques of oppression.

To gender feminists nothing institutionalizes patriarchy's oppression of women quite like the family. It is the central site for women's oppression because of the way it has touched the young lives of so many women. The family, the theory goes, is where women have been assaulted, demeaned, and abused emotionally. The family teaches women to accept heterosexuality as the norm. Eventually women learn to internalize their subordination *à la* Foucault. Women are thus engaged in nothing less than a war for their survival, made all the more sinister and dangerous by the fact that patriarchy functions in ways that are not obvious. According to gender feminists, this is a major reason why the conflict is literally a matter of life and death for women. Patriarchy disarms women (and to a large extent its male accomplices). It keeps people unaware of what is actually going on. It keeps their minds off the ways in which patriarchy conditions their personal lives, turning women into unwitting enemies of their own sex.

Hence the popularity among gender feminists of the slogan "The personal is the political." As a student at the University of Pennsylvania told Christina Hoff Sommers, "If you feel the whole world is on top of you, then it is." According to gender feminism, this kind of insight often comes in a "click experience," the sudden revelation when a woman sees with unerring perception that the world is arranged by men to serve men's interests solely. Women see in this instant that their suffering is necessary for such an unjust social and cultural system to endure. Every migraine, every mood swing (to say nothing of misfortunes such as the loss of a job or the death of a friend) can be blamed on patriarchy.

Little wonder, then, that the hyperbole of gender feminism is taken literally by its followers. By making every woman's life a microcosm of macrocosmic events, it helps women in the 1990s make sense of lives they believe are deeply dissatisfying. Unfortunately, if all personal problems are the problems of entire societies, then there is no limit to the extent to which people can project their own unhappiness onto society itself. The result is outrageous exaggeration. Thus, among gender feminists, few eyebrows arch when one of them states that a "Fourth Reich" is in the works if women don't do something dramatic and revolutionary right away. These women aren't interested in typically revolutionary activities like kidnapping industrialists or robbing banks to subsidize a coming armed struggle. Like the paranoids in a Pynchon novel, they know that doesn't work any more. But they haven't lost hope and they haven't entirely rejected the reality principle they castigate so freely. The solutions they prefer don't jeopardize their positions as bestselling authors or highly paid academics, at least not in the long run. What they recommend is consciousness-raising and self-fulfillment through therapy or New Age spirituality. If they are academics, they preach gender feminism to their students. In any case, they are careful not to leave noticeable bite marks on the hands that feed them. They practice "symbolic politics, a replacement for, and diversion from, the gritty politics of community and street," as the UCLA professor Russell Jacoby notes.

Still, there's no mistaking the revolutionary intent here. As the Canadian journalist Donna Laframboise points out, there is no reason to disbelieve leading gender feminists like Catharine MacKinnon who claim that the feminist movement intends to change the world. Their theories share disturbing similarities with other paranoid totalitarianisms that have cost so many lives and produced so much injustice in the twentieth century. MacKinnon and her ilk assert they want nothing less than "to transform language, community, the life of the spirit and the body and the mind, the definition of physicality and intelligence, the meaning of left and right, right and wrong, and the shape and nature of power." They imagine themselves a band of feminist Lenins working assiduously to destroy all institutions, tearing down all of society to rebuild it from scratch. If that analogy seems far-fetched, consider that MacKinnon herself told a sympathetic audience at New York University Law School, "There are more people at this conference than it took Bolsheviks to topple the czar." MacKinnon is as likely to overthrow contemporary society as today's Marxist-Leninists. But her remarks demonstrate gender feminism's hubris, its indebtedness to the paranoid totalitarianism of Communism, and its self-perception as a small group of persecuted warriors dedicated to overthrowing an entire regime.

Thus, gender feminism shares many of the features seen in other examples of cultural paranoia: the same hyper-vigilance, boundless resentment, sensationalist language, wild exaggerations. There are the familiar apocalyptic visions, belief in conspiracies, persecution complexes, delusions of grandeur, and ingrained reflex to accept the gnostic faith in one's own innocence and goodness. As Christina Hoff Sommers says, gender feminists are "prone to self-dramatization and chronically offended." They preach that women are under constant attack. They stress the systemic victimization of women, and one of the most heavily traveled avenues of victimization is sexual harassment.

Gender feminists, of course, take a hard-line stance on sexual harassment. They argue that the crucial factor in all heterosexual encounters is the balance of power, always tipped heavily in men's favour. When it comes to a president and an intern, there can be no greater disparity in power dynamics. No matter how flirtatious Monica Lewinsky was, no matter how willing, only Clinton had the power to make their Oval Office trysts reality. In effect, his power and privilege transformed her yes into a no, rendering him culpable of sexual harassment. Monica Lewinsky was the ultimate big-haired victim. Everything about her personal relations with the president was political.

This theory of sexual harassment caused no end of consternation in the Clinton camp during the Lewinsky affair. The scandal raised questions about Hillary Clinton's attitude toward the very gender she wishes to defend. To defend the Clinton presidency, the White House, including Mrs. Clinton, had to rally around the president. Clinton's supporters had to denigrate the many women Bill Clinton is alleged to have propositioned. They were expected to believe, in Michael Kelly's words, that Paula Jones, Kathleen Willey, and Monica Lewinsky were cheap tramps who were asking for it. Paula Jones, the Clintonite James Carville said, is what you get when you drag a hundred-dollar bill through a trailer park. As for Lewinsky, Democrats took to dismissing her as a victim of "emotional problems," someone who hadn't "played with a full deck in her other experiences." She was caricatured as "pure *Melrose Place*."

Gender feminists faced even bigger problems. Until Kathleen Willey's appearance on network TV, gender feminists had either said nothing or tried to exonerate the president. The National Organization for Women (NOW) refused to comment. Gloria Steinem pleaded laryngitis, though some asked how that kept her, a prolific author, from writing something. In the aftermath of the Willey interview, she did find her voice. Borrowing from victimology's deep well of rationalizations, she said that if all the allegations about Bill Clinton were true he'd be a suitable candidate for sex-addiction therapy. But her main point was that since the president seemed to be able to take Willey's no for an answer, his sexual harassment was excusable. Unfortunately Steinem seemed to forget that she and her allies in gender feminism had been responsible for broadening the parameters of sexual harassment far beyond "no means no" in the first place. When you live by the sword of paranoia, you die by the sword of paranoia.

The backtracking of other gender feminists and loyal Democratic women has been equally glaring. Notable Democratic Party women Pat Schroeder and Barbara Mikulski, who championed Anita Hill's cause when President George Bush nominated Clarence Thomas for the Supreme Court, either refused to "finger-point" or began making exquisite distinctions between valid and invalid cases of sexual harassment. Even feminist scholars took to saying things like "Being a feminist doesn't mean you believe everything every woman says," conveniently forgetting that for most feminist leaders that's precisely what it meant. These remarks, and the smear campaign against Lewinsky, left many Clinton admirers with a sour taste in their mouths. Maureen Dowd of the *New York Times* warned that assassinating the character of these women set "a dangerous precedent." It reeked of the worst hypocrisy. More seriously, it reminded us of the knee-jerk demonization that appeals to paranoid minds.

This hypocrisy of gender feminism has become increasingly evident as the 1990s wind down. Like all movements founded on paranoid premises, it ends up doing incalculable harm. Besides the damage it does to its stock (and frequently innocent) enemies, it ends up persecuting its own constituencies. It now runs the risk of grinding to a halt, having alienated growing numbers of thoughtful and concerned women. In recent years gender feminism has given every indication of collapsing under its own weight of absurdities and ironies. The Clintonites' antics merely shifted this drama onto the most visible stage in the nation. Whether gender feminists remain silent about "Zippergate" or try to excuse it, they can't help discrediting their own movement.

IN THE EVERYDAY WORLD, paranoia often gets revealed for what it is. But on university campuses things are different. Several scandals over alleged sexual harassment have broken out at Canadian universities in recent years. The stories behind these scandals brought to national attention the Inquisitional nature of sexual harassment policies. These scandals also demonstrated vividly how the indulgence of gender feminist paranoia solves little and ruins innocent lives. But what else should we have expected from policies that from the beginning depended on paranoid logic and theory? When a process is in place to smoke out the paranoids and indulge their delusions, should we be surprised to see gross violations of natural justice?

One such violation was the case of Dalhousie University mathematics professor Alan Surovell. In June 1993 he was accused of sexually harassing a female student. Nine months later a five-person panel made up of representatives of the faculty, staff, and students at Dalhousie voted unanimously to dismiss the complaint. It found no evidence that Surovell had threatened the student with reprisals for failing to comply with his alleged sexual requests.

Surovell's troubles had begun during the academic year 1992–93. A student in his entry-level mathematics course had approached him with her worries about succeeding in the course. They struck up a friendship and twice over the Christmas break he invited her to his home. On both occasions Surovell's ten-year-old son was present and on the second occasion so was his brother. The student received a grade of C– for the first term. They kept in touch during January 1993 but in February she began to miss

classes. After Surovell reminded her that consistent attendance was important for a struggling student, she approached him in mid-March and angrily
told him there would be no more social contact between them. She con-
tacted Barbara Harris, who was both the university's sexual harassment
officer and the university president's advisor on women's issues. In June,
when the student learned that Surovell had given her a D in the course, she
filed a formal complaint of sexual harassment with Harris.

An outspoken gender feminist, Harris began serving as investigator,
prosecutor, magistrate, and advocate/advisor to the student, an obvious
conflict of interest. The entire process took place in secret, and Harris
appeared with the student at a hearing before a panel whose members were
drawn from the committee she chaired. The student, perhaps distressed at
the way her complaint was now caught up in an Orwellian bureaucratic
maze, suggested that a formal apology from Surovell would be enough to
induce her to drop all charges. Surovell justifiably refused and the inquisition continued. Ultimately the complaints were dismissed, but not before
Surovell had to take medical leave because of the stress of the entire episode.

Dalhousie's sexual harassment policy, implemented in 1984, was one of
the first at Canadian universities. To Dalhousie officials it was a source of
pride. One might have thought that since its introduction those involved
would have worked any kinks out of the system. But the Surovell case shows
this hadn't happened. The complaint against him should never have been
taken seriously. But that didn't faze Barbara Harris; she seemed quite comfortable with the notion of "zero tolerance" when it came to allegations of
sexual harassment. In the words of the University of Toronto's sexual
harassment officer in 1994, zero tolerance means taking every "whiff of a
sliver of a rumor" and going in "with police escort." Every complaint, no
matter how trivial or badly founded, deserves the full arsenal of punitive
weapons available to the university. Besides consuming time and resources,
this approach is also akin to trying to kill a gnat with a machine gun. It is

systemically flawed. As Parker Barss Donham wrote in the Halifax *Daily News*: "Defenders of speech codes may try to portray Surovell's ordeal as a good process gone amiss. It is nothing of the kind. The abuses he suffered are the inevitable result of secret judicial procedures administered by ideological zealots." They are what happens when paranoia guides policy on and off campuses.

If Surovell had been the only casualty of the paranoid reasoning underlying sexual harassment policies the public might be justified in forgiving and forgetting. But the fireworks did not end with his case. While he was undergoing an inquisition at Dalhousie, controversy over sexual harassment was brewing on the other coast. In June 1992 a group of graduate students at the University of British Columbia had alleged that at least fourteen members of UBC's political science department were guilty of racism and sexism. The graduate students charged that female students, both white and non-white, had been marginalized, demeaned, and silenced. The students followed up these accusations with a memo in November 1993, complaining that the relationship between faculty and students in UBC's political science department was "authoritative" (they meant authoritarian). The racism and sexism of the faculty, they alleged, made them feel as if they weren't "partners in the learning experience." Staking out the paranoid's inviolable position as seen in the controversy over repressed memory, they stated that the "first symptom of racism is to deny it exists." In other words, if one dared dispute their charges one was automatically a racist.

The UBC scandal gathered its morbidly comical momentum as university officials and faculty made one mistake after another. In 1994 Lorraine Rigo, a graduate student, ratcheted up the tension when she resorted to an old student radicals' tactic of the sixties. She confronted the university with a list of "non-negotiable requests." The incident that had prompted her complaint was a conversation with a white, male, limited-term member of the political science department. Momentarily forgetting the fanciful students' rhetoric about student-faculty partnership, Rigo had mentioned that her students were taking her more seriously now that she had given out her first marks. The faculty member had replied: "Yeah, now they probably think you are just one big, bad, black bitch." She had promptly filed a formal complaint of sexual/racial harassment. Despite a letter of apology from the chairman of her department and two apologies from the faculty member in question, she demanded $40,000, six letters of reference, and the upgrading of two of her marks to passes. When she upped her demand to $50,000 and automatic admission into a doctoral program, the dean of arts, Patricia Marchak, recommended forming a committee of inquiry. In a move most would regret later, the feminist labor lawyer Joan McEwen was hired to investigate all the allegations of systemic racism and sexism.

As Sandra Martin wrote in the *Globe and Mail*, "giving a feminist labour lawyer *carte blanche* to find racism and sexism is like asking someone from the Flat Earth Society whether it's possible to fall over the edge of the world." Predictably, in June 1995, after ten months of interviews and study, and at a cost of about $250,000, McEwen submitted a 174-page report that essentially upheld the students' grievances. Though she found no more than five actual complainants, McEwen concluded that the mostly male department was guilty of "intolerance towards non-mainstream perspectives, the silencing of women and people of colour in the classroom, and gender differentiation." Among other things, she recommended shutting down admissions to the political science department until "all of the students in the department, both existing and prospective, will be accorded educational equity, and will be afforded a learning and working environment which is harassment- and discrimination-free."

An environment that is pristinely harassment- and discrimination-free is a paranoid's dream world. It's not the real world. Whoever thought such a report would end the crisis was dreaming in Technicolor. Marchak discovered there can be no peace with paranoids. Having done what she thought was the right thing, she was startled to find that the McEwen report called her a "negligent administrator." She promptly tendered her resignation in protest. She published her account of the controversy in 1996, saying McEwen's ideological bias led her to ignore due process and crucial evidence that contradicted the students' complaints. In the meantime, UBC president David Strangway had accepted the McEwen report. He ordered admissions to the political science department halted until it was "harassment- and discrimination-free," in effect smearing all its members. The *Globe and Mail* swiftly attacked the report for failing to provide "one solid proof" that any student had been treated as inferior because of race or sex. The CBC Television show *The National* descended on campus to cover the story. Civil rights groups were in an uproar. A former judge of the B.C. Supreme Court resigned in protest from UBC's board of governors. Strangway decided not to seek a third term as university president.

The McEwen report was fairly typical of the paranoid mindset that is allowed to flourish on university campuses. Marchak had given McEwen the go-ahead in the first place to file a report. If she didn't know what was likely to be in it, she should have known. Marchak later admitted that McEwen told her (after Marchak had appointed her) that white, successful, middle-class women (e.g., Marchak) cannot possibly understand racism and sexism, which in a saner atmosphere might have cast aspersions on McEwen's objectivity. McEwen was quite prepared to accept the idea, so dear to the paranoid, that perceptions of discrimination and harassment were enough to start collective scapegoating. Her report made no effort to verify any of the allegations made about any of the individual political science professors. Indeed, to some at UBC the whole scandal had nothing to do with ordinary rules of evidence. One university administrator told Marchak she really didn't care whether the male members of the department were guilty. Punishing them was a good way to send the signal across campus that sexism would not be tolerated. In other words, presumption of innocence until proof of guilt had been superseded by a new principle, one a distressingly large number of gender feminists accept: guilty even when innocent.

Finally, the whole affair ground to its predictably absurd halt. A group of graduate students relied upon the paranoid logic behind the McEwen report to draw up a list of demands. These demands called for nothing less than a revolution in post-secondary education. Graduate students were to be granted a majority vote in departmental decisions, "unlimited" letters of references, and the right to choose a "pass" designation if they were disappointed with a grade. Ranking of graduate students was to stop in order to end the practice of distinguishing between "winners" and "losers." Each professor was to sign a "formal apology," accepting the McEwen report, acknowledging the "racism, sexism, [and] harassment" of the department, and explaining the difference between these and academic freedom. Further, professors were to submit to a faculty-only, twelve-week, twelve-step "recovery" program intended to convince them they had abused their power and must relinquish it. Those who did not acquiesce were to be given early retirement.

A university spokesman had no alternative but to turn down the students' demands. The suspension on admissions was soon lifted. But the UBC atmosphere was still charged with paranoia. The new acting head of the political science department had in the meantime become engaged to the *Vancouver Sun* reporter who had covered the story. Graduate students insisted that he should have been excluded from the ongoing negotiations between professors and students. In response, on the eve of their wedding, both faxed their colleagues and news organizations that in marrying neither was harassing the other. In UBC's paranoid environment matrimony itself had become a cause for mistrust. When every social relation is reduced to a struggle over naked power, heterosexual love is grounds for suspicion.

Just as the UBC fracas was cooling down another was heating up not far away at Simon Fraser University in Burnaby, British Columbia. The cause célèbre again was sexual harassment policy and codes of conduct. The central figures were Liam Donnelly, a swim coach, and a student, Rachel Marsden. The charges at SFU were more serious than those at UBC. Marsden accused Donnelly of raping her during a date in September 1995, as well as other charges of unwanted sexual attention, intimidating behavior, and psychological sexual harassment. What followed after Marsden laid her charges was a drama that demonstrated in its own way how ideological paranoia had poisoned campus life through the theory of sexual harassment.

Initially it looked like an open-and-shut case. A formal harassment panel heard the case in the fall of 1996. Donnelly, believing himself innocent and acting on legal advice he later regretted taking, refused to take part in the hearing. After five days of deliberation, the university panel found him guilty of sexual harassment. When Donnelly requested a private interview with SFU president John Stubbs, Stubbs refused. On May 23, 1997, Donnelly was fired. Shortly thereafter, Marsden was awarded $12,000 in compensation and full credit for a course she hadn't completed.

Time and again, however, life defies the tendency to stereotype and oversimplify. The hearing itself, like so many other sexual harassment proceedings, was held in secret. Marsden's word was taken as fact without any effort to corroborate it. Moreover, Marsden had developed a close friendship with Patricia O'Hagan, the university's sexual harassment officer, who had handled the case up to the hearing. A draft of the panel's report was said to have been given to Marsden before being released. Just as seriously, Stubbs turned down Donnelly's request that Stubbs view lewd e-mail messages and provocative photos Marsden admitted sending to Donnelly.

All this was revealed to the shocked SFU community in June 1997 by acting president David Gagan. Stubbs was then on a three-month academic leave and unreachable. Later it was disclosed that he was suffering from depression and was on medical leave. The following month SFU acknowledged that the process had been unfair and Donnelly was reinstated. SFU also agreed to pay up to $35,000 to cover Donnelly's legal costs. Remarkably, it declined to take back the $12,000 originally awarded to Marsden.

The SFU case and others we've looked at reveal how epidemic paranoia can grip a campus over the issue of sexual harassment. Like sexual abuse theorists in general, people start with the recognition that something unpleasant – in this case sexual harassment – exists. Then the fanatical minority takes over, spreading the message that its incidence is far greater than the public thinks. Task forces and committees of inquiry are struck, usually dominated by the fanatics themselves. The recommendations of their studies often call for bureaucrats to be hired with the mandate not only to investigate complaints of sexual harassment, but to both encourage complainants to come forward and actively take their sides. A bureaucracy takes shape headed by equity officers and harassment counselors, whose careers rest on their zeal in ferreting out cases. They become part of what Margaret Wente of the *Globe and Mail* called "the harassment *apparat*," the countless consultants, lawyers, and coordinators across the continent who claim expertise about sexual harassment. Procedures of investigation are drawn up to minimize discomfort for complainants. A fast-track system is thus created that is stacked against the accused. After a while, the system's mere existence is sufficient to convince people that there's a problem. The benefit of the doubt is given to the very people whose occupational interests lie in magnifying the issue. The call goes up for more bureaucracy, which ensures that scandals such as those at SFU and UBC will erupt. When the roof falls in, most people look around, scratch their heads, and wonder how it all transpired. The answer lies in paranoia's unique capacity to disarm even the most rigorous of minds.

Why have universities become the principal battleground on which radical gender feminism and other paranoid philosophies thrive? Why does paranoia prosper precisely where it ought to meet the most resistance, where in theory our most critical minds are clustered and where paranoia's patent absurdities and exaggerations run the greatest risk of exposure? There are two main reasons. One is the very nature of university life in the 1990s. The university of today embodies the intimate symbiosis between bureaucracy and paranoia. All institutions and corporations today have a tendency to expand their purely administrative functions, but lately the university has been in the forefront of this trend. At one time a university or college was a place where professors taught students to master a body of knowledge and learn how to evaluate it critically. Now it is a place where students expect to be shuffled effortlessly from one program of studies to another until they graduate. Their teachers are increasingly made to feel that the onus is on *them* to make this transition successful. The notion that students are there to learn from their professors has been supplanted in recent years by the idea that students are there to have their self-esteem and their own opinions validated. A new wrinkle has it that students are mere consumers who pay a fee and have a right to expect the flawless delivery of certain services. But education is never a flawless experience, reducible to the satisfaction of consumer desires. It is an emotionally bumpy, often unsettling, potentially rewarding process that demands as much from students as from teachers. Where the mind is challenged, disappointment and satisfaction alternate. To expect otherwise is to yield to paranoia-mongers who like to capitalize on demoralization and magnify grievances.

This may sound as if students are to blame, but the main responsibility for this state of affairs lies with the universities themselves. Many faculty and staff have shown over the last four decades a reflexive willingness to comply with this approach to education. What was once a relatively unmediated, straightforward relationship between student and professor is now viewed as a vexing association fraught with troubling possibilities and in need of constant monitoring. The practical result? Institutional sclerosis. More bureaucracy. More rules, committees, administrators, and paperwork.

More counselors, equity officers, sexual harassment officers, conflict resolution mediators, and the like. Once things could be accomplished simply and quickly. Now they are accomplished slowly and with complications, if at all.

Bureaucracy doesn't just inject a high level of incompetence and inefficiency into an organization. It also creates a paranoid atmosphere. Bureaucracy exponentially breeds further bureaucracy. The more guidelines, committees, and administrators you add, the more guidelines, committees, and administrators you need to monitor the first batch. Ostensibly intended to make the system fairer and more accountable, proliferating bureaucracy instead makes it hard to know who's doing what to whom. As an institution's flow chart becomes more complex, real lines of responsibility blur, which is just fine for the kind of person bureaucracy requires. It welcomes a certain type of administrator, someone who is ever-vigilant about the dizzying rule changes and people's compliance with them, someone who enjoys working within a labyrinthine organization where individual accountability and initiative vanish into thin air like the Cheshire cat in *Alice in Wonderland*, leaving only the bureaucrat's anodyne smile. By privileging an apparatchik mentality, bureaucracy also alienates the many conscientious administrators who are just trying to do their jobs.

The Kafkaesque quality of bureaucracy is neatly captured in the means used to prosecute sexual harassment. Persons accused of sexual harassment, as we've seen, are confronted with a largely secret process. Committees render decisions that administrators, staking out arm's-length distance, refuse to question, lest the paper trail end on their desks. Is it any wonder that bureaucracy engenders paranoia in the people caught up in it? Because bureaucrats, like paranoids, shun face-to-face encounters, people trying to wend their way through bureaucracies continually feel frustrated. Suspicions multiply. Hatreds simmer. Intrigues are plotted. In other words, bureaucracies are ideal Petri dishes for culturing paranoia. Bureaucracies will cease to foster paranoia only when general agreement is reached that they are a necessary evil incapable of solving major social problems.

The institution top-heavy in administration and bureaucracy is the perfect environment for nurturing paranoid ideologies. Nowhere else have the theories of gender feminism enjoyed so much popularity as in the hallowed halls of academia. The growing respectability of gender feminist theory in academic departments such as literature, history, sociology, and political science testifies to the infinite tolerance for paranoia in post-secondary institutions. And the crucial engine behind the acceptance of gender feminism has been the creation of women's studies departments.

Starting in the 1970s, universities and colleges rushed to introduce these departments, to the point where scarcely a university exists without one today. Many discount the importance of women's studies feminism on campuses, alleging that it is a distinctly minority presence without any real clout. Some justifiably claim that women's studies programs actually work against gender equity and other goals of feminism, that they ghettoize women by clustering them in a gender-specific department, thus strengthening the anti-feminist argument that women are capable only of teaching women about women. In the long run such ghettoization probably takes place. But as John Maynard Keynes once said, in the long run we're all dead. In the short run the gender feminists wield considerable power within universities. In a classic example of the squeaky wheel getting the grease, gender feminists on and off campus are listened to carefully by university administrators. Gender feminists are largely responsible for the introduction and continued operation of sexual harassment tribunals. They have successfully pressured campus officials to remove putatively offensive art, revise curricula, change academic standards, hire underqualified job candidates, and in general spend incalculable amounts of money on projects of dubious value. As Christina Hoff Sommers noted in 1994, "Gender feminists have proved very adroit in getting financial support... They hold the keys to many bureaucratic fiefdoms, research centers, women's studies programs, tenure committees, and para-academic organizations. It is now virtually impossible to be appointed to high administrative office in any university system without having passed muster with the gender feminists."

A measure of gender feminist influence was an incident at the University of Nebraska, when the department of psychology ordered a male graduate student to remove from his desk a small photo of his wife on a beach in a bikini because two female graduate students who shared the same office complained it created a "hostile work environment." Gender feminists are so powerful that criticism of them has itself been ruled as grounds for censorship. Debating gender feminists, like debating paranoids, inevitably invites the charge that one oppresses them.

Perhaps no event galvanized the gender feminist movement on Canadian campuses as much as the Montreal Massacre of December 6, 1989, when a lone gunman, Marc Lépine, killed fourteen young women at the École polytechnique in Montreal. Before turning his gun on himself, Lépine said that he wanted to kill the feminists. Patently unbalanced and probably mentally ill, Lépine, like Fabrikant, was motivated by the utter hatred for others that characterizes the paranoid's outlook.

Every December 6 in every city in Canada and on every campus in the country, in a ceremony as solemn and emotional as any Remembrance Day commemoration, men and women gather to remember the Montreal Massacre. Officially a protest against male violence against women, it has been exploited by gender feminists to draw attention to their views and agenda. In attacking male violence against women, gender feminists have publicized studies like the 1993 Statistics Canada survey that found that 51 percent of Canadian women reported being victims of violence. Almost a third of women who had ever been married reported being assaulted by a current or previous husband. A closer analysis of the data shows that Statscan used an extremely broad definition of violence when it surveyed the opinions of some 12,000 women. When computing the rate of spousal assault, the most common form of violence, it in effect equated acts like throwing a plate or uttering a threat with knife attacks. Even then, because multiple responses were permitted, there was bound to be plenty of overlap among the answers. How many women who are or were ever married reported violent incidents? Eleven percent said they had been beaten up, seven percent choked, six percent hit with something, and five percent threatened with a knife or gun.

Findings by Statscan four years later showed a much different picture. A 1997 study found that incidents in which women were assaulted by their husbands or ex-spouses had declined by 18 percent from 1993 to 1996 across Canada. In big cities like Toronto (30.9 percent) and Montreal (22.5 percent) the drop was even steeper. Such a slide conflicts with the stock gender feminist theory that violence is actually getting worse. Clearly the problem of spousal assault, while still a matter of concern, is not as serious as the gender feminists would lead us to believe. And with mounting evidence that women also abuse males both sexually and violently, the scientific foundations of gender feminism are beginning to totter.

This form of statistics abuse has been the stock-in-trade of gender feminist groups for years. Christina Hoff Sommers has documented the many examples of statistics abuse in the U.S., including the "findings" that Super Bowl Sunday is "the biggest day of the year for violence against women," and that 150,000 American women die of anexoria each year. Each assertion is a falsehood presented as scientific fact. In Canada, Donna Laframboise and Margaret Wente have played the same role as Sommers in the U.S. They protest that these claims, far from being harmless or just grist for an ongoing societal debate, actually go unchallenged and end up swaying politicians and other government officials. In 1995, for example, Quebec's women's issues minister, Jeanne Blackburn, used the Montreal Massacre to justify more spending on programs to end spousal violence against women. What concrete connection there is between Marc Lépine's machine-gun rampage and a husband who swears at his wife remains a mystery, though Blackburn seems to be drawing on the gender feminist theory of a continuum of violence that links insults to murder. How sensitivity training could have stopped the likes of Marc Lépine also baffles the imagination. The unfortunate consequence of Montreal Massacre exploitation is the paranoid vision that all men are toxic, just coiled springs ready to strike violently at the nearest woman. Such a notion is precisely what gender feminists want us to believe.

The overall message of gender feminist propaganda about the Montreal Massacre is that all women not only are oppressed but also live in physical as well as emotional danger from men every day of their lives. These men can be husbands, fathers, uncles, brothers, lovers, friends, strangers, even women's own children. I have heard a Canadian gender feminist maintain seriously that women were literally dying on her university campus because of male violence. Some dismiss these statements as the witting exaggerations of people trying to win support for their cause, and there is no doubt some truth to that. When a cultural icon like Gloria Steinem says things like "Patriarchy *requires* violence or the subliminal threat of violence in order to maintain itself . . . The most dangerous situation for a woman is not an unknown man in the street, or even the enemy in wartime, but a husband or lover in the isolation of their own home," it's hard to know if she truly believes what she's saying. What about a sex-addicted president in the Oval Office? If Steinem is in fact trying to con us, there's little reason to hope that her many followers in the ranks of gender feminism are equally clever. What's most troubling is that this fondness for partisan hyperbole is so tolerated on campuses, precisely where it ought to be challenged for its distortion of the truth.

Women's studies paranoia should not mislead people into thinking that the main targets of gender feminist suspicion and hatred are men. If anything, other women end up being victimized as grievously as men by radical feminists. As numerous courageous refugees from women's studies departments have testified, the brand of feminism taught in such departments has reached ridiculous extremes. Christina Hoff Sommers's *Who Stole Feminism?* (1994) and Daphne Patai and Noretta Koertge's *Professing Feminism: Cautionary Tales From the Strange World of Women's Studies* (1994) document the paranoia of recent women's studies thinking, barely hidden beneath the glib phrases and impressive degrees of its articulate spokeswomen. Other women on and off U.S. campuses who have spoken out against 1990s gender feminism include Elizabeth Fox-Genovese, Elizabeth Powers, Camille Paglia, Karen Lehrman, Ruth and Wendy Shalit, Ruth Wisse, Margaret Talbot, Katie Roiphe, and Carol Iannone – the list gets longer virtually every day. Their Canadian counterparts include Laframboise, Wente, Patricia Pearson, Kate Fillion, Sandra Martin, and Senator Anne Cools.

When these women have tried to air their criticisms, they have found themselves the target of vicious attempts to silence them. Gender feminists have heaped scurrilous abuse on their heads, using defamatory tactics that rival those of the worst hate groups. In doing so, they simply mimic what used to go on in innumerable Communist organizations and states across the globe. In the paranoid little worlds of cults and Communist cells it's the heretics, the dissenters, more than the official enemies, who are earmarked for special punishment. As Arthur Koestler and other renegades from Communism have recounted, life within Communist parties was dominated by particular suspicion of other party members. Instead of camaraderie and solidarity, party members encountered inveterate mistrust. Individual opinions counted for nothing. Only the party could be right. Those who couldn't follow all the twists and turns of the official party line were considered more dangerous than Communism's stock foes. Dissident members were either drummed out of the party or, in Communist-run countries, eliminated by more violent means. In the final analysis, those who didn't submit to total party discipline were vilified.

The world of gender feminism works much the same way. It's not the defenders of patriarchy who suffer most. It's other women, often successful, independent individuals who have risen to prominence thanks to their wits and grit. Sometimes it's women who once were part of the movement but now have doubts about it. Paranoids may direct their hatred against abstract entities, but they save their real venom for those who once shared their delusions but now threaten to expose them. If, as Susan Faludi argued in 1991, feminism is suffering from a "backlash" today, then the backlash includes growing numbers of thoughtful and brave women who have discovered that gender feminism is dictatorial and exclusive in its methods, intolerant of questioning and criticism, and just plain incoherent when it comes to serious philosophizing.

The examples of gender feminist "silencing" of their sisters, feminist or not, are legion. In Canada the major bastion of off-campus gender feminism and the principal agent of silencing is the National Action Committee on the Status of Women (NAC). Founded in 1971, NAC is the rough Canadian equivalent of the National Organization for Women (NOW) in the U.S. While NOW has always depended on private money, NAC enjoyed strong governmental support right up to the mid-1990s, when politicians began cutting its public funding ($270,000 from Ottawa and $250,000 from Ontario in 1994). NAC always contended that it was a huge umbrella organization that spoke for 550 member groups and some three million Canadian women. That claim has now been revealed as a myth. Only 173 of these groups sent delegates to NAC's 1996 annual convention.

Such symptoms of NAC's decline aren't due solely to cuts in government subsidies. In an effort to be more "inclusive," NAC policies, ironically, have made it decreasingly attractive to most Canadian women. By pushing for greater representation from lesbians, immigrants, aboriginals, and women of color, NAC has made some women feel unwelcome. White, middle-class, heterosexual women, no matter how impeccable their feminist credentials, are told repeatedly by the new wave of NAC activists that they are part of the problem. They share the racist baggage of all whites and people of their social class. This is what happened to the longtime activist and fundraiser June Callwood in 1992. A founder of Nellie's, a Toronto hostel for battered women, Callwood was compelled to resign from its managing board amid charges of racism laid by women of color. The charges were bogus, but because of their magnitude they were enough to eclipse the substantial contributions Callwood had made to Nellie's. It is another symptom of the paranoid nature of contemporary culture that the accusation of racism, like the charge of sexism, is considered heinous enough to override any protestations of innocence.

One letter-writer to the *Globe and Mail* in 1995 identified herself as white, middle-class, able-bodied, heterosexual, with a management position. She had stayed at home with her child and admitted using new reproductive technologies. This, she charged, had made her a virtual enemy in the eyes of NAC. Though a feminist, she was told her problems on the job were of "no consequence." She claimed she stopped attending International Women's Day events because she was made to feel guilty for "the supposed sins of my peers." Finally, she broke with NAC over its family policy, which strongly suggested that her baby was better off in daycare than at home.

It's a familiar scenario played out in all paranoid groups seeking unrealizable utopias: nasty name-calling and infighting develop. The most fanatical and unscrupulous take over. An exodus of moderates ensues. Those who are left eye one another suspiciously, readying themselves for a new purge. Such has been NAC's sad history in recent years.

Other stories of gender feminist silencing reinforce the conclusion that it is widespread. In 1994 Gloria Steinem used her considerable media clout in an attempt to prevent CBS-TV from airing Connie Chung's taped interview with Christina Hoff Sommers, who wanted to talk about her new book on gender feminism. When Elaine Showalter tried to question the reality of recovered memories in a 1994 lecture at the Dartmouth School of Criticism and Theory, she received a rude reception.

Showalter describes what happened next: "Some of the women in the audience were so outraged by my remarks that they organized lunches and workshops; I was invited to defend myself against their anger and distress. They asked me how, as a feminist, I could wash our dirty linen, so to speak, in front of men, including Dartmouth undergraduates who might use my words against any women complaining of any kind of abuse. How could I live with myself, knowing I was making it harder for women to be believed? How did I dare challenge the authority of therapists and psychologists? A few of the women asked me to take the chapter out of my book [*Hystories*]. They looked stunned when I said that, on the contrary, I planned to expand it."

Things got worse after *Hystories* was published. A year after her book tour she still found herself the target of what she calls "avengers" who told her by e-mail they wanted her punished for her sins. "Almost all were female," she sadly observed. "I hate you, you fucking anti-feminist bitch" was among the most printable of these messages. She continues to receive feminist hate mail for things she writes, such as a *Vogue* magazine article in which she talked about her love of shopping.

Showalter had run smack up against the broad gender feminist allegiance to the theories of repressed memory and multiple personality disorder, long championed by Steinem and other luminaries of the movement. Some might say that Professor Showalter, who is a well-paid faculty member at Princeton University and a media star, ought to have a thick skin about such criticism, especially when it comes from "disempowered" students or less affluent and less privileged women. But gender feminist harassment of other women doesn't stop when the accuser is much wealthier and better connected than the accused. Donna Laframboise knows. She and four other women writers – Patricia Pearson, Danielle Crittenden, Kate Fillion, and Sandra Martin – were the target of virulent character assassination at the hands of one of Canada's grandes dames of gender feminism, Michele Landsberg. Their sins? They had dared to question multiple personality syndrome, cast doubt on the reality of recovered memory, write about domestic violence against men, argue that women are capable of terrible crimes, and contend that sexual harassment is not a simple, straightforward matter.

Landsberg, who writes a regular column for the *Toronto Star*, is the wife of Stephen Lewis, former leader of the Ontario New Democratic Party and Canadian ambassador to the United Nations. Like many spokeswomen for gender feminism, she has lobbied hard for what she thinks are the needs and rights of women. But apparently that doesn't include women journalists in their early thirties who are barely managing to earn a living, who "don't have full-time employment largely due to the huge number of baby-boomers who preceded us into the job market," in Laframboise's words. To Landsberg, Laframboise and her peers are little more than prostitutes for patriarchy and the anti-feminist, male-orchestrated backlash. Trying to sound like an announcer in a strip club, Landsberg wrote: "Yessiree, folks, here they are: our very own bouncing, bodacious babes of backlash! Perky Patricia; Dee-lectable Danielle; Kommando Kate; Sassy Sandra and (again and again) Double-trouble Donna." "Why can't we shake any neocon mag or rag without their flaky prose showering out like so much dandruff?" she asked. In Landsberg's view these writers are the paid hacks of the "conservative ideologues [who] own most of the media" and conspire to oppress women.

Landsberg's gender feminism takes on starker colors in light of the efforts of one of her targets, Patricia Pearson, to highlight the outrageous plea bargain of Karla Homolka. The 1995 deal resulted in a twelve-year sentence for Homolka's part in the sexual assault and murder of two teenage women by her husband, Paul Bernardo, in 1991 and 1992. Homolka also participated in the rape and inadvertent murder of her younger sister Tammy at Christmas in 1990. But when she testified in court in 1995 she and her lawyers claimed she was actually a victim herself – of battered woman's syndrome. Despite the overwhelming evidence provided by the Bernardos' home videos, shown only in court, Homolka contended that her husband's physical abuse had intimidated her into helping him commit sadistic torture and murder. Pearson courageously questioned Homolka's lawyers' exploitation of a condition that applied to countless less-fortunate women but came nowhere near fitting Homolka herself. She charged Homolka with "renounc[ing] her own claim to be an adult" and "insult[ing] women generally, who want to be judged as moral actors, accountable for our deeds." Meanwhile, Canadian feminists who had done so much to popularize the notion of battered woman's syndrome were silent about a tremendous miscarriage of justice, just as silent as feminists during the Clinton scandal.

Women are deserting gender feminism today because, as Daphne Patai insists, in the late 1990s it has also embraced "heterophobia." Patai, who once taught women's studies at the University of Massachusetts at Amherst, defines heterophobia as "the feminist turn against men and against hetero-sexuality." Like many women, Patai believes that feminism, which started as a movement to introduce pragmatic and equitable reforms, is in a state of crisis. Feminism is in danger of being hijacked by the extremists, and especially the male-bashers, as the examples of Dworkin, MacKinnon, Steinem, and French attest. To Patai, feminist criticism of patriarchal insti-tutions already has "derailed into a real, visceral, and frightening antago-nism toward men and a consequent intolerance toward women who insist on associating with them."

As Patai discovered, surfing the Web introduces us to hate messages against men as vicious as those against minorities. There are calls for ending men's participation in the rearing of children and accusations of wholesale incest. Gender feminist male-hatred on the Internet, however, is very different from cyberspace expressions of neo-Nazi racism or the millenarian ravings of Bob Fletcher's militia crowd. It's similar to what feminist leaders say pub-licly and without much critical feedback. It also finds its way into the corri-dors of judicial and political power. Steinem's references to "testosterone-poisoned men" are taken seriously in some quarters, including government. MacKinnon co-wrote the legal brief that served as the basis for the Supreme Court of Canada's Butler decision in 1992, in effect authorizing Canada Customs to practice censorship at the border. She was also a consultant to the federal government on the issue of sexual assault legislation.

The notion that men are a toxic influence on women has led to events such as Womenfolk, a 1996 women's festival co-sponsored by the Ontario government and the federal Department of Canadian Heritage. Billed as "a grand celebration of women's culture, heritage and dreams," Womenfolk made it clear that not only adult men but all males over the age of five were unwelcome. Educators have jumped on the women-only, men-are-toxic bandwagon. The tony private Linden School in Toronto justifies offering girls-only education on the basis that girls deserve to "go to school unafraid of sexual harassment." Mary Daly, a well-known gender feminist and professor at Boston College, refused to admit male students to her classes in religious studies until finally ordered by school administrators to do so in 1999. Other examples of sexual segregation due to anti-male bias are easy to find and are rooted in the paranoid delusions that have gripped gender feminism in the 1990s.

Equally worrisome is the growing distrust within gender feminism of heterosexuality itself. How could it be otherwise, given the intemperate rhetoric that has passed for "debate" within gender feminism in recent years? Dworkin and MacKinnon, who are greeted by standing ovations when they speak at feminist conferences, have long asserted that "the major distinction between intercourse (normal) and rape (abnormal) is that the normal happens so often that one cannot get anyone to see anything wrong with it." To Dworkin, marriage is "a legal license to rape." As Patai asks, "What . . . is a heterosexual woman to do in a climate that tells her that male potency is a threat? That the penis is an instrument of domination? How many heterosexual feminists fail to challenge heterophobia out of a secret belief that only lesbian feminists are The Real Thing? How common is it for heterosexual women who call themselves 'feminists' to find their heterosexuality complicated by their feminism?" To this last question, she answers that it's very common indeed. Heterophobes may have failed in many respects to achieve the kind of world they emphatically want, but "they have succeeded in introducing an element of genuine paranoia into the relationships of ordinary men and women... Their ideas need to be seen for what they are: a project posing as utopian that, were it ever to become reality, would instead be a nightmare."

Heterophobia infuses yet another variety of cutting-edge gender feminism. As the Canadian academic Philip Davis reveals in his book *Goddess Unmasked* (1998), one of the most outlandish trends in modern society is the growth of a respectable form of witchcraft or "Wicca." Largely female in membership and surprisingly concentrated among urban and suburban well-educated whites, Wicca is based on many of the phenomena described in this book: serial scapegoating, cultish ghettoization, delusions of grandeur, New Age psychotherapy. Wicca feminists worship the goddess within all women. This deity, they claim, endows them with special magical powers of healing. They feel empowered by the belief that they are continuing a long tradition of nature worship that was once proscribed and persecuted by patriarchal society. Unfortunately, there is no historical evidence that any society has ever worshipped a single, benign, nurturing goddess. Today's neo-pagan goddess feminism is an entirely modern invention. It's more indebted to the febrile theories of male thinkers than female thinkers. None of this hard evidence has shaken the faith of the goddess feminists, however. If anything, there is every sign that goddess feminism is becoming fairly conventional through such practices as "croning." Croning, or becoming a crone, refers to the onset of menopause. Groups of women get together to celebrate croning as a momentous stage in personal development. At its most prosaic, croning is an opportunity for women to offer each other emotional support, but as it grows more popular it mainstreams gender feminism and its fundamental distrust of heterosexuality.

These recent developments within gender feminism confront us with a good-news/bad-news scenario. The good news is that, because of its extremism, gender feminism is marginalizing itself. Causes that gender feminism promoted for years are falling into disrepute. Recovered memory and multiple personality disorder have been lambasted in publications like *The New Yorker* and *The New Republic*. In the wake of mounting criticism from psychiatric associations on both sides of the Atlantic, Canadian justice minister Anne McLellan told the president of the Criminal Lawyers' Association in May 1998 that the issue of people being convicted based on recovered-memory testimony warrants study. The self-esteem movement and the theory of separate education for girls, which feminism in decades past did a lot to popularize, are faltering. Growing numbers of erstwhile supporters defect as each day passes. Gender feminism's paranoid characteristics are there for everyone to see: its sensationalist rhetoric, its demonization of men and heterosexuality, its insistence on the systemic victimization of all women, its irresponsible manipulation of data, its gleeful cultivation of a siege mentality, its malicious prosecution of innocent people on sexual harassment charges and on the basis of repressed memories, its quasi-comical reliance on New Age psychobabble and psychotherapy, its shrill self-dramatization, its censorious attitudes toward anyone who questions even the most outlandish feminist assertions. Last but not least, gender feminism's dishonesty and hypocrisy became obvious to millions of Americans as the Zippergate story unfolded in 1998.

The bad news is that the Clintons' legacy, like that of gender feminism, may never be erased. Their involvement in the Lewinsky scandal will simply accelerate the trend, ongoing since Watergate, which has seen Americans increasingly lose respect for the highest office in the land. Analysts shake their heads in disbelief when they see the poll numbers showing Americans' high approval of the job done by the president but low estimation of him as a role model and trustworthy figure. It's hard to minimize what he has done to the office of the presidency. Moral outrage aside and Bill's acquittal notwithstanding, the Clintons' stint in Washington has reinforced the sharp cynicism and hip paranoia about politicians and the political process. They came to Washington with high hopes of reintroducing integrity in presidential politics. Hillary will leave with her dignity intact, "the only winner." But after Bill, will anyone be able to think about the Oval Office without smirking?

Similarly, no matter how delusional its ideology, gender feminism has shaped some aspects of the law and social policy, to say nothing of conventional language and everyday behavior between the sexes. Feminism alone can't be blamed for the way in which heterosexual communication, like verbal communication, has become a paranoid experience in the 1990s, but there's no mistaking how gender feminist theories have blighted sex by depicting it as a matter of raw power politics. These theories stress a pseudo-realistic interpretation of sex that strips it of romance and redeeming emotional significance. Gender feminism's grim views on heterosexuality, when combined with fear of AIDS, herpes, and other venereal diseases, have helped to produce the widespread perception of sex as frightening, dehumanizing, and degrading. Growing numbers of musicians, artists, and writers have expressed the terror that lurks beneath the surface of what was once thought to be normal interaction between individuals.

In the 1990s sex has also become the cause for rampant exhibitionism, blatant, defiant acting-out in public, such as the "do-me" feminism of someone like Scary Spice of the Spice Girls rock group. Reflecting the loss of confidence in our former view of sex, performers flaunt sexual behavior, the more bizarre and obscene the better. Rock stars rap about sexual violence or sing in unflattering, candid tunes about all varieties of sexual practice. Alanis Morissette rancorously sings, "Does she go down on you in the theater?" or "Are you thinking of me when you fuck her?" Gone are the innocent, sweet expectations that used to surround sex. In destroying naïveté, we have replaced it with anger. As far as sex is concerned, the motto appears to be: Trust no one and nothing. As Tina Turner sang, "What's love got to do with it?" Catharine MacKinnon couldn't have scripted a better anthem for the gender feminist movement.

Thus, though gender feminism has fallen far short of its stated revolutionary goals, its impact has been substantial. Largely because of its teachings, we think, sing, write, and talk about the relations between the sexes as if they were fraught with nothing but violence, subordination, and exploitation. That this perception rarely matches normal experience doesn't seem to subvert its popularity in the academic, corporate, government, and entertainment worlds. This success of gender feminism testifies to the marked indulgence of paranoia in North American society. In particular, gender feminism has staked out a formidable position in everyday Canadian life. As the next chapter contends, it is just one of several disturbing paranoid trends that have gripped the country as it heads into the new millennium.

CHAPTER FIVE

Only in Canada?

H IS NAME WAS Louis Riel. Handsome, eloquent, charismatic, and well educated, he lived more than a century ago on the sprawling Canadian prairies. He was fluent in Greek and Latin as well as English, French, and a variety of Indian languages. His ancestors included French Canadians and Indians. Among the 210,000 Métis people of Canada, he has attained folkloric status. He helped to usher the province of Manitoba into Canadian Confederation in 1870. To acknowledge these accomplishments, a group of members of Parliament from all five political parties have drafted a bill, expected to pass in 1999, to declare Riel a Father of Confederation. Calling it the ultimate Canadian millennium project, the MPs hope to have July 15 set aside as Louis Riel Day.

At first glance, Riel's legend would seem an unlikely subject for political controversy. His memory looks made to measure for a country which has always bemoaned its lack of heroes. Like almost all figures from the past, however, he comes with baggage. Riel once ordered the execution of a political opponent. He was exiled from Canada and returned to lead an armed rebellion against the Canadian government. He was hanged for treason in 1885. Turning him into a national hero means transforming a traitor into a nation-builder.

For some time the accepted view was that Riel was a rebel and dangerous promoter of seditious ideas. But now Riel is seen as the ultimate Canadian victim. In this version of history, his tragedy epitomizes the distinctive oppression of minorities that have suffered at the hands of a white, racist, Eurocentric, male-dominated civilization. Riel and the Métis were just defending their homes, the new historical script goes. Canada and its government were the criminals.

Riel's official rehabilitation is an apposite sign of the times. As a symbol Riel has become a lightning rod for a wide variety of interest groups who nurse paranoid grievances against Canadian society. The wide latitude given to these groups underscores the ineffable indulgence of the paranoid mindset by society's leaders. "Canada's very impossibility is its hope and possibility," the critic and essayist Bruce Powe wrote in *A Tremendous Canada of Light* (1992). With a few exceptions, the country's intelligentsia celebrate the way Canada appears to have self-consciously broken with the past, leaving modernism behind with its reliance on traditional democratic principles, institutions, and modes of expression. Science, reason, progress, and universal norms have no meaning in today's post-industrial Canada. Postmodernism is the new orthodoxy. As Powe, Robert Fulford, Richard Gwyn, and others have argued, Canada may be the first postmodern nation. Pluralism, eclecticism, diversity, impermanence, irony, and dissonance reign supreme in today's Canada. A country, like an individual, has no stable and autonomous identity, the postmodernists maintain. In a sense, a nation gets an identity only when it concedes it hasn't one. Canada's postmodernist elites see this as a virtue; they imagine that by turning Canada into a nation with no common identity they are blazing a path for the rest of the globe to follow. So just as postmodernist theory privileges paranoid psychology, Canada can be described as the world's first postwar paranoid nation.

Though most of the examples of cultural paranoia cited in these pages refer to the United States, Canada is probably the more systematically paranoid country. This is a hard message to swallow for many Canadians, who normally display more reticence and sang-froid than most Americans, conveying the impression that over the years nothing much has changed north of the border. Canadians still like to think of themselves as moderate, law-abiding, non-violent, public-spirited, cosmopolitan, compassionate, peaceful, phlegmatic, and deferential to authority. Some of this may still be true. But no Canadian in the late 1990s can deny that things are changing with dizzying speed, that the Canada of old is becoming a foggy memory. Events like the collapse of the East Coast fishery, or the 1995 Quebec referendum, or the pepper-spraying of student protestors in Vancouver in 1996 and the government cover-ups that followed it, or the malfeasance surrounding the tainted-blood scandal, with its literally lethal consequences, have alerted many Canadians to the possibility that their Canada no longer exists. The new Canada, in the words of the political scientist Mark Wegierski, is a country "in the throes of a tangled skein of pathologies." It is rapidly changing into a litigious, fractious, abrasive, adversarial, self-pitying, and grudge-nursing nation. Tempers are fraying, anger is growing, resentments are festering. Public discourse is increasingly dominated by a hypersensitive censoriousness which effectively shuts down real debate, leaving the field to those willing to recycle bureaucratically approved nostrums. The centrifugal forces of paranoia-driven, identity-group politics are alive and well, destroying Canada's already fragile sense of community and inching the country toward a crisis of national unity and social cohesion. United in hatred toward a virtually mythical Canadian power structure, the country's minority groups will soon realize that the emperor in Ottawa has no clothes. Sooner or later Canadians will be saying of Ottawa what the writer Gertrude

Stein once said about Oakland, California: there is no there there. They will discover that Canada is indeed "de-centered." It is a Lacanian ego: paranoid and desiring what it knows not.

The world is taking notice of Canada, even if some Canadians aren't. Internationally, more and more eyes are shifting to the ongoing Canadian experiment with multiculturalism and multiethnicity. It's an experiment with global implications, for what happens to a nation like Canada will reverberate around the globe. World history is being written in small letters in Canada, with no conclusion in sight. Canada's postmodern apologists shrewdly acknowledge this, but most of the nation's elites don't realize the magnitude of the crisis. If Canada, so proud of its traditions of civility, tolerance, justice, and good government, can't survive in the twenty-first century as a united nation-state, then its trials augur poorly for the many other nations with similar challenges. If Canada can't make it, what country can?

The case of Riel highlights the paranoid dimensions of Canada's crisis. The facts of his life tell the tale of a contradictory and highly complex person. Much of his life was spent among his Métis people in the Canadian west, then a sparsely populated and economically backward region. No stranger to jails on both sides of the border, he was also hospitalized in at least two asylums for the insane. In the judgment of several leading Canadian psychiatrists of the time he was certifiably psychotic. Certainly he reported having visions and voices that told him he was an inspired prophet destined to lead his people and establish a New Jerusalem on the prairies. He viewed his mission as heavily tinged with religious meaning, sometimes believing God had told him to appoint himself pope and found a new religion. When he went to the gallows he was initially unmourned by the vast majority of Canadians. In a day and age when society took a much dimmer view of paranoia than it does today, few thought of him as a hero.

With the passage of time, thanks to political pressure from Manitobans, Quebec nationalists, Métis organizations, and Canadian intellectuals keen on rewriting the past, Riel's reputation has undergone a facelift. As these groups loudly proclaim Riel their hero, politicians are scrambling to get on the bandwagon. Early in 1998 Jane Stewart, the federal minister of Indian affairs, praised his contribution to Canadian history. The separatist Bloc Québécois heralded him as an early defender of distinct society status. Even Reform Party leader Preston Manning, ever looking to broaden his national support, called him a bridge-builder. Every public official seems to want a piece of Louis Riel.

The sad truth is that Riel ought never to have been hanged. His conviction and execution were largely the result of shady and politically expedient maneuvering. The federal Conservative government of Prime Minister John A. Macdonald bowed to pressure from English-speaking Ontario when it rejected the jury's recommendation for mercy. In a contemporary courtroom he would have been declared mentally ill and sent to a psychiatric institution. How Canadian history might have been different if only lithium had been available in Riel's day.

But all that doesn't mean that Riel was a saint. He was indeed a rebel against duly constituted political authority, and his political and religious philosophy mark him indelibly as a nineteenth-century descendant of those self-proclaimed medieval prophets whose paranoid conceptions of cosmic strife led to so much chaos and violence. By the time of the 1885 Rebellion he was in the grip of apocalyptic delusions. As Ottawa's army headed west Riel imagined that the coming military conflict was a colossal showdown between his forces of good and the federal government, which he believed was evil incarnate. It was to be a war of millenarian extermination. "It is blood, blood, we want blood," he told one of his followers. His mind succumbed to a strange mixture of euphoria and foreboding. He began to overrule his military leadership, with fatal consequences for his cause. The delusions and hallucinations that serially clouded his thinking marked him as a man who, though urbane and articulate, was under the spell of paranoia.

Riel's rebirth as an official political hero in today's Canada, then, is a sign of the times. He is the paradigmatic historical icon for delusional times, a role model for a paranoid citizenry. It is no coincidence that this misguided and unfortunate paranoid besotted with millenarian fantasies should receive accolades from the country's leaders in the paranoid 1990s. Riel wins both ways today. He not only subscribed to paranoid ideas popular today. He is also widely viewed as a victim at the hands of powerful, hegemonic interests. In the eyes of his supporters he was both visionary and martyred saint. Nationalist Quebeckers who nurse resentments against English-speaking Canada, westerners who feel alienated from central Canada, aboriginal people who blame all their social problems on white society, multiculturalist critics of traditional Canadian assimilationist value systems: all see in him a potent symbol incarnating their rage, frustration, complaints, and feelings of being exploited and persecuted. He died to redeem their hopes and dreams, just as his memory keeps them alive. If Riel had never existed, Canadians in the 1990s would have had to invent him.

The most obvious cause served by the rehabilitation of Louis Riel is that of the Métis themselves. In recent years they have lobbied hard for official recognition that, in the words of Minister for Foreign Affairs Lloyd Axworthy, a longtime Manitoba MP, "promises were made to the Métis that were not kept." The supposed breach of faith refers to land grants issued to the Métis when Manitoba became a province in 1870. Half-breed adults and children were each given scrip with which to buy land set aside for distribution to the Métis at a dollar an acre. This arrangement was intended to replace Métis title to prairie territory, which they allegedly inherited from their Indian ancestors. Now Métis organizations claim either of two things. Either their forebears did not receive the land and scrip, or the government permitted them to sell their land and scrip to speculators for pittances. As the University of Calgary historian Tom Flanagan insists, neither claim is true. Myth or not, the story resonates as a drama of conspiracy, betrayal, and persecution. Like most paranoid narratives popular today, it casts the Métis as innocent victims, deserving of almost limitless restitution. In this scenario Riel is not the unbalanced traitor of traditional history books but a righteous crusader for Métis rights.

The success of the Métis project depends heavily on the popularity of the victimhood syndrome. Few trends in recent cultural history promote paranoid thinking more than the victimology industry, and nowhere does victimhood take its claimants further than contemporary Canada. As the journalist and author Richard Gwyn laments in *Nationalism Without Walls: The Unbearable Lightness of Being Canadian* (1995), fewer and fewer things unite Canadians as the end of the twentieth century approaches. But Canadians do have one thing in common: "We're all victims," he writes. When he states that "unquestionably" there are more victims in Canada than in any other country, he's not joking. Canada is a country of people who believe themselves terribly persecuted. It's worth quoting him at length on the subject:

All francophones are victims of all anglophones, all natives of all non-natives, all ethnic groups of all WASPs. Also, as a consequence of today's identity perceptions, all women of all men, all people of colour of all whites, all disabled of all abled, all gays and lesbians of all straights. Distinctive to Canada, and quite aside from the endless "humiliations" the Québécois have suffered, has been the victimization of the West by the East and of the Atlantic provinces by central Canada. Indeed, the depredations of the "pale, patriarchal, penis people," as they've been memorably called, have been inflicted upon an extraordinary number of victims by extraordinarily few victimizers. Excluded from the "dominant majority" must be all those WASPs who are homosexual or disabled, poor or unemployed, all those underdeveloped regions, and within the wealthy provinces, all those in small towns and on farms, and all those in the metropolitan suburbs who are patronized by the clever sophisticates of the inner cities. This equation leaves thirty million Canadians being victimized by roughly three thousand well-off metropolitan WASP males.

Thanks to the perception that virtually every Canadian is a victim of some variety, Métis attempts to acquire this same status fit squarely into the nation's postmodern mainstream.

Like so many other paranoid myths of victimhood, the Métis and Riel sagas come with sizable price tags, a sign that Canadian paranoid politics is big business and has been sustained artificially to some extent by the country's courts and governments. The Métis leaders apparently want the same things status Indians have: a land base, trust funds, a registry, Ottawa money, their own legislation. If they get these, it will be expensive. Ottawa already earmarks more than $6 billion a year for approximately 550,000 registered (status) Indians. When word spreads that there will be federal funding for the Métis, the many thousands of Canadians with Indian ancestry who have declined heretofore to identify themselves as Métis will be sorely tempted to do so. The impact will not just be monetary either. According to conventional socioeconomic indicators, on average the Métis have tended to do better than Indians. Many Métis have viewed themselves as Canadian citizens with the same rights as any other Canadians, not as dependants of the Crown. That may end if governments accede to Métis demands as they have to Indian lobbyists. The Métis could discover that playing the paranoia card is ultimately self-defeating. Like the paranoid politics of self-esteem, there can be no healthy resolution to situations where one group seeks limitless validation – financial or otherwise – from others. In the meantime, though, the politics of paranoia can be remunerative.

Of course, the Métis story is just a footnote to the much larger problem posed by the relations between white governments and Canada's aboriginal peoples. As any Canadian history textbook will tell you, the arrival of white settlers was not conflict-free. On the prairies the conjuncture of a variety of events – the arrival of the settlers and the railway, the disappearance of the buffalo, the shift of Indian tribes to reservations – led many to believe that this chapter in the country's history could be reduced to a tale of white oppression and native victimization. The subsequent sorry history of aboriginal residential schools reinforced this interpretation. For years aboriginal children were taken from their communities and placed in schools where they were cut off from their culture and language in an effort to assimilate them into non-native society. In the 1990s revelations surfaced of sexual, physical, and emotional abuse at these schools. A powerful myth has now crystallized in the official Canadian consciousness: historically and relentlessly whites have been cruel, corrupt, depraved, materialistic, and criminally cunning; aboriginals have been innocent, intuitive, spiritual, and environmentally responsible. Such a stark antinomy frames virtually every discussion today of policy toward Canada's aboriginal peoples.

For the most part Ottawa has accepted this theory. In November 1996 the Royal Commission on Aboriginal Peoples, at $58 million the most expensive study of its kind in Canadian history, issued its 3,500-page report. Among its many sweeping recommendations to change Ottawa's dealings with aboriginal communities were the creation of an aboriginal parliament and an aboriginal university, the abolition of the federal Department of Indian Affairs, and an increase of $2 billion in annual spending for native people within five years of the report's release. Ottawa's response was to issue a widely publicized "statement of reconciliation" in which the federal government expressed its regret over policies like the residential school system and the forced relocation of aboriginal communities. Symbolizing the shift from an assimilationist to a self-government policy, this statement also pledged about half a billion dollars to be administered by a board of aboriginal leaders at arm's length from the federal government. Much of the money will go to a "healing" fund, targeted for such things as language training and counseling for former students of the residential schools. It's true that the wording of the statement fell short of an outright apology. Ottawa had to be careful about saying something that might make it liable to lawsuits for abuse at residential schools. But there was no mistaking the message: present-day non-aboriginal Canadians – whether or not they are descendants of the whites responsible for the original anti-native abuse – were to accept the blame for past injustice and pay up accordingly.

In one sense, Ottawa's "statement of reconciliation" could be an opportunity for turning the page, for moving on rather than obsessively dwelling on isolated events in our past. There is no excuse for forgetting history simply because we don't like to think about it; totalitarian regimes, we know, prefer rewriting history and airbrushing out uncomfortable facts because it makes citizens more docile. But it's quite another thing to fixate on past horrors as if they were all there is to history. Nursing grievances from the past does the descendants of neither the victims nor the victimizers any good in the long run. It reinforces the trap that the victimhood culture falls into consistently. It encourages people to think of victims as all good and everyone else as tainted. It supports the old Rousseauian notion, dating back to the eighteenth century, that the native peoples were noble and pure while Europeans were decadent and evil. Thus, rather than generate further discussion about the past, it replaces one orthodox interpretation of history with a one-dimensional ideology geared to closing down debate. The practical consequences of this attitude include the current move to aboriginal self-government in Canada. After all, if Eurocentric whites contaminate everything they touch, the solution must lie in giving native peoples complete sovereignty over their own affairs, acknowledging their "inherent" right to self-government.

Recent developments should give Canadians pause before they buy into such a simple solution. Opponents of aboriginal self-government point to the examples of the Samson Cree reserve near Hobbema, Alberta, and the

Stoney Indian reserve just west of Calgary. By the late 1990s the Stoney reserve was one of Canada's wealthiest. In 1996 the 3,300-member Alberta band received $20 million from Ottawa and another $13 million from resource royalty payments, or about $10,000 per man, woman, and child. Somehow it ran a deficit of $5.2 million. Like many First Nations reserves it is also afflicted with unemployment, alcoholism, high crime and suicide rates, and general despair, especially among the young. Roughly 60 percent of all residents were on social assistance, despite the proximity of Banff and other nearby resorts desperately short of labor. By late 1997 Ottawa had placed the Stoney band under the financial trusteeship of an accounting firm and ordered a forensic audit of its books.

If anything, conditions are even worse at Samson Cree. Like Stoney it is one of the richest of Canada's reserves. In 1996 the band had revenue that exceeded $97 million, including more than $47 million in federal and provincial spending. The reserve also benefits financially from oil and gas holdings and a substantial investment portfolio including real estate and a trust company. Yet close to 80 percent of its 5,100 residents are on welfare. The unemployment rate is estimated to be 85 percent. Many of the residents live in unimaginable poverty and squalor. At the same time, a small group of band leaders who control its affairs and finances enjoy a globe-trotting existence. According to a federal audit of Samson Cree, tax-free compensation packages and other economic privileges enable the band leaders to live in a style that contrasts sharply with the rest of the reserve's inhabitants.

The point is not that the country's First Nations should be singled out as congenitally incapable of solving their current problems. The challenge is to discover the best means of doing so in the face of conventional wisdom as articulated by groups like the Royal Commission on Aboriginal Peoples. Its report says that the problems of the country's native peoples can be solved once they achieve economic self-sufficiency and erase their past dependence on white paternalism. Only then, goes the reasoning, will their learned helplessness, which Indians and whites both condemn, disappear. Many think a system of transfer payments and self-directed economic management will do the trick. But critics are skeptical, pointing to the failures of federal and provincial economic development programs across the country. There are even fewer grounds for optimism when the systemic nepotism and venality of tribal leaderships are taken into consideration. Nonetheless, the country seems hell-bent on moving toward granting all 1.5 million aboriginal Canadians the economic, political, and constitutional power to govern themselves. How this can be done without erecting an apartheid-like hodgepodge of sovereign communities from one coast to the other remains to be seen. Native self-government means establishing yet another level of government in a country that many Canadians believe needs fewer politicians, not more. How can all this actually strengthen national unity and improve relations between aboriginal and non-aboriginal Canadians? Steps are now being taken to address the countless land claims of native peoples across the nation. In British Columbia these claims amount to about 95 percent of the province. The difficulties involved here too are so immense that more and more Canadians – including natives themselves – have been rethinking the entire enterprise. Ultimately, that process of rethinking is bound to spark recognition of the paranoid foundations of Canada's whole approach to the problems of its aboriginal peoples.

The sobering fact is that the debate over aboriginal land claims and rights to self-government is only one chapter in a much larger drama surrounding the official Canadian policy of multiculturalism. Defining multiculturalism is notoriously hard. But to most people it means acknowledging, tolerating, and respecting the diversity represented by the many ethnic groups that make up Canada. To some it also means recognition that this diversity is one of Canada's strengths. So far so good. Most educated and compassionate Canadians would go that far. But a minority go further. They elevate multiculturalism from a position of being one of several strengths characterizing Canada to the position of being *the* basis for national unity. Combining the twin themes of diversity and unity may seem a paradox, conceded Hedy Fry, the federal minister of state for multiculturalism and the status of women, in 1996. But that doesn't keep Canada from trying to live that paradox. Canada, she stated, is the only country in the world to stress differences in an effort to unify the whole. Multiculturalism is "an inherent Canadian value." She and other multiculturalists inexplicably endorse state encouragement for the perpetuation of differences in the face of challenges that confront all individuals.

Ottawa and the provinces have proven to be eager listeners. Thanks to them, multiculturalism is a multimillion-dollar business. Once limited to dances and parades, it has now assumed a ubiquitous, in-your-face quality. Five-year-old preschool children are given lectures on racism. Protesters demand the dismantling of public crèches and nativity scenes during the Christmas season. "The Maple Leaf Forever" is no longer sung because it mentions General James Wolfe, whose victory at the 1759 Battle of the Plains of Abraham helped to seal the fate of French Canada. In 1997 some $16 million was spent in Toronto schools to offer classes in seventy "international" languages. No TV channel-surfer can miss the presence of multicultural television networks preaching awareness of cultural diversity. Sikhs in British Columbia insist on wearing their kirpans, or ceremonial daggers, at school; Muslim girls demand their right to wear the hijab to classes. Government money in Toronto goes to groups like Pino Sa Canada, the Sekyereman Society of Ontario, the Ethno-Racial People with Disabilities Coalition of Ontario, and the Ethiopian Association. In 1993–94 federal multicultural grants found their way to the Retired Black Miners ($5,500) and the Lao Association of Manitoba ($10,000). Recently federal money to the tune of over $10 million also went to a four-city project studying why Tamil women over fifty in Canada avoid breast cancer screening.

While several nations around the world proclaim a pious belief in multiculturalism, only Canada has made it official policy. In 1971 the Liberal government under Pierre Trudeau declared multiculturalism state policy, a move followed in 1973 by the creation of a Ministry of Multiculturalism. The 1982 Charter of Rights entrenched multiculturalism in the Canadian Constitution. And in 1988 the Conservative government under Brian Mulroney adopted the world's first multiculturalist law, supported by all three national parties.

Instead of congratulating themselves, perhaps Canadians ought to suspect that the rest of the world knows something they don't. There are good reasons why multiculturalism does not enjoy global assent, least of all in the Third World regions celebrated by Canadian champions of diversity. The primary reason is its reliance on outdated and fundamentally paranoid notions. It implicitly says that traditional Western, democratic institutions, customs, and laws can never serve as the common ground on which diverse groups can reach consensus. Multiculturalism is in fact an *invented* Canadian value. Far from being "an inherent Canadian value," it is an ersatz repudiation of almost all historical Canadian ideals and values. To multiculturalists, freedom of speech and expression is a racist swindle. White writers – especially if they're deceased – are condemned by the likes of Toni Morrison for "appropriating" the voices of the downtrodden. In 1993 black groups in Toronto protested the staging of the musical *Show Boat*, and in the process one black community newspaper expressed anti-Semitic opinions about the show's producer, Garth Drabinsky.

Multiculturalism declares that any assimilation into a common culture or American-style "melting pot" is not only bad but a huge con job perpetrated by a powerful ruling elite at the expense of disadvantaged groups. Multiculturalism is dear to the hearts of identity-group political leaders like Louis Farrakhan, Gloria Steinem, and the First Nations leader Phil Fontaine, who militantly oppose assimilation and favor social balkanization. Multiculturalism dovetails with other paranoid, late twentieth-century ideologies like gender feminism which depict all human interaction as mired in some apocalyptic struggle between the privileged and the disenfranchised. This struggle can be mediated only by state intervention designed to "teach" tolerance. But this is tolerance with a twist. To multiculturalists, tolerance doesn't mean everyone putting up graciously with things we don't agree with. Grudging tolerance is not enough. In reality, multiculturalism means positively affirming individuals or groups that claim victim status. *They* determine the terms for tolerance.

Unsurprisingly, then, multiculturalism as state policy breeds defensiveness, suspicion, wariness, and hostility, for both those who demand tolerance and those expected to ceaselessly extend it. It frays the very nerves it is meant to soothe. In multicultural, homogeneous civil society, no one can dissent from or opt out of the ideological public square with its formal and abstract matrix of rules. To do so is a virtual crime against the principle of mandated diversity. When the Trinidadian-born Canadian author Neil Bissoondath criticized multiculturalism in his 1994 book *Selling Illusions*, the vicious backlash he experienced sent strong signals to everyone else who thought of doing the same. So in a macabre example of the law of unintended consequences, multiculturalism, meant to end the silencing of voices, silences voices as never before. People eventually learn the advantages of self-censorship and dissimulation. Compliance increasingly translates into expediency, with people interested only in what they can get away with instead of doing what they think is right. People don't change their minds as much as they teach themselves to sanitize what they say and do. Predictably multiculturalism collapses because the whole effort is so transparent. Everyone knows that the enterprise is fake.

In this sense, multiculturalism apes the conditions under East Bloc Communism described by the Czech poet and politician Vaclav Havel. People learn how to be hyper-alert about what others are thinking, rarely accepting things at face value or crediting others with good intentions. The result

is a paranoid public square disturbed sporadically by the impatiently escalating demands of the multiculturalists as they see their experiment fall short
of expectations. It's no coincidence, then, that multiculturalism enjoys government approval in Canada. It's the perfect paranoid doctrine for a paranoid
nation. Little wonder that Gina Mallet described Canada in 1997 in the *Globe
and Mail* as "the proverbial Spanish shawl, one big fringe." Multiculturalism,
designed to unify, is actually creating a gaping hollow where once was the solid
core of a great country. Instead of creating a new communitarianism for the
twenty-first century, it has fostered social fragmentation.

AS A RELATIVELY RECENT paranoid ideology in Canadian history,
multiculturalism has nowhere near the lineage of Quebec nationalism. As
the journalist Gwynne Dyer observed in early 1999, Quebec nationalism,
like the Scottish independence movement, may trigger debates about taxes,
rights, and constitutional issues, but it's really "a psychodrama about self-
esteem." French-Canadian nationalism is almost as old as Quebec itself.
Like all ethnic nationalist ideologies, it is based on a skewed version of
history that depicts French Canadians as the perpetual victims of English-
Canadian chicanery and outright exploitation, dating back to Great Britain's
conquest of New France in 1763. Down through the years Quebeckers'
sense of victimhood has bred resentment, suspicion, and a form of self-
imposed apartheid. Well into the twentieth century Quebec politicians,
clerics, academics, intellectuals, and artists trumpeted the province's fundamental separateness from English-speaking Canada. And indeed Quebec,
with its different language, predominantly rural society, and overwhelm-
ingly Roman Catholic religion, *was* separate from largely Protestant,
English-language Canada.

With the so-called Quiet Revolution of the 1960s, however, Quebec
made a speedy transition to the modern, industrial, commercial, and secular
era. In a stunning reversal, Quebeckers turned their backs on their church

and now claim the lowest church-attendance rate of all the Canadian provinces. At the same time, a separatist political movement began to coalesce, a political party preaching secession from Confederation was formed, and in 1976 the Parti Québécois was first voted into power as the provincial government. A referendum on separation was held in 1980 and the federalist forces won by a healthy margin of 60 to 40 percent. Determined to snuff out separatism forever, federal politicians in the 1980s accelerated efforts to reach federal-provincial agreement on constitutional amendments designed to satisfy Quebec's demands for a special status within Canada. But in 1988 and 1993 the Meech Lake and Charlottetown Accords fell short of ratification. Another PQ government was elected shortly thereafter, and it announced that a new provincial referendum would be held in 1995.

The 1995 referendum was a loud wake-up call for English-speaking Canadians, showing that the politics of paranoia had come perilously close to destroying the country. The winning, whisker-thin margin was only about 53,000 votes. The separatist Yes side won 49.4 percent of the votes. True, a number of factors artificially improved the fortunes of the Yes forces in the campaign, suggesting the sovereigntists may never have it so good again. The PQ government had recently won a provincial election, ousting the unpopular Liberals, and had yet to make any unwelcome economic cuts to public spending. The premier, Jacques Parizeau, had handed out ridiculously favorable contracts to the provincial public service unions, among the biggest supporters of sovereignty. Mario Dumont and his Action Démocratique party, a splinter group of soft nationalist Liberals, also came over to the Yes side. By October 1995 the ingredients were all in place for a Yes victory. A vague, loosely worded referendum question was chosen to encourage moderate nationalists to think that a Yes vote was only a mandate to start negotiations with Canada for what was called "sovereignty-association." And when Parizeau faltered early in the campaign, the Yes side parachuted Lucien Bouchard, the charismatic chief of the federal separatist party, the

Bloc Québécois (BQ), into the post of leader of the sovereigntist forces. The effect was to pump new blood and impassioned rhetoric into what had been an otherwise enervated campaign. As a result the Yes side steadily gained support until the last week before the critical vote. On referendum day, as later investigations revealed, thousands – and possibly tens of thousands – of anti-separatist ballots were rejected by PQ scrutineers in electoral ridings with a significant proportion of No voters. More than 12 percent of all ballots cast in some ridings with large ethnic and anglophone communities were rejected. In four ridings the average rejection rate of No ballots was an incredible 89.3 percent.

By contrast, the federal side was woefully unprepared to fight the campaign. When it looked to be a close battle Ottawa quickly elbowed aside Lucienne Robillard, the desultory generalissimo of the No forces. Federalists panicked, harping negatively on the economic and social consequences of a Yes vote. Finance Minister Paul Martin, in a burst of ill-considered fearmongering, said Quebec would lose one million jobs if the Yes side won. Thanks to his gaffe the federalist campaign lost credibility among wavering voters.

The Yes forces apparently had everything going for them and still lost. This has led some Canadians to insist that another referendum might never be held, much less lost. Some say that even if the separatists manage to pull off a victory in another referendum, it won't matter. In the event of a Yes vote, Quebec, needing a prompt return to normality as soon as possible to quiet the nerves of international bankers and financiers, would have to negotiate with Ottawa on the federalists' terms. Such an outcome runs the risk of disillusioning the many moderate nationalists who voted Yes and who assumed that sovereignty-association would include things like the integrity of present-day Quebec's borders, the continued use of Canadian passports and currency, MPs in Ottawa like always, and a lucrative "golden handshake" from Ottawa. Should negotiations come close to breaking down and Quebec unilaterally declare independence, as Parizeau claimed he would have done in 1995 with a Yes victory, the economic and social upheaval would be so great as to spark massive public protest and effectively threaten to return the process to the status quo ante. Either scenario would constitute a political fiasco for the nationalists, so the argument goes, leaving Bouchard and his followers with no option but to avoid a referendum at all costs.

Then there is the specter that terrifies virtually every separatist: with each passing day the birthrate of Quebec francophones declines relative to that of immigrants and ethnics, weakening the numerical strength of the Yes cause. Bouchard, who followed his referendum campaign coup against Parizeau by taking over leadership of the PQ, expressed this hegemonic view in 1995 when he lamented that Quebeckers were "one of the white races with the least children. It doesn't make sense." What the sovereigntist cause needs is more Yes babies.

In addition, Bouchard has been forced to practice a kind of economic conservatism since 1995. He has had to cut public spending drastically in an effort to bring down the bloated provincial deficit. Reductions in spending, particularly on health, have alienated his chief constituencies, the provincial civil service and the public-sector unions.

Some claim that these realities will undercut the appeal of separatism; still, it would be unwise to underestimate the powerful attraction of paranoid victimology for Quebeckers. The resort to blaming English Canada for the province's ills is a favorite tactic of nationalist politicians in Quebec. It's true that the old-style grievances are wearing thin for recent generations of Quebeckers who never experienced the admittedly very real discrimination their forebears suffered at the hands of chauvinist English Canadians. After all, Quebeckers have been increasingly "maîtres chez nous" since the 1960s. Also, at the federal level, francophones have been privileged by essentially a massive official affirmative action policy that has provided employment for Quebeckers in the biggest employer in the Canadian economy, the federal civil service. In the cold light of day, scapegoating

English Canada for Quebec's problems in the 1990s looks ludicrous.

But the hyperbole continues. The provincial motto on license plates reads "Je me souviens" (I remember), and what nationalists like to remember is a selective, adversarial, and Manichean version of history that has now become gospel in Quebec public schools. In one respect the history taught to Quebec schoolchildren is similar to that taught to students all across Canada. It harps on grievances and victimization. But what distinguishes Quebec history teaching is that it concentrates almost obsessively on events in Quebec, as if the rest of Canada did not matter. On the few occasions when English Canada enters the story it is treated as monolithic, "perpetually united in word, thought, and deed," and intent on humiliating Quebec, says the historian Jack Granatstein in *Who Killed Canadian History?* (1998). Anglo-Quebeckers become imperialist exploiters who refuse to recognize the French language. The October Crisis and the use of the War Measures Act in 1970 are treated as if the Front de libération du Québec (FLQ) had never thrown bombs or kidnapped and killed hostages. Repatriation of the Constitution without the concurrence of Quebec shines as a classic example of the evil motives of English Canada. Federalists are painted as villains in a version of the "stab-in-the-back" conspiracy theory that ideally suits paranoid minds.

Figures like Parizeau similarly echo widespread sentiments when it comes to economic matters. He traces the economic troubles of the province in the late 1990s not to the fiscal irresponsibility of provincial governments but to Ottawa's debt reduction programs, which cut transfer payments to the provinces and forced Quebec to raise the sales tax. Parizeau and his avid listeners ignore the fact that in 1994–95 the federal government, in addition to providing many services to Quebec's seven million residents, transferred $12.5 billion to the province, including $3.9 billion in equalization payments (while Ontario, with its 11 million residents, received $11.4 billion and was one of three provinces that didn't receive equalization). In 1996

Quebec paid 23 percent of all unemployment insurance premiums and received 31 percent of the benefits. The list could go on; the fact is that Quebec benefits immensely from Confederation. Of course, to paranoid ideologues, these data mean nothing. Their rhetoric has paid off handsomely. It has gotten them elected, and it has wrung huge amounts of money from Ottawa. Why change?

Even things that might justifiably spark Quebeckers' outrage evoke a reaction in nationalists that's completely disproportionate. For example, in May 1998 the bilingual health administrator David Levine was appointed president and chief executive officer of the new, amalgamated Ottawa hospital. When it surfaced that he had once run as a PQ candidate, some Ontario politicians and community groups protested long and vociferously. As a separatist, Levine was labeled a traitor. To English Canadians a protest was warranted because, it was alleged, Levine's appointment to the job was directly due to official favoritism toward bilingual candidates. Critics correctly pointed out the fact that non-francophone bilingual Quebeckers were dramatically underrepresented in Quebec civil service hiring. Why should bilingual francophones be privileged in English Canada when linguistic minorities suffer from public service employment discrimination in Quebec? Memories were still fresh too of news leaked shortly after the referendum that a BQ member of Parliament had "invited" francophone members of the Canadian Armed Forces, nearly 30 percent of all enlisted men and women, to defect to an independent Quebec in the event of a Yes vote. Nonetheless, Quebec journalists condemned the protests against Levine as "ridiculous, gross and rabid denunciations." Pierre Bourgault, sovereigntist columnist for *Le Journal de Montréal*, could hardly restrain his invective. "The mad dogs of English Canada are leading us down the road to catastrophe," he wrote. "I will dare to say what others are thinking. Their virulent racism is leading straight to civil war."

The ugly dimension to nationalist paranoia became clear to all

Canadians both before and after the 1995 referendum. For years sovereigntist animosity toward anglophones and "allophones" had been growing ominously. Before the referendum there were separatist calls to deny "ethnics"
the right to vote. During the referendum campaign, matters were not
improved by Bouchard's comments about Quebeckers being part of a "white
race." Then Parizeau, in his speech conceding defeat, blamed the Yes side's
loss on "money and the ethnic vote." Later that same night Bernard Landry,
deputy premier of Quebec and minister for cultural communities, subjected
the Mexican-Canadian clerk behind the registration desk at the hotel where
he was staying to a splenetic, xenophobic tirade. "Why is it that we open the
doors to this country so you can vote No?" he asked. Landry became so agi-
tated that security had to be called. Not to be outdone, Pierre Bourgault in
a post-referendum interview identified Jews, Italians, and Greeks as casting
"ethnic votes."

The outrage separatists felt about the referendum defeat found an outlet
in Raymond Villeneuve. Villeneuve is a convicted FLQ terrorist whose bomb
was responsible for killing a security guard in 1963 at an army recruiting
center. He made headlines in 1996 when he formed the Mouvement de libération nationale du Québec, an organization dedicated to harassing
people and businesses who may have voted No. Threatening violence if the
circumstances did not improve for separatism, Villeneuve called immigrants
and anglophones the "enemies of the Quebec people." Quebeckers who considered themselves Canadians first were advised ominously "to go home
before it's too late."

It doesn't help matters that the current premier of Quebec and chief of
the PQ is a man inveterately predisposed to vitriolic hatred of other people,
especially former allies. Canadians learned this in 1996 when a psychiatrist's
report on Bouchard was released to the press and made public. Dr. Vivian
Rakoff, one of Canada's leading psychiatrists, never talked to Bouchard, but
upon being asked by a Liberal MP to draw a psychological profile of

Bouchard, Rakoff agreed. He concluded that Bouchard was suffering from "aesthetic character disorder," a term to describe a kind of emotional zoning, in which a person is able to forget the past entirely, concentrate blindly on the present, and thus lose all sense of continuity or discontinuity. This means powerful feelings of the moment, like the hatreds which Bouchard is prone to, can grip an individual without any mitigating factors sapping his fury. Opponents are transformed into demons, even if they were once friends or associates. Pierre Trudeau, whom Bouchard once admired, is now an enemy of Quebec. So is Brian Mulroney. Others, like Daniel Johnson, the former leader of the provincial Liberal Party, and his successor, Jean Charest, are, in Bouchard's eyes, beneath contempt. Though politics can be a rough-and-tumble business sparking strong personal dislikes, writes journalist Lawrence Martin, "rarely has the vitriol reached such a sustained level, with every public figure who failed to meet Lucien Bouchard's ever-shifting standards blasted as unworthy or disloyal." With Bouchard, the independence movement has found a leader naturally adept at voicing its passions.

There is another dimension to nationalist political paranoia in Quebec worth mentioning. Even if the sovereigntists were to win another referendum, the likelihood is that a majority of Quebeckers would be no more in favor of separatism than they were in 1995. Polls continue to show that support for secession from Canada hovers around the 30 percent mark, whereas most Quebeckers seem to want their province to remain part of Canada. The 1998 provincial election, which returned a majority PQ government, did nothing to change the situation. But with their infatuation with a unilateral declaration of independence the separatists threaten to turn a Yes vote in favor of a renegotiated alignment with Canada into a revolutionary coup d'état, an outright act of insurgency. In that event, Quebeckers would be, in Parizeau's own words, like lobsters in a pot of boiling water. It would be too late to protest. In other words, a small class of Quebec's social elite, playing on paranoid fears, hatreds, and dreams, would have engineered the ultimate feat of social irresponsibility. Providing another graphic example of the treason of paranoid intellectuals, they would have succeeded in leading over seven million people into a situation few of them wanted in the first place. Like latter-day Lenins, the separatist leadership would have hoodwinked an entire Canadian province into mandating a process that could make the Riel Rebellion look like a schoolyard tussle.

Perhaps it's only fitting that a province whose politics has descended to such paranoid depths should also be mired in a host of social pathologies. Quebec's suicide rate is the third highest in the industrialized world, higher than that of any other Canadian province. Worldwide, only Hungary and Finland have higher rates. Almost half of Quebec children are born to unwed mothers. Almost 65 percent of Quebeckers aged 25 to 29 are in common-law relationships, twice as many as in Ontario. Between 1971 and 1991 the marriage rate declined by 18 percent in Ontario but by 49 percent in Quebec. Quebec's divorce rate is one of the highest in Canada. Quebec has the highest number of high school dropouts in Canada, especially among young males.

Is it coincidence that a province afflicted with so many social problems should also be gripped by so many collective delusional fantasies and persecution complexes? As the *La Presse* columnist Lysiane Gagnon has noted, in Quebec New Age ideas, "miracle therapies, and various mushy instant-philosophies abound. Quebec is the province with the most sects and cults." She traces many of these problems to the void left by the retreat of Catholicism since the 1960s. Into that vacuum paranoid ideologies like Marxism, feminism, separatism, and labor unionism have spilled, says Gagnon, exploiting the religious emotions traditionally contained by the church. Yet for decades the country's political and constitutional energies have been focused on accommodating the supposed interests of this province.

Some contend that Quebec nationalism is simply part of a worldwide trend. This trend sees ethnic and linguistic communities challenge the authority of large, centralized federal systems, like the defunct Soviet Union.

An independent Quebec in this view is almost a healthy alternative to the technocratic system of social domination necessary to keep such federal states together. The implication is that Quebec separatism is a ripple in the wave of a global future and Canadians ought therefore to accept it. Some argue that Canada should simply let Quebec go. Perhaps Canadians should. But that doesn't disguise the paranoid, parasitic nature of Quebec separatism. Nationalists seek to actualize in a new, autonomous Quebec the same statist worldview as their federalist counterparts in Ottawa, a polity run by a bloated, meddlesome, and publicly funded bureaucracy headed by a class of managerially trained mandarins answering only to their deracinated imaginations. Years of playing the victimology and humiliation game have left Quebec unable to disengage itself psychologically from the mentality engendered by ritualistic warring with federalists who often are francophones themselves. The debate over separatism has assumed a kind of surreal, in-house quality, like the venomous spatting among siblings – which in a sense it is. Animosities and paranoid distrusts escalate in inverse proportion to the reality quotient of the issues. Candid separatists acknowledge this peculiar co-dependency and claim only independence can cure it, but a glance at the core nationalist constituencies would seem to dispel such a hope.

The spectacle of Quebec paranoid politics would be less threatening to the rest of the country if the English-Canadian elite didn't appear to be infected with the same intellectual and emotional virus. Perhaps it's necessary to fight separatism by engaging in the same tactics, but fighting paranoia with paranoia is a losing proposition. It was perhaps inevitable that the politics of Quebec separatism would provoke a backlash. Years of the separatist intelligentsia propagating the cult of victimhood and demonizing anglophones and the rich, when combined with the alarming spectacle of the 1995 referendum, culminated in the election of the firebrand journalist and activist William Johnson to the presidency of Alliance Quebec, the province's anglophone-rights organization. Johnson, a thoroughly bicultural and bilingual Quebecker, in many ways represents Pierre Trudeau's ideal Canadian. A person (like Trudeau himself) of mixed ancestry and blended cultural traditions, Johnson is the kind of "New Man" Trudeau and the Liberal Party have tried to invent since the 1960s, cosmopolitan yet rooted, multicultural in a distinctly central-Canadian way. But in today's Quebec he is a pariah, even in the eyes of other anglophones, striking proof that Trudeau's vision of Canada is out of date.

For some years Johnson has been writing about troubling examples of rights violations at the hands of Quebec provincial governments. In the process he has acquired the reputation of someone unafraid to speak out and protest against indignities heaped on anglophones and allophones. His margin of victory in the Alliance Quebec election was slim, triggering fierce debates within the province's anglophone precincts. Many anglophones distrust his in-your-face tactics, believing they would simply make life more difficult for minorities.

One of Johnson's biggest backers is the American-born Ontario journalist Diane Francis. The former editor of the *Financial Post,* now a columnist at the *National Post,* Francis too was appalled by the closeness of the referendum result and the antics of Canadians on both sides of the national unity debate. In her 1996 book *Fighting for Canada* she argues courageously that at the heart of the separatist cause was a poisonous constellation of lies, ruthlessness, racism, and intolerance. Unless fought and defeated, she contends, the separatist movement would spell the end of a united Canada and the onset of a calamitous political and economic crisis. The time for muddle and passivity is over, Francis concludes; expecting the separatist threat ultimately to disappear is inviting disaster. Federalists must use extreme prejudice to counter the separatists, employing every weapon at their disposal, through the courts, the ballot box, the airwaves, the country's political and social institutions. "Canada," she admirably asserts, "is worth fighting for."

All this is understandable and, from a federalist perspective, noble. But clearly engagement in the hothouse world of Quebec nationalist politics has infected Francis and others on her team; they have adopted the tactics of their opponents. Quebec separatism, she writes, is "not a legitimate struggle for self-determination." It is a threat to national unity for Francis, an illegal and unscrupulous effort to destroy the country. "It is a racially motivated conspiracy that has run roughshod over human rights, fair play, the Quebec economy, and democracy." She traces the conspiracy back decades to xeno-phobic, ethnocentric, and corporatist Quebec organizations that opposed assimilation into Anglo-Canadian society. Relentlessly these clandestine groups exploited the anti-Semitism and medieval Catholic prejudices of Quebec culture, irreversibly poisoning Quebec's cultural climate long after the influence of the Catholic church had dwindled. The separatists of the 1990s, according to Francis, with their disdain for constitutional rights and their affection for demagogic politics, are the secular heirs to this conspir-acist tradition.

To Francis, the conspiracy doesn't end within the ranks of the national-ist movement. She accuses the Canadian media and non-Quebec politicians of either wittingly or unwittingly abetting the separatist cause. The federal Liberal Party comes under particular censure for its cowardice and oppor-tunism. Obsessively worried about their seats in Quebec, Francis argues, the Liberals have refused until recently to stare down the separatists and chal-lenge their propaganda.

Much of what Francis has to say about the nationalist movement is true. While both Ottawa and Quebec nationalism can be blamed for the present state of national unity affairs, however, there is a lot less plotting and a great deal more sheer dottiness and self-interest than Francis acknowledges. Quebec already has more or less separated emotionally from the rest of Canada, and to accuse the separatists of grand conspiracies to destroy Canada may be like trying to shut the barn door after the horse has bolted. What has brought Canada to the brink on the eve of the millennium is not conspiracy but a collective failure of will, loyalty, and common sense on the part of many influential Canadians on both sides of the unity debate. Resorting to charges of conspiratorial intent misses this critical point. Quebec separatism is just the most graphic example of a kind of fashionable delusional ideology that has driven the country's identity politics for decades. It is not unique to Canada or to the rest of the developed world. What has made it particularly toxic within our own borders is the failure of educated and otherwise informed Canadians to resist its blandishments. To mimic the paranoia-mongers is to play the paranoid's game, one that brave and prudent individuals (like Francis herself) can never win.

But at least Francis sees the threat posed by the paranoid politics of Quebec separatism. Most of Canada's elites think the danger lies elsewhere. They help to sustain a peculiar kind of state-of-siege, grievance-ridden, victimhood culture, different than but every bit as delusional as that of Jacques Parizeau, Lucien Bouchard, or Raymond Villeneuve. Their self-delusion extends to the point of complacency. Despite appearances to the contrary, they believe their vision of Canada to be the perfect antidote to national disunity. Like Canada's left, which for decades believed nationalism could be defeated by an appeal to the solidarity of the country's working class, they fail to recognize their own paranoia in the adversarial paranoia of Quebec separatists. They are condemned to perpetual surprise every time they encounter the consistent refusal of Quebec nationalists to sign on to their version of reality.

To understand the Canadian elite's failure to provide real intellectual leadership in the age of paranoia one need look no further than the author John Ralston Saul. Saul is an international Canadian success story, a celebrated and accomplished writer, in both official languages. His non-fiction work *Voltaire's Bastards* (1993) was a bestseller, published in nine countries. In 1995 he was invited to deliver the Massey Lectures, broadcast in November 1995 as part of CBC Radio's *Ideas* series. Out of these lectures came another bestseller, *The Unconscious Civilization* (1996).

Saul is hardly a social pariah; indeed, someone in his shoes might be for-given for thinking that the world wasn't such a bad place after all. Such commercial success and literary adulation for a writer with an uncomfort-able, self-consciously subversive message would hardly be possible in most other societies. For Saul, however, all this is incidental. The truth, he claims, is that we live in an oppressive society not unlike Red China. Canada has been hijacked by a tiny group, a "technocratic managerial elite." In Ontario, as he told the *Hamilton (Ont.) Examiner*, the victory at the polls of the Progressive Conservatives led by Mike Harris in 1995 was really "a quiet coup d'etat from the inside by a group of what are essentially right-wing ideologues." These ideologues, according to Saul, are intent on brainwash-ing people and making them into so many Manchurian candidates.

Saul correctly maintains that people "sense that our civilization is in a long-term crisis." This sense of crisis reaches down to the level of the private individual. In an era of rapid information delivery and communications technology, people are disoriented, numbed, fearful of reality, and largely unconscious of the things that truly influence their lives. As Saul argues, we retreat into a mental world ruled by ideology, illusion, and displaced self-loathing, a realm defined by abstract patterns of language that reinforce our detachment from reality. We are captive to "the recurring delusion of a safe haven in both the grandiose and microscopic aspects of our lives." Retreating into our own mental worlds, he contends, is dignified by the romantic "myth of the triumphant, unattached individual." The trouble is that this sort of individual is neither triumphant nor unattached, merely unconscious of reality. He seeks refuge in the corporatist atmosphere of the group, searching for personal fulfillment by immersion within a collective identity. As a result, Saul concludes, democracy suffers because genuine indi-vidualism, the bedrock of a truly free state, cannot withstand the passivity, conformism, and raw self-interest cultivated by late twentieth-century corporatism. Society needs to learn to condemn ideology, denounce verbiage, reconnect language to reality, and define what we mean by individualism and democracy.

Who could dispute Saul's call to renounce sloppy ways of thinking and speaking? Who doesn't believe that professional specialization has produced an avalanche of impenetrable prose that mystifies more than it enlightens? Saul is on shaky ground, though, when he tries to answer the question: How has all this come to pass? What has produced the psychological complex that continues to cripple the effective functioning of democracy? It is here that he betrays his own weakness for paranoid thinking. Having diagnosed the problem with some accuracy, he only makes things worse with his proposals for solving it.

In Saul's view, the blame for our present crisis lies with the "neo-conservatives." Neo-conservatives like to call themselves "liberals mugged by reality," but to Saul they are ideologues, apologists for the marketplace, utopians who claim that minimizing government intervention in the economy will produce paradise. Like those of all utopians peddling ideology, their true interests lie in feathering their own nests while duping others into believing that it will all work out to the public's benefit in the long run. Although Saul is never clear about how conscious the neo-conservatives are of plotting this massive scam, readers are bound to conclude that there is a huge conspiracy afoot to fool and beggar the public.

Now one can say some caustic things about neo-conservatives, but calling them utopians is so far-fetched it's almost libelous. Neo-conservatism is hardly restricted to a defense of free markets and the global economy. Pro-capitalism may not even be its most important belief. There are real tensions within neo-conservatism between those who hail free-market economics as a bulwark against bloated governmental bureaucracy and socialist regimentation and those who stress sociocultural issues, like crime, drugs, abortion, and euthanasia. Almost all neo-conservatives, men and women, agree that economic and social concerns are inseparable. Individualists more than libertarians, neo-conservatives repeatedly emphasize free will and personal responsibility, hardly the things a corporatist tyranny wants. Many would agree with Saul that we should never ignore the potential dangers that unbridled free-market capitalism poses to communal existence by fostering avarice, consumerism, and social atomization. It's precisely because neo-conservatives are so aware of this potential that they stress the importance of religion as a force constraining the rootlessness and individualism bred by an unfettered global capitalism.

Neo-conservatives most certainly are not utopians; conservatism itself has been described as the enemy of ideology. Conservatism is the nemesis of ideological infatuation, which is the wellspring of utopian thought. In fact, neo-conservatism gets most of its headlines by attacking the utopianism of the political left, many of whose members believe that something as complex as race relations can be solved by policies like multiculturalism and affirmative action. Genuine utopianism, as we've seen, is alive and well in gender feminism, hardly a bastion of neo-conservatism. Neo-conservatives actually pride themselves on challenging the very premises of utopianism, like the notion that paradise is achievable through social engineering and messianic ideologies such as Marxism. They seem to take the collapse of Communism between 1989 and 1991 far more seriously than Saul; they see it as a sign that *all* utopianism is intellectually bankrupt and that all future philosophizing about economics, society, and culture must resist the siren call of ideology. If they prefer the free market it's not because they see it as a way of resurrecting paradise here on earth. Nor is it because they are "economic determinists," as Saul maintains. It's because they see it as superior to state-managed economics, a more sober approach to the challenges of generating productivity, prosperity, and real growth. The admiration of market capitalism derives not from unrealistic expectations but from the unblinking conclusion in the wake of global events over the last ten years that millenarian ideologies exact a huge human cost when put into practice.

Saul is also off-base when he insists that neo-conservatives like Mike Harris exploit populist fears in order to engender support for NAFTA, free trade, and the global economy. This, he contends, is "false populism" which only serves the interests of corporatist big business. But what about the leading American neo-conservative Pat Buchanan and his campaign against NAFTA? As one of the most vocal critics of globalism's impact on the American worker, Buchanan demonstrates that populism, neo-conservatism, and defense of open markets don't always go together.

Perhaps Saul's most bizarre charge is that 1990s neo-conservatism is part of a political tradition stretching back to Hitler and Mussolini. He alleges that Harris's Tories are "neo-fascist," heirs to the corporatist movements of the 1920s and 1930s that culminated in the Nazi takeover of Germany. Such an accusation will come as a surprise and insult to the many Jewish Americans and Canadians in the neo-conservative movement. They quite properly point instead to the far more solid totalitarian affinities among German national socialism, Italian fascism, and leftist regimes such as Pol Pot's Cambodia, Mao's Red China, and the Soviet Union. One is entitled to dislike Harris government policies, but lumping his Tories with the Nazis and Italian Blackshirts smacks of the kind of rhetorical exaggeration paranoids love to indulge in. By using sensationalist terminology he wins over kindred minds but effectively shuts down real debate over the many legitimate points he raises. Were there not enough evidence to the contrary, one would be forgiven for thinking that Saul labors under a delusional belief as skewed as the old McCarthyite suspicion that Communists were everywhere plotting to overthrow America.

In other words, Saul is an expert at the demonization game. Again and again he lambastes what he calls "right-wing ideologues" for somehow grabbing control of modern society. Infuriatingly, he rarely says who these ideologues are, except to round up the usual suspects: Newt Gingrich, Milton

Friedman, the Chicago School of Economics. The rest of the time he relies on abstractions, a curious tactic for someone so adamant about concretizing thought.

Above all, there looms the sinister leviathan of market capitalism. To Saul, and like-minded Canadian nationalists such as Maude Barlow and Bruce Campbell, national affairs are no longer run by elected officials responsible to the citizenry but by a "network of unaccountable institutions that . . . include the World Bank, the International Monetary Fund, and the World Trade Organization." This scapegoating of international finance not only fails to explain the whole story, it implies that Canada's future as a cohesive nation lies in protectionism, the erection of a kind of "Fortress Canada" that protects the values and principles Canadians hold dear. But when pressed, Saul and company can cite as examples of these values and principles only a commitment to compassion or a fondness for the public sector, with national health insurance figuring prominently. The bankruptcy of Canadian paranoid politics could hardly be more obvious. To claim that our national narrative is all about constructing "public services and universal social programs" is a serious misreading of Canadian history. The more the Canadian intelligentsia fixates on global economic trends as the primary reason for Canada's crisis in the 1990s, the more brightly shines its failure to come up with effective solutions.

Like Michael Lerner, Saul knows that 1960s counter-cultural politics won't sell in this day and age. But fear and loathing of capitalism taps into a visceral strain in the modern psyche. People no longer respond to the call to give up their cars, VCRs, and homes in suburbia. They can't be taught to return to the land and join communes. Some have already been there, done that. But like the militiamen, they can easily be incited to hate the banks, international investors, the IMF, and so on. They can easily be convinced that there is a handful of wealthy moguls plotting to dispossess and disenfranchise them. When someone with the fame and smarts of a John Ralston

Saul fosters these anxieties and animosities, it amounts to irresponsible para-noia-mongering on the part of an intellectual who probably knows better.

THINLY DISGUISED in Saul's attack against capitalist corporatism is the hegemonic anti-Americanism of Canada's intellectual trendsetters. Nothing knits them together like America-bashing. As the U.S.-born historian Michael Fellman has said, "Anti-Americanism has been the chief ideological manner in which Canadians have attempted to hold at some remove the colossus to the south." Historically Canadians have harbored a deep ambivalence about America. On the one hand, Canadians get misty-eyed about the long border between them and the United States that doesn't need defending. On the other, Canadians are keenly aware of elements in U.S. republican politics, society, and culture that they don't like. Canada did not achieve nationhood until 1867 and long after retained sentimental as well as constitutional ties to Great Britain. Its parliamentary political institutions confirm this British con-nection; indeed, until 1947 there was no such thing as Canadian citizenship and Canadians were British subjects carrying British passports. As late as 1982, Canada's constitution was a legislative act of Great Britain's parliament.

Well into the twentieth century Canadians remained wary about American intentions, fearing plans were under way for U.S. hegemony over the continent. But in recent decades the anti-Americanism has assumed a different tint. As Canada's links to Britain have shrunk, thanks to Liberal governments' policies designed to end them in the 1960s, anti-Americanism has become more paranoid. What once was a Tory, conservative sentiment securely rooted in the past became in the 1960s a left-of-center ideology, stripped of its historical underpinnings. Reflecting Canadians' growing uncer-tainty about who they really are as a country, anti-Americanism has increas-ingly scapegoated Americans for what ails Canada. Canadian nationalists today blame U.S. corporate capitalism and its media giants for dismantling Canada's borders and leaving its citizens vulnerable to unemployment, low wages, environmental degradation, the high costs of living, and the mounting incivility of public life. Eerily echoing Quebec nationalists' charges against the rest of Canada, they even blame Americans for the insolvency that spend-crazy Canadian governments created in the first place. This recent anti-Americanism, according to the historian Jack Granatstein, has been at the core of the Canadian identity. Canadians have come to define themselves, he says, "not as they were and are, but in contradistinction from that great and grasping neighbour." Like a paranoid who has no concrete sense of self, who is not anchored in any firm sense of community or tradition, Canadians project their insecurities and especially their doubts about national unity onto the United States in an attempt to prove to themselves that they can teach the Americans civil virtue. Paranoid anti-Americanism sees the United States as the consummate bully and source of all pathologies, a classic case of collective denial if ever there was one.

Canadian anti-Americanism shows up in the weirdest places. During the terrible ice storm that hit eastern Ontario and much of Quebec in January 1998, a VIA Rail passenger train left Ottawa for Toronto. It took eighteen hours to reach its destination instead of the usual four and a half. Numerous trees laden with ice had fallen across the track. Each time the train encountered one, the tree had to be removed by emergency crews. The train hit a downed power line at one point. Then it was ordered to travel in reverse. Food began to run out and alarm mounted about children and passengers who might have health problems. Through it all the passengers stuck together, organizing services until VIA Rail officials were able to help. When the passengers arrived bleary-eyed in Toronto at 3:30 a.m., VIA Rail had arranged to have them put up at the Royal York Hotel. Passengers felt a mixture of relief, anger, and consolation. As one said, "I felt happy I was on a Canadian train. If it had been an American train, people would've responded differently. We're less confrontational. There was a sense we all had to pitch in together."

Canadians often outdo even Third World or European anti-Americans in their vilification of the United States. Canada's stance toward Castro's Cuba, for example, has always had a perverse anti-American element to it, starting with Pierre Trudeau's visit to the island in 1976 and continuing right up to Prime Minister Jean Chrétien's junket in 1998. So pathological was the Canadian government's anti-Americanism that Chrétien was willing to sit through a typical Castro rant about American "genocide." Castro drove home the anti-American message of the 1998 meeting by donning the old army uniform he had mothballed after the collapse of Communism. Recognizing a glorious photo op for what it was – a chance to disguise his international pariah status – he exploited it to the point of embarrassing Chrétien. That few in Ottawa were appalled shows how far Canada's governing elite will go to score paranoid points. Anti-Americanism has taken on such a self-evident and gratuitous quality in Canada that it's obvious only to Americans who emigrate to Canada or to Canadians who return to their homeland after living in the States.

The main pitfall of this type of paranoid anti-Americanism lies in its capacity to blind Canadians to nearer and clearer dangers. As Canadian intellectuals nurse their ill-founded anxieties about American annexation and the encroachment of American values in Canadian life, they have surprisingly little to say about Quebec nationalism. Denouncing separatist sentiment sounds too much like racism directed against a minority identity group; better to castigate the Brobdingnagian yet largely benign and indifferent superpower to the south. As Fellman shrewdly observes, the enemy is not outside Canada's borders; it's within her own frontiers. "Obsessive anti-Americanism is fiddling while Montreal burns."

Fellman is right in drawing a link between anti-Americanism and the delusional denial of Canada's opinion-makers in recent years. Few have contributed more to this trend than Margaret Atwood, internationally renowned author of such novels as *Surfacing, Lady Oracle*, and *Alias Grace*.

Atwood attended Harvard University as a graduate student in the early 1960s. There she developed the kind of self-indulgent national navel-gazing that Canadians mistake for profundity. As her biographer Rosemary Sullivan notes, Atwood herself recognized that Harvard "was personally very important. It was the place where she started thinking of Canada as a country with a shape and culture of its own. And it was the place where she recognized that writing was a political act." At Harvard, Atwood encountered what she remembered as the typically American taste for hypocrisy, puritanism, arrogance, and violence. She later based the setting of her novel *The Handmaid's Tale* on Harvard. In the novel she depicts "a terrifying vision of patriarchy: sterile, unable to reproduce itself, it turns murderous and enslaves the young men and women under its control." According to Atwood's ex-husband, this nightmarish vision captured the stifling oppression they had felt within Harvard's walls.

Living among Americans for that brief period obviously affected her deeply as a young Canadian. Others might have developed a larger curiosity for Americans and their country, might have asked what accounted for the American mentality. Eventually they might have concluded that like all nationalities Americans were far more complex than the caricatured impressions she ultimately drew. But not Atwood. Her encounter with Americans triggered instead in her a primal urge to search for the Canadian national identity. "We knew perfectly well," she reminisced, that Canadians had a national identity. "We just didn't quite know what it was ... We knew nothing about ourselves."

Atwood's search ended in the conclusion that Canadians were "paranoid, fearing invasion from without." Armed with this insight, and seeing a prophecy she couldn't resist fulfilling, she began convincing other Canadians. Ten years later she codified her thoughts in *Survival*, her 1972 survey of Canadian literature, which went on to sell over 80,000 copies, an extraordinary total for Canadian non-fiction. *Survival* quickly became orthodox reading for the emerging wave of Canadian literary nationalists in the 1970s. Atwood slaked the thirst of Canadians who believed that the country had a literary tradition of its own. Canadians were enjoined to "read Canadian." University faculties transformed curricula to include ever more examples of Canadian writing. The Canadian state stepped in to massively subsidize the arts and culture. The subtext to English-Canadian literary nationalism, however, was the self-righteous notion that Canada's unique cultural identity had been forged in defiance of American influence. Canadian paranoia was vindicated. Suspicion of Americans was built into the very foundations of literary nationalism. At its center, this movement was mostly made up of a group of Toronto writers, "and at the centre of that group was Margaret Atwood," writes the literary critic Andy Lamey.

Survival is full of ideas of unquestionably lasting value. But some haven't weathered the years well. One was Atwood's thesis that victimhood was the overriding theme of the Canadian experience. There was "a superabundance of victims in Canadian literature," she writes. "Canada is a collective victim," she adds, tracing this sense of victimization to the country's past as an outpost of France and England and then as an economic colony of the United States. Chapters follow that describe victimized immigrants, families, aboriginal peoples – even animals. Anticipating the nineties rage for therapy, Atwood offered a four-part taxonomy of "victim positions" which presumably enable the victim to cease denying he's a victim and become "a creative non-victim." The whole thing is written in a slightly ironic tone, but the irony barely disguises the note of seriousness. One year after the publication of *Survival* Atwood made sure people knew she wasn't really kidding when she lumped Canadians with other colonists, citizens of "emerging nations," and Holocaust survivors. To Atwood, the Canadian "habit of mind" was an identity shared with refugees from genocide; the frost-bitten Canadian with cabin fever was as much a victim as an Auschwitz survivor.

The point is not that Atwood's statements are open to question, though they are. It's that they proved to be so persuasive. Her statements are possible only in an age attuned to surreality and gross hyperbole, an age that sees nothing implausible in the wild literary plots of writers like Thomas Pynchon. Their plots make sense only to people morbidly conscious of their own imagined inferiority. And in a rare and unaccountable way such statements become self-fulfilling. Since the publication of *Survival* Canadians have been taught in schools and universities to internalize such a message. Many have come to believe it, including Canadian writers. They form a sort of priestly tribe whose collective mentality is a strange combination of literary noblesse oblige and paranoid distrust of the average Canadian. Never before has an aristocracy of wealth or talent felt such a paradoxical need to lead and loathe its alleged inferiors. As the literary critic Philip Marchand and others have argued lately, this "tribe" is animated by an "us-against-them attitude." The tragedy is that they may be united less by soaring talent than by cliquish and stock sentiments, nurtured by the funding practices of a sympathetic Canadian state.

THE INFLUENCE OF the nation's literary "tribe" is nowhere more evident than on the Internet. Showing that they've internalized the tribe's value system, Canadians in cyberspace indulge their worst anti-American fears. Most paranoia-inclined Canadians worry about a gigantic U.S. plot to take over the country. Thanks to sources like Jeff Koftinoff's "Main Canadian Conspiracy" Website, Canadians can learn that their politicians are selling out the country to a natural resources–starved America. To those Canadians who complacently believe that only Americans are paranoid about New World Orders, NAFTA, and the IMF, a visit to Koftinoff's Website is sobering.

The story behind Koftinoff's Website takes us into Canada's conspiracy-minded subculture, where political boundaries and definitions blur. Koftinoff is a computer programmer from Grand Forks, British Columbia.

He burst onto the cyberspace scene in the mid-1990s when he set up his own Website for those who think America wants to annex most of Canada. His inspiration had come from Glen Kealey, a former commercial developer in the Hull, Quebec, area, whom Koftinoff had met in 1991. Kealey may be Canada's most visible conspiracy theorist. He became a conspiracist, he explains, after Roch LaSalle, Brian Mulroney's minister of public works, allegedly demanded a $5,000 bribe from him in exchange for government support of one of Kealey's projects. (The charge Kealey brought against LaSalle was eventually dropped.) Kealey investigated and claims to have found evidence of a massive bribe and kickback scheme operated right out of the Prime Minister's Office, involving the Tory party, the RCMP, and the Justice Department. To publicize the scandal Kealey camped out on Parliament Hill for 1,000 days. He and his wife, the former Shelley Ann Clark, were married in a First Nations ceremony on Parliament Hill in 1994. Mrs. Kealey was an executive assistant with the Canadian NAFTA delegation and claims to have been ordered to falsify and shred briefing books to smooth the pact's acceptance. Though she has no hard evidence, she insists that the deleted sections contained references to a plan whereby Canada would become the fifty-first American state by 2005.

Since the Kealeys' marriage they have traveled the country telling everyone who listens that a huge plot is afoot behind government's closed doors to sell out Canada. They formed the Assembly of Independent Canadians (AIC), supposedly because so many First Nations people told them that the country could be saved only if the Kealeys were able to create a critical mass of angry Canadians willing to oppose such treason. After meeting the Kealeys, Koftinoff decided to set up his cyberspace clearinghouse for messages about this crisis. Within a few months he'd gathered over fifty documents. Over 500 computer users were accessing his site every week. To this day Koftinoff denies believing in conspiracy theories himself, stating only that he finds many of them fascinating and worthy of investigation.

The Kealey tale of a mammoth strategy to destroy Canada from within shows that political paranoia is not peculiarly American, not restricted to the delusional fantasies of the American militia. It indicates that Canadian conspiracy theories are both homegrown and highly akin to American-style fusion paranoia, obliterating customary distinctions between right and left. They defy all familiar political labels. Conspiracists accuse Mike Harris and Alberta premier Ralph Klein as readily as former Ontario premier Bob Rae of complicity in the destruction of Canada. Conspiracist theories echo themes that have cropped up in the rhetoric of countless social groups and political parties from across the political spectrum. In tone and content they strongly resemble what respectable nationalists like Maude Barlow and Bruce Campbell have also said. They warm the hearts of multiculturalists when they celebrate Canada's aboriginal peoples as the country's last great defenders, and they contain just enough factual material to appear plausible at first glance.

The Kealey conspiracy story begins with the Free Trade Agreement (FTA), a treaty he says Mulroney, the premiers, and Mulroney's allies in the multinational corporate world managed to sneak by Canadians in 1989. The FTA, according to Kealey, allowed American banks to snap up Canadian assets. To Canadian conspiracy theorists, the FTA was the first act in a carefully scripted scenario that would culminate in Quebec separation, the U.S. annexation of Canada, and the building of the Grand Canal Project. This project has as its goal the damming of James Bay in order to make it a freshwater lake. Next this water will be diverted south through a complex system of dams so it can eventually flow into arid American regions hit hard by global warming and non-sustainable farming methods. All this is being done to satisfy the needs of giant U.S. agribusiness companies that stand to lose a lot unless Canadian water can be exploited. Behind these enormous corporations lie the United Nations–centered engineers of the New World Order who seek to demolish national borders like Canada's and erect a world government determined to annihilate personal freedom.

The key event in such a conspiracy theory is Quebec separation. Secession will weaken Canada, making it easier to unite with the U.S. It will also lead to a showdown between the Cree Indians of Ungava and a newly sovereign Quebec government eager to go ahead with the second phase of the James Bay hydroelectric project. Violence would give American troops located just across the Canadian border – and disguised as United Nations peacekeepers – the pretext to enter Quebec's northlands and subdue the Cree, paving the way for total U.S. control of the entire region. Quebec will be reduced to its old boundaries, a narrow strip on either side of the St. Lawrence River. The rest of Quebec and Canada will be in American hands. Just like the visions of Bob Fletcher and the U.S. militia, these theories feature troops donning blue UN helmets, parachuting out of helicopters, and launching an orgy of bloodletting.

It would be a mistake to write Glen Kealey off totally. Thanks to Stevie Cameron's investigation of the graft and corruption of the Mulroney years in *On the Take* (1994), we know there were traces of fire behind the smoke of his wild allegations. Kealey was exposed to just a fraction of the very real venality that punctuated Mulroney's government, but through the infectious paranoia of Canadian politics and the mounting frustration felt by countless citizens in the 1990s as the country lurches toward some kind of reckoning, Kealey has succumbed to the Canadian curse. In a sad transformation, he has gone from fighting a noble cause to pursuing a conspiracy-drenched theory that impresses only the converted and the grudge-ridden. As he admits, he'll speak to any groups that will listen, including right-wing hate groups. In Cameron's words, "Like many whistle-blowers who are alienated from the mainstream ... his conversation has become infused with descriptions of the evils of the Rothschild banking empire, and his once-tolerant listeners have begun to drift away."

If Canadian conspiracist anxieties about a coming New World Order focus on anyone, they focus on Maurice Strong. Strong's life and career are a genuine rags-to-riches story. Born in poverty and raised in Manitoba during the Depression, he is a billionaire today, thanks to hard work and judicious investments. He has headed Ottawa's foreign aid program, Petro-Canada, and Ontario Hydro. At present he works for the United Nations and advises the president of the World Bank.

It is eminently fitting that Strong arouses Canadian paranoia; in true Canadian style he almost asks for it. He is himself one of the most publicized and respected alarmists in the world today. As an environmentalist dooms-day prophet he makes Al Gore look soft on the environment. Just as political paranoids claim that the earth is constantly in crisis or at an unprecedented crossroads, so Strong preaches that our fragile planet is doomed unless revo-lutionary changes take place. A new "eco-industrial revolution" is in order, he argues, to redress the terrible inequality of wealth between the globe's rich and poor. Only an environmentally benign and resource-sustainable approach to the economy will do the trick. This will entail a "renewed role of the United Nations," a pioneering policy sponsoring globalization, "uni-versalization," and national interdependence. If not, there's always Plan B. Strong has helped to finance a second Ark in preparation for the next deluge. To Canadians who fear the loss of sovereignty and statehood his views are calculated to heighten anxiety.

Besides saying the wildest things, Strong also does things that make people shake their heads. As chairman of Ontario Hydro in 1994, he opened talks with Costa Rican officials to buy over 30,000 acres of rainforest. According to the few who knew anything about the proposed deal, Strong was pursuing the plan to preserve rainforest land to offset the emission of greenhouse gases. Understandably, the Tory opposition at Queen's Park raised objections. Hydro had just cut 10,000 jobs and had a $34-billion debt. Then news leaked that Strong had business interests in Costa Rica, including a hotel complex. The NDP government swiftly canceled further talks. The fact that the government had been blindsided by Strong on this and other occasions simply sparked more speculation about his conspiratorial, New Age motives.

The conjunction of Strong's paranoia-mongering about the environment and the paranoia of Canadians fearful of globalization and world governments reveals how public discourse has been reduced to a dialogue of the deaf. Each side is the captive of a particular delusion; each expresses genuine distrust of forces at work in the world today. In some respects it's a healthy distrust. Why should we trust international bankers or powerful figures like Strong? Conversely, why should we ignore the environmental ravages of air and water pollution, overpopulation's effects in some parts of the planet, the degradation of non-renewable natural resources, the loss of soil, forest cover, and important species of plant and animal life? These are legitimate concerns, of course, and warrant concerted and informed debate from citizens and their elected representatives.

Unfortunately, in such a heated cultural climate it's almost impossible for the non-paranoid to get a word in edgewise. A kind of hyperbolic inflation has set in, debasing the language of measured debate. Discussion is dominated by the shrillest and most sensational voices. Those who patiently challenge outlandish claims find that in a paranoid, oppositional culture they end up as targets for the chronically offended, or they discover that no one's listening for very long. Few are interested in the laborious task of extracting the tiny specks of truth embedded in the fool's-gold nuggets of paranoia.

Similarly, Canadians suspicious of their politicians, governments, and institutions have grounds for being so. There is much truth to the theory that federal, provincial, and local politics over the last half-century have come close to unraveling the country. Irresponsible economic policies have led Canada to the brink of bankruptcy. Measures designed to accommodate Quebec and other grievance groups have merely produced constitutional gridlock. Multiculturalism has created artificial fault lines throughout society, pitting Canadians against Canadians. To the American political observer Paul Piccone, "Canada provides a perfect example of a country where New Class excesses have brought a previously stable and peace-loving society to the brink of disintegration." This "top-down" type of New Class paranoia has finally settled at the bottom levels of Canadian society. Canada's opinion-makers, seeing their reflection in grassroots paranoia, naturally applaud it as an inchoate form of subversion directed against people and things that deserve contestation. But this merely validates it, upping the ante in an already paranoid culture of suspicion and distrust.

Will Canada's elites wake up from their dogmatic slumber? There is reason for some hope. As Lawrence Martin points out, Canadians increasingly reject the "debate psychology" that has characterized the country's prolonged struggles to appease Quebec. Up to the late 1990s this psychology "conferred a sort of moral superiority" on Quebec nationalists. The consensus was that Quebeckers were perfectly entitled to share a "defensive victim complex." Canadian collective guilt made this possible. But mounting numbers of Canadians refuse to play this perverse game any longer. As they realize that the Quebec imbroglio is just a graphic example of the larger malady that affects Canada, they lose patience with the struggle. They wonder if there isn't a better way. They wonder if Canadians outside Quebec haven't "demeaned" themselves enough in trying to placate the separatists.

Still, the emergence of a more clear-sighted approach to Quebec separatism probably comes too little, too late. And even if the problem of Quebec nationalism could be licked, the larger pathology remains undiagnosed. The Canadian condition reveals that paranoia escalates wherever a sense of community declines. Canada's intelligentsia, with some notable exceptions, remains obsessed with the belief that the nation is a loose collection of victims deserving of infinite compensation and compassion. They rail about corporate capitalism, neo-conservatives, and the bigotry of Albertans and the tractor-pull crowd. They claim Preston Manning is a bigger threat to national unity than Quebec separatists. Or they play the reliable anti-American card. All the while they try to forge a new national identity, a new sense of community stressing inclusivity and diversity, but oddly out of touch with most individual Canadians. This effort at self-conscious social engineering began with Pierre Trudeau's theory of the multicultural, cosmopolitan "New Man" and has culminated in the postmodern ideal, the "de-centered," mutable, impermanent individual, playfully and ironically open to character modification. Just as paranoia thrives in a telecommunications environment based on simulated images, so postmodern paranoia has a sort of counterfeit quality, less heartfelt than stage-managed. Too often it is the product of opportunistic and disingenuous preaching on the part of an officialdom whose very survival depends on paranoia-mongering. Be that as it may, by promoting the postmodern, social constructivist notion that all reality is simulated anyway, conditioned by other people and things, the intelligentsia simply encourages all-too-real paranoid ways of thinking.

As a citizenry, we live amid the detritus produced by endeavors such as Trudeau's and the postmodernists'. Our task in the new millennium will consist of rejecting similar projects and launching a reasoned yet firm civic debate about how to erect a genuine community. That doesn't mean censorship, the proscription of free speech so dear to paranoid hearts. It means revealing transparently foolish popular delusions for what they are. It means immunizing ourselves against the many trends in current society that nurture a delusional mentality. Only then will the lazy yet diffuse tolerance of paranoia begin to disappear. But it won't be easy. Warding off the seductive charms of paranoia takes an intellectual effort of the first magnitude.

FOR SUCH AN EFFORT to succeed, leadership is essential. Today's intelligentsia must help us negotiate our way amid the overheated rhetoric of today's culture. Reasons for optimism stem from the example of Jean Bethke Elshtain. Elshtain is a distinguished professor at the University of

Chicago, the first holder of an endowed chair in social and political ethics. In 1993 she gave the CBC Massey Lectures, titled *Democracy on Trial*. Her thoughts provide a valuable corrective to the ideologies that have hamstrung life in Canada and elsewhere.

Yet as important as what she has to say today is the path she took to get to the University of Chicago and attain national notoriety. Her life defies stereotypes. A small-town success story, Elshtain grew up in Tinmath, Colorado, population 185. At the age of ten she overcame childhood polio and the opinions of her doctors who said she would never walk again. At eighteen she married; five years later she divorced, becoming a single mother with three children, one of whom is retarded. Somehow she managed to obtain a PhD. She has now been married for thirty years to her second husband, with whom she has had a fourth child.

Elshtain would appear at first glance to be the perfect poster girl for the victimhood movement. Had she wanted to, she could have become a professional griever, that all-too-familiar paranoid character on our current cultural landscape. With her smarts, she would have been embraced unctuously by what Elshtain and others call "the chattering classes," not for what she had accomplished but for what she *was*, not for what she had done but what had *happened* to her. In paranoid culture it is the passive, not the active, state that truly qualifies someone for honors.

But Elshtain wants no part of victimhood. She sees little dignity in the way our paranoid age celebrates helplessness. On the contrary, she has eloquently and powerfully protested against many of the paranoid features of modern culture described in this book. Like a growing number of thoughtful observers across the political spectrum, she feels highly uneasy about the state of North American society. She worries that democracy is on trial, that civil society is breaking down. Though she abhors the mainstream sensationalist alarmism that captures the headlines, that doesn't mean she doesn't hear alarm bells ringing loudly. As a student of history and political theory, she doesn't suffer from the rampant cultural amnesia of our time, the precondition for so much of today's identity-group politics of self-delusion and narcissistic insulation.

As a concerned citizen, she is aware of the high rates of divorce, premature sexuality, teenage motherhood, youth violence and suicide, alcohol and drug abuse, the widespread neglect and abuse of children. It's her keen sense of what ails civil society today that sets her apart from the fearmongers of paranoid culture. She refuses to go along with the cant about organized denominational religion being a mass neurosis, a threat to free speech, or an obstacle to discovering the god/goddess lurking in all of us. She refuses to blame the family for society's woes or herald the "redefinition" of society as a community of "families." She attacks the attempt to address the great spiritual malaise so many feel today through victim-oriented psychotherapy or self-esteem and sensitivity training. Perhaps most important, she objects strenuously to the "sentimental simplification" of politics that has claimed a kind of bipartisan approval. She feels that the crippled actor Christopher Reeve's appearance and Vice-President Gore's talk of his sister's death from lung cancer at the 1996 Democratic Party convention corrupted the political process. These spectacles capitalize on emotion to disarm criticism. By limitlessly extending the boundaries of sympathy they basically mimic the paranoid's debating tactic of transforming one's opponents into nasty, uncaring creatures.

Instead, Elshtain thanks her family and credits their Lutheran faith for giving her the emotional resources to overcome her disability. As she tells the story now, her early life taught her that the family, small towns, and organized religion are hardly perfect. But they provide an education in the fullest sense of the word to young people growing up. Village neighbors are a "mixed blessing." They can be meddlesome, judgmental, and gossipy. But they can also be supportive in times of adversity, setting examples of prudence, integrity, and generosity whose memory can last a lifetime. If their opinions about teenage dress and behavior look hopelessly outdated to adolescent boys and girls, over time these sentiments make more and more sense.

At the core of small-town life is marriage and the family, topics that continue to fascinate Elshtain. She and the Rutgers University sociologist David Popenoe recently issued "Marriage in America: A Report to the Nation." When Hillary Clinton preaches greater government spending on interventionist strategies in family matters so trained experts can spend more and more time with other people's children, Elshtain balks. She is hardly against government programs to help the family. She simply distrusts fashionable language that essentially validates child and family welfare methods that have been tried for decades and found seriously wanting. In their place, she invokes the views of thinkers from the past such as Saint Augustine, who argued that at the root of society's problems is the gnostic search for the self. The big difference between Saint Augustine and most pop psychologists today is his insistence that self-understanding is indissolubly associated with an outward love of one's neighbors. Self-help therapists tend to stress that obsessive, exclusive preoccupation with one's own personality will ultimately lead to a benign, loving attitude toward those around oneself. But that simply leads to paranoid delusions of grandeur, a self-serving covetousness that inevitably conflicts with the demands of social existence. Seeking one's inner child or inner goddess breeds a selfishness that acknowledges no impersonal authority. How this is supposed to improve social cohesion is anyone's guess. The more we think of ourselves as divine-like, worthy of admiration, the more we are bound to devalue others who can never fully share our enthusiasm for ourselves. In the end, that kind of personal process of discovery can only pit people against people. Elshtain follows Saint Augustine and the others in the Western philosophic tradition who have taught the folly of privileging self-love over neighborly love. She rejects the fundamental narcissism of paranoid culture. She enjoins people to turn outward first to seek the communitarian spirit on which genuine self-identity is based.

Not surprisingly, all this has made Elshtain a pariah in the eyes of a good many academics. She is distinctly unpopular among gender feminists. They accuse her of being an apologist for neo-conservatism, an unwitting pawn of right-wing Republicans. When interviewed in 1990 at Duke University for a post in political science and women's studies she was met with open hostility from women's studies professors and her candidacy was ultimately vetoed by the same individuals. What makes her unpalatable to her opponents is her refusal to be taken in by their petulant demand, central to all strands of contemporary multiculturalism, that society both acknowledge their equality in all things and privilege their status on the basis of group difference. Homogeneity and uniqueness: the paranoid personality wants it both ways, demands to be freed absolutely from the fear of persecution without giving up the fantastical dreams of grandeur. Hence the insistent demands of identity groups that they be embraced for their commonality and rewarded for their dissimilarity. The patently nonsensical quality of such a stance is something that Elshtain has labored to expose in a variety of current media.

Elshtain refuses to partake in the paranoid's polarized, binary, oversimplistic worldview. She rejects the paranoid's way of seeing the universe in terms of absolute moral and political opposites, preferring to stress the world's paradoxes and ambiguities. To quote Vaclav Havel, life is "unfathomable, ever-changing, mysterious, and every attempt to confine it within an artificial, abstract structure inevitably ends up homogenizing, regimenting, standardizing and destroying life." The same could be said for Elshtain's own stereotype-defying life. Human existence is not dominated by fossilized political concepts like right and left. Instead it is characterized by moral dimensions that are recognizable only through concrete human experience. These dimensions need to be disentangled from the verbiage of present-day politics. As Havel says, language today all too often becomes an end in itself, an exercise in self-indulgent wordplay. It's no coincidence that the further down the path of ideology we travel, the more we employ artificial language.

We can learn a lot from thinkers like Elshtain. Like her, they mix genuine iconoclasm with a reverence for the accumulated wisdom of the past. Elshtain and others preach tirelessly that the popular effort to reconstitute ourselves anew is folly. The past does mean something. While many follow the advice of paranoia-mongers and search their personal histories for the events that account for their unhappiness, others see the past as a storehouse of supportive emotions and memories that can help to sustain us as we advance in years. The past also contains the wisdom of our ancestors, those who have both succeeded and failed when faced with similar problems. History tells the story of men and women, some more fallible than others, some more courageous than others, engaged in an effort to make society more civil and just. All were part of the historical drama perhaps best described by the Canadian historian Donald Creighton as the encounter between character and circumstance. While their and our lives are far from identical, they nonetheless share enough features for us to draw inspiration from them. The bond between past and present reminds us of the continuities that join the different generations. In turn these continuities remind us that the present is not totally alien from our own experiences. The myriad paths running backward and forward between past and present teach us the complexity of life itself. Its nuances and subtleties, shading one into the other, don't mean that human experience is unintelligible. They simply mean that the customary divisions employed by the paranoid ideologies that have dominated the modern and postmodern ages are like the proverbial square pegs. They can be fitted into the round holes of reality only by denying reality itself.

But then again, that's precisely what the paranoid does. The paranoid is a study in emotional and intellectual immaturity. The paranoid hates to be reminded of history because it reminds him that, as Cicero said, those who don't know history are destined to remain children forever.

This form of knowledge can't be acquired without, first, an affection for history and, second, a discerning and patient study of the past. If we are to hold paranoia in check it will be through a revival of interest in historical knowledge. Such a view seems to be taking shape. Thoughtful educators like Jack Granatstein and Arthur Schlesinger Jr. have warned about the temptation to pluck selectively from the record of the past whatever appears to flatter our personal or group identities. This is not merely a miscarriage of the historical method. It is a one-way street to self-ignorance. In other words, though paranoids think they are on a voyage of self-discovery, without a worldview grounded in history they are merely adrift. Or they are on a treadmill, running fast but going nowhere.

Ultimately, the study of history is key to recovering the ties that once bound us together as communities. For what else is the current plague of paranoia but a reflection of the rampant anomie of today's society? What better place for paranoia to thrive than in a society of disconnected and anxious selves, whose belief in history has been shattered? With the family in crisis, neighborhoods in chaos, and nations divided, we might appear to have good reason to be paranoid. But as this book has argued, there is no good reason for paranoia. The search for new communities through reconstructed group identities, notions of irreconcilable difference, and categorical sepa-rateness is vain. It will only destroy what semblance of community still exists.

NOTE ON SOURCES

RECENT INDICATIONS of paranoia's impact on society, politics, and culture are examined in Robert S. Robins and Jerrold M. Post, *Political Paranoia: The Psychopolitics of Hatred* (New Haven and London: Yale University Press, 1997), and Daniel Pipes, *Conspiracy: How the Paranoid Style Flourishes and Where It Comes From* (New York: The Free Press, 1997). Many of the phenomena described here as paranoid are defined as symptoms of mass hysteria in Elaine Showalter's *Hystories: Hysterical Epidemics and Modern Media* (New York: Columbia University Press, 1997). Further evidence of modernity's paranoid temper can be found in John Farrell's *Freud's Paranoid Quest: Psychoanalysis and Modern Suspicion* (New York and London: New York University Press, 1996). Farrell argues that Freud was distinctly paranoid, something that will come as no surprise to those who have studied the founder of psychoanalysis and his writings. The term "fusion paranoia," used to describe how extremists at either end of the political spectrum are joined by their similar paranoid fantasies, was coined by Michael Kelly in "The Road to Paranoia" (*The New Yorker*, June 19, 1995: 60–75). Jeet Heer addresses the question of why conspiracy theories are on the rise in an age of science and mass education in "Comfort in Lies," *Gravitas* (Autumn 1997: 22–28).

The impact of World War I on twentieth-century fiction is superbly described by Paul Fussell in his *The Great War and Modern Memory* (New York and London: Oxford University Press, 1975). Chapter Three, titled "Adversary Proceedings," warrants close attention. For the paranoid dimensions of Don DeLillo's *Underworld*, see James Wood, "Black Noise," *The New Republic* (November 10, 1997: 38–44).

For the "paranoid streak" in human nature, see Paul D. MacLean's essay in Arthur Koestler and J.R. Smythies, eds., *Beyond Reductionism: New Perspectives in the Life Sciences* (London: Hutchinson, 1969). Ronald K. Siegel offers useful examples of delusional psychoses in *Whispers: The Voices of Paranoia* (New York: Crown Publishers, 1994). Other commentary on the status and history of the delusional disorder diagnosis can be found in the psychiatric periodical *The Psychiatric Clinics of North America* (volume 18, 1995), which includes clinical descriptions of various delusional patients. For a slightly dated account of paranoia, see David W. Swanson, Philip J. Bohnert, and Jackson A. Smith, *The Paranoid* (Boston: Little, Brown, 1970). Katharine A. Phillips describes "body dysmorphic disorder" in *The Broken Mirror: Understanding and Treating Body Dysmorphic Disorder* (New York and Oxford: Oxford University Press, 1996).

Peter Marin reflects on Michael Lerner's National Summit on Ethics and Meaning in "An American Yearning: Seeking Cures for Freedom's Terrors," in *Harper's* (December 1996: 35–43). The history of the multiple personality diagnosis is described in Ian Hacking's *Rewriting the Soul: Multiple Personality and the Sciences of Memory* (Princeton, NJ: Princeton University Press, 1995). The unmasking of "Sybil" was first announced in *Esquire* (March 1994); see also Mikkel Borch-Jacobsen's "Sybil – The Making of a Disease: An Interview with Dr. Herbert Spiegel," *New York Review of Books* (April 24, 1997: 60–64). Paul McHugh's attacks on repressed memory syndrome and related psychological treatments are found in *American Scholar*, volumes 61 (1992) and 63 (1994). Frederick Crews, Berkeley professor of literature, in a series of 1994 articles in *The New York Review of Books*, blames Freud for the repressed memory fad and its injustices. Other powerful critiques of repressed memory and its abuses include Richard Ofshe and Ethan Watters, *Making Monsters: False Memories, Psychotherapy and Sexual Hysteria* (New York: Charles Scribner's Sons, 1994); Elizabeth Loftus and Katherine Ketcham, *The Myth of Repressed Memories: False Memories and Allegations of Sexual Abuse* (New York: St. Martin's Press, 1994); and Mark Pendergrast, *Victims of Memory: Incest Accusations and Shattered Lives* (Hinesburg, VT: Upper Access, 1995).

The legacy of the 1960s and its impact on contemporary life are drawing increasing attention. Among the many insightful accounts that have been published in recent years, see Robert H. Bork, *Slouching Towards Gomorrah: Modern Liberalism and American Decline* (New York: HarperCollins, 1996); David Horowitz, *Radical Son: A Journey Through Our Times* (New York: Free Press, 1997); and Richard J. Ellis, *The Dark Side of the Left: Illiberal Egalitarianism in America* (Lawrence, KS: University of Kansas Press, 1998). Ellis's book came to my attention just as I was finishing this book; it deserves close reading.

There is a considerable literature on the ideas and influence of Lacan, Derrida, and Foucault. James Miller's controversial biography of Foucault, *The Passion of Michel Foucault* (New York and London: Anchor, 1993), deftly combines Foucault the thinker and Foucault the man. *Jacques Lacan*, by Elisabeth Roudinesco (Barbara Bray, trans., New York: Columbia University Press, 1997), suffers from Roudinesco's admiration for her subject but ably documents the principal people and events in Lacan's life. Other useful accounts of Lacan's and Derrida's views include J.G. Merquior,

From Prague to Paris: A Critique of Structuralist and Post-Structuralist Thought (New York: Verso, 1986), and Mikkel Borch-Jacobsen, *Lacan: The Absolute Master* (Douglas Brick, trans., Stanford, CT: Stanford University Press, 1991). The definitive biography of Derrida has yet to be written.

The growing discontent with gender feminism has reached impressive proportions, evident in magazines and journals such as *Commentary*, *The New Republic*, *First Things*, *Partisan Review*, *National Review*, and *Saturday Night*. The most significant accounts detailing the extremes of gender feminism and its allies in women's studies are Christina Hoff Sommers, *Who Stole Feminism? How Women Have Betrayed Women* (New York: Simon and Schuster, 1994); Daphne Patai and Noretta Koertge, *Professing Feminism: Cautionary Tales From the Strange World of Women's Studies* (New York: Basic, 1994); and Donna Laframboise, *The Princess at the Window: A New Gender Morality* (Toronto: Penguin, 1996). Ellis's *The Dark Side of the Left* has a revealing chapter on what he calls "radical feminism." Patai's most recent contribution to this literature is "Heterophobia: The Feminist Turn Against Men," *Partisan Review* (volume 62, 1996: 580–94). For a trenchant analysis of the flawed statistical studies conducted and publicized by Canadian radical feminists, see John Fekete, *Moral Panic: Biopolitics Rising*, second edition (Montreal and Toronto: Robert Davies Publishing, 1995).

Lately there have been signs that American interest in Canada is picking up, a sign of mounting concern that Canadian current affairs contain lessons for non-Canadians. Perhaps the first salvo was fired by Peter Brimelow in his *The Patriot Game: National Dreams and Political Realities* (Toronto: Key Porter, 1986). See also Charles F. Doran, "Will Canada Unravel?" *Foreign Affairs* (September–October 1996). The U.S.-based journal *Telos* has conducted a lively and thoughtful debate on the political future of Canada in the twenty-first century. See Mark Wegierski, "The Reform Party and the

Crisis of Canadian Politics," *Telos* (Spring 1998: 163–72); Frederick Johnstone, "Canadian Federalism: The Decline and Fall of Quebec Separatism," *Telos* (Fall 1996: 141–58); Paul Piccone, "Secession or Reform? The Case of Canada," *Telos* (Winter 1996: 15–63); and Wayne A. Hunt, "The First Peoples and the Quebec Question," *Telos* (Summer 1996: 139–48). More and more Canadians are beginning to suspect that Canada's doomsday clock has struck two minutes to midnight. One example is Kenneth McDonald's *His Pride, Our Fall: Recovering From the Trudeau Revolution* (Toronto: Key Porter, 1995). See also William D. Gairdner, *The Trouble With Canada* (Toronto: Stoddart, 1990); Mordecai Richler, *Oh Canada! Oh Quebec!* (Toronto: Penguin, 1992); Richard Gwyn, *Nationalism Without Walls: The Unbearable Lightness of Being Canadian* (Toronto: McClelland and Stewart, 1995); and Diane Francis, *Fighting for Canada* (Toronto: Key Porter, 1996). Jeff Koftinoff's Canadian conspiracy Website can be accessed at http://www.jdkoftinoff.com.

For examples of recent critiques of Margaret Atwood in particular and Canadian fiction in general, see Philip Marchand, *Ripostes: Reflections on Canadian Literature* (Erin, ON: Porcupine's Quill, 1998); Andy Lamey, "The Wacousta Syndrome: Literature, Nationalism, and Lousy Taste," *The New Republic* (June 24, 1996: 33–40); Scott Reid, "Survival According to Atwood," *National Post* (April 10, 1999: B7). Rosemary Sullivan's biography of Atwood is *The Red Shoes: Margaret Atwood, Starting Out* (Toronto: HarperCollins, 1998).

Index